WRITING THE RESEARCH PAPER

A HANDBOOK
With Both the MLA and APA Documentation Styles
Fourth Edition

Anthony C. Winkler
Jo Ray McCuen
Glendale Community College

HARCOURT
BRACE

HARCOURT BRACE COLLEGE PUBLISHERS
Fort Worth   Philadelphia   San Diego   New York   Orlando   Austin   San Antonio
Toronto   Montreal   London   Sydney   Tokyo

Publisher	•	Ted Buchholz
Acquisitions Editor	•	Stephen T. Jordan
Developmental Editor	•	Tia Black
Project Editor	•	Jeff Beckham
Production Manager	•	Debra A. Jenkin
Book Designer	•	Don Fujimoto

___

Acknowledgments

p. 51 From July 1992 *Readers' Guide to Periodical Literature.* Copyright H. W. Wilson, New York.

p. 52 From 1990 *New York Times Index.* Copyright New York Times Index, New York.

p. 53 From October-November 1991 *Art Index.* Copyright H. W. Wilson, New York.

p. 53 From March 1991 *Psychological Abstracts.* Copyright American Psychological Association, Washington, D.C.

p. 54 From January-April 1992 *Book Review Index.* Copyright Gala Research, Detroit.

p. 54 From April 1991-March 1992 *Social Sciences Index.* Copyright H. W. Wilson, New York

Printed in the United States of America

ISBN 0-15-500166-3

Library of Congress Catalog Card Number 92-076185

Preface

Writing the Research Paper: A Handbook was originally intended to provide specific information on the conventions of the research paper in a readily accessible handbook format. The fourth edition is still structured to be used without being read from cover to cover. We explain research conventions as briefly as possible; we partition our explanations into digestible topics that can be read separately without any loss of continuity. To find the answer to any particular question on the research convention or process, a student merely has to scan our exhaustive table of contents.

Nevertheless, those familiar with previous editions of this book will notice two changes immediately.

First, in previous editions the chapter on "Doing the Research" preceded the one on "The Thesis and the Outline." We have reversed the sequence of these two chapters in this edition. Whether a writer will draft a thesis before doing the research or do the research before drafting the thesis depends as much on temperament as it does on any imagined necessity. But we have made the change because we have been persuaded that it is more typical of student writers to first draft a thesis and then research the topic than vice versa.

Second, we have added a chapter on "Style" (Chapter 7), in which we discuss how to write objective prose that doesn't sound stuffy. Here we also suggest some common tactics for beginning and ending a paper.

Our discussion of the library now takes into account the popularity of computerized retrieval systems and guides the student to an understanding of how the systems work. For those libraries that still mainly rely on manual systems, we retain our original explanation of the card catalog.

In Chapter 5, "Doing the Research," we now cover and include examples of the general and specialized indexes students are most likely to consult. In Chapter 6, we have added a lengthy section advising students on how to use research material to explore and discover their own ideas. Here we urge students not to function merely as passive collators of uncovered opinions, but also to incorporate their own interpretations and views into the paper.

One of the most substantial changes in this edition has been made to the appendix, which presents an annotated list of general and specialized references. Marshall Nunn, formerly of Glendale College, has exhaustively catalogued and updated the many reference sources listed. He has added information on available databases for computer users and included material on video and audio sources. Researchers who begin by consulting the appendix of this book will, as before, find a cornucopia of useful references at their fingertips.

Finally, as always, we have been guided in this revision by suggestions from users. Numbered among them are Vicki Adams, Beth Basham, Joan Bolden, Theresa Brychta, Virginia M. Jones, Delma Porter, Alice H. Tanner, Henrietta S. Twining, and June Zimmerman. To them and to other unnamed colleagues who suggested ways of streamlining and improving this book, we offer our thanks.

Anthony C. Winkler & Jo Ray McCuen

Contents

BASIC INFORMATION ABOUT THE RESEARCH PAPER

1a Definition of the research paper

1b Format of the research paper

1c Reasons for the research paper

1d The report paper and the thesis paper

1e Steps and schedule involved in writing a research paper

1a Definition of the research paper

The research paper is a typewritten paper in which you present your views and research findings on a chosen topic. Variously known as the "term paper" or the "library paper," the research paper is usually between five and fifteen pages long, with most teachers specifying a minimum length. No matter what the paper is called, your task is essentially the same: to read on a particular topic, evaluate information about it, and report your findings in a paper.

1b Format of the research paper

The research paper must conform to a specific format such as the one devised by the Modern Language Association (MLA), a society of language scholars, or the American Psychological Association (APA), a society of scientific scholars. The format governs the entire paper from the placing of the title to the width of the margins, and to the notation used in acknowledging material from other sources.

The format of scholarly writing is simply an agreed-upon way of doing things—much like etiquette, table manners, or rules of the road. For instance, in literary articles published recently you are likely to run across passages similar to this one:

> Brashear considers Tennyson to be at his best when his poetry is infused with "that tragic hour when the self fades away into darkness, fulfilling all of the poet's despairing pessimism" (18).

This citation is in the style of "parenthetical documentation" used by the Modern Language Association. The author of a quotation is introduced briefly, the quotation cited, and a page reference supplied in parentheses. In the alphabetized bibliography of the article will appear this listing:

> Brashear, William. *The Living Will.* The Hague: Mouton, 1969.

This sort of standardization is as time-saving to scholars as standardization of pipe fittings is to plumbers. To do research, or even to read articles about it, you must become familiar with the major citation styles used by scholars—all of which are covered in this book.

1c Reasons for the research paper

One obvious reason for writing a research paper is that the experience will familiarize you with the conventions of scholarly writing. You will learn accepted styles of documentation, the ethics of research, and a great deal about the chosen subject.

A second reason is that you will become familiar with the library through the "learn by doing" method. Even the simplest library is an intricate storehouse of information, bristling with indexes, encyclopedias, abstracts, and gazetteers. How to ferret out from this maze of sources a single piece of needed information is a skill that you learn by doing actual research. The ability to use a library is a priceless skill, because sooner or later everyone needs to find out about something: a mother needs to know how to stop her child from biting his fingernails; a physician, how to treat a rare illness; a lawyer, how to successfully argue an unusual case. Everyone can profit from knowing how to do research.

There are other benefits. Writing the research paper is an exercise in logic, imagination, and common sense. As you chip away at the mass of data and information available on your chosen topics, you learn

- how to think
- how to organize
- how to discriminate between worthless and useful opinions
- how to summarize the gist of wordy material
- how to budget your time
- how to conceive of a research project from the start, manage it through its intermediary stages, and finally assemble the information uncovered into a useful, coherent paper

1d The report paper and the thesis paper

The two kinds of papers usually assigned in colleges are the report paper and the thesis paper. The report paper summarizes and reports your findings on a particular subject. You neither judge nor evaluate the findings, but merely catalog them in a sensible sequence. For instance, a paper that listed the opinions of diplomats during the debate over the Panama Canal treaty would be a report paper. Likewise, a paper that chronologically narrated the final days of Hitler would also be a report paper.

Unlike the report paper, the thesis paper takes a definite stand on an issue. A thesis is a proposition or point of view that you are willing to argue against or defend. A paper that argues for the legalization of abortion would therefore be a thesis paper. So would a paper that attempts to prove that Hitler's political philosophy was influenced by the writings of the philosopher Nietzsche. Here are two more examples of topics as they might conceivably be treated in report papers and thesis papers:

Report paper: A summary of the theories of hypnosis.
Thesis paper: Hypnosis is simply another form of Pavlovian conditioning.

Report paper: The steps involved in passage of federal legislation.
Thesis paper: Lobbyists wield a disproportionate influence on federal legislation.

Teachers are more likely to assign a thesis paper than a report paper, for obvious reasons: writing the thesis paper requires you to exercise judgment, evaluate evidence, and construct a logical argument, whereas writing the report paper does not.

1e   Steps and schedule involved in writing a research paper

Generally, there are seven distinct steps requiring you to produce at least five hand-ins over a period of five weeks. With some variations, many instructors will more or less observe this schedule:

WHAT YOU MUST DO	WHAT YOU MUST PRODUCE	WHEN IT IS DUE
1. A topic must be selected that is complex enough to be researched from a variety of sources, but narrow enough to be covered in ten or so pages.	Two acceptable topics, one of which will be approved by the instructor.	At the end of the first week. _____ Date due
2. Exploratory scanning and in-depth reading must be done on the approved topic.	A bibliography of all titles to be used in the paper.	At the end of the second week. _____ Date due
3. The information gathered must be recorded (usually on note cards) and assembled into a coherent sequence. 4. A thesis statement must be drafted, setting forth the major idea of your paper. 5. The paper must be outlined in its major stages.	Note cards, a thesis statement, and an outline. (Papers following the APA format will require an abstract rather than an outline.)	At the end of the third week. _____ Date due

WHAT YOU MUST DO	WHAT YOU MUST PRODUCE	WHEN IT IS DUE
6. The paper must be written in rough draft and the thesis argued, proved, or supported with the information uncovered from the sources. Borrowed ideas, data, and opinions must be acknowledged.	A rough draft of the paper.	At the end of the fourth week. _____ Date due
7. A bibliography must be prepared, listing all sources used in the paper. The final paper must be written.	The final paper, complete with bibliography.	At the end of the fifth week. _____ Date due

CHOOSING A TOPIC

2a   How to choose a topic

Ideally, you should choose a topic that interests you, that is complex enough to generate several research sources, and that will neither bore nor stultify your reader.

- Pick a topic that you are curious about, or that you are either an expert on or in which you are genuinely interested. For example, if you have always been intrigued by the character of Rasputin, the "mad monk" of Russia, you can learn more about him by using him as the topic of your paper. Similarly, an interest in the career of Elvis Presley might lead to a paper analyzing and evaluating his music.

- If you are utterly at a loss for a topic, have positively no interest in anything at all, and cannot for the life of you imagine what you could write ten whole pages on, then go to the library and browse. Pore over books, magazines, and card catalogs. An encyclopedia can be a veritable supermarket of possible topics. Browse through its entries until you find an appealing subject. Check the two-volume *Library of Congress Subject Headings* (LCSH) for some heading that might appeal to you. Even a general idea can be whittled down to a specific topic (see Section 2c). But you must first arrive at the general idea.

- Take your time as you search for a topic. Do not latch on to the first workable idea that pops into your head. Mull it over. Ask yourself whether you would really enjoy spending five weeks on that topic. If you have any qualms, keep browsing until you get an idea that really excites you. All of us are or can be excited about something (thankfully, not the same thing). So whatever you do, do not make the mistake of choosing "any old" topic merely for the sake of getting on with it. Choose carelessly now and you will pay dearly later. But choose carefully and you will be rewarded with the age-old excitement of research.

2b   Topics to avoid

Some topics present unusual difficulties; others are simply a waste of time. Here is a summary of topics to avoid:

2b–1 Topics that are too big

Though it may be the longest writing assignment you will receive during the semester, the research paper is still scarcely longer than a short magazine article. Obviously, you can neither review the evolution of man nor completely fathom the mysteries of creation in ten pages. Do not even try. Regrettably, we cannot give you a good rule of thumb for avoiding impossibly broad topics. Use your common sense. Check the card catalog. If you find that numerous books have been written about your topic, then it is probably too big. The signs that you may have bitten off more than you can chew usually come only after you are already deeply mired in the research. Reference sources that multiply like flies; a bibliography that grows like a cancer; opinions, data, and information that come pouring in from hundreds of sources—these signs all indicate a topic that is too big. The solution is to narrow the topic without darting to the sanctuary of the trivial. Here are some examples of hopelessly big topics: "The Influence of Greek Mythology on Poetry"; "The Rise and Fall of Chinese Dynasties"; "The Framing of the U.S. Constitution."

2b–2 Topics that can be traced to a single source

Research papers must be documented with opinions drawn from different authorities and sources. One reason for assigning the research paper in the first place is to expose students to the opinions of different authorities, to a variety of books and articles, and to other reference sources. Consequently, if the topic is so skimpy that all data on it can be culled from a single source, the purpose of the paper is defeated. Choose only topics that are broad enough to be researched from multiple sources.

Biographies are numbered among those topics that must be chosen with care lest they lead to a one-source paper. If you choose to write about a person, use an approach that allows the use of a variety of sources. You might focus on his or her contributions, motivation, or development. For instance, if you were to write about James Monroe you might narrow your focus to an evaluation of the Monroe Doctrine, which would require research of multiple sources. Avoid becoming so charmed by any single account of the person's life that you end up merely parroting that source.

2b–3 Topics that are too technical

A student may have an astonishing expertise in one technical area and may be tempted to display this dazzling knowledge in a research paper. Resist the temptation. Technical topics often require a technical jargon that the teacher might not understand and might even dismiss as an elaborate "snow job." The skills that a research paper should instill in you are displayed better in a paper on a general topic. Stick to some area broad enough to be understood by any decently educated reader. The following are examples of overly technical topics: "The Use of Geometry in the Perspective of Paolo Uccelo"; "Heisenberg's Principle of Indeterminacy as It Applies to Subparticle Research"; "Utilitarianism versus Positivism in Legal Rights Cases Involving Minorities."

2b–4 Topics that are trivial

Obviously, your own common sense and judgment must steer you away from such topics, but here are some that teachers would reject as too trivial: "The Use of Orthopedic Braces for Dachshunds Prone to Backaches"; "The Cult of Van Painting in America"; "The History of the Tennis Ball"; "How to Get Dates When You're Divorced."

2b–5 Topics that are overused

The prudent writer will avoid topics that repeatedly have been overused in public debate. Opinions on such topics tend to harden into familiar postures, and the effort to pen something original about them can lure a writer into wild exaggeration. Numbered among these shopworn topics are abortion, teenage marriages, legalization of drugs, euthanasia, capital punishment, substance abuse, and cruelty to animals. We do not mean to say that these topics are unimportant; indeed, their popularity is a measure of their importance in the public consciousness. But writers who tackle overused topics often unconsciously will parrot well-known and commonplace prejudices as if they were unique opinions. If you cannot help yourself and must write about an overused topic, at least try to approach it from a new angle. For instance, if you intend to write about abortion, comparing the effects of the Ru486 pill with traditional surgical abortions would be a tack different enough to keep you from being sucked into the whirlpool of platitudes. Or, if you feel compelled to write your paper on euthanasia, you might avoid the emotional hot spots by dispassionately analyzing the laws of your state that govern medically assisted suicide.

2b–6 Topics that are contemporary

Contemporary topics are best avoided for two reasons: first, it often is difficult to locate unbiased sources on them; second, what sources are available will usually come from newspapers and magazines whose speculative reportage may make your documentation seem suspiciously flimsy. Intellectually solid papers should reflect opinions culled from a variety of sources—books, periodicals, reference volumes, specialized indexes, video materials, and the like—which require a topic that has weathered both the passage of time and the scrutiny of scholarly contradiction. If you find yourself drawn to a too contemporary topic, our advice is that you try to locate an equivalent in the past and write about that instead. So, for example, rather than writing about a revolutionary war that broke out yesterday in some Baltic state, you might turn your attention to a well-documented equivalent such as the Castro revolution in Cuba.

2c Narrowing the topic

Once a general subject is found, the first step is to narrow it down to a suitably small topic. There is no easy or set way of doing this. You simply must be guided by the available sources and information; again, common sense must come into play. No python knows the exact dimensions of its mouth, but any python instinctively knows that it cannot swallow an elephant. Experiment with your topic: pursue one train of thought and see where it leads and whether or not it yields an arguable thesis. Pare down and whittle away until you have something manageable. Bear in mind that ten pages amount to a very modest length—some books have longer prefaces. Here are a few examples of the narrowing that you will have to do:

GENERAL SUBJECT	FIRST NARROWING	FURTHER NARROWING
Mythology	*Beowulf*	Courtesy codes in *Beowulf*
Migrant workers	California migrant workers	Major California labor laws and their impact on Mexican migrant workers
Theater	Theater of the Absurd	Theater-of-the-Absurd elements in *Who's Afraid of Virginia Woolf?*
Jack Kennedy	Jack Kennedy's cabinet	The contribution of Averell Harriman as U.S. Ambassador to Russia
Russia	The Bolshevik Revolution of 1917	The role of Grigory Efimovich Rasputin in pre-revolutionary Russia
China	Chinese agriculture	The effect on China of Chinese agricultural policies during the past ten years
Indians	Famous Indian fighters	Major Rogers's Rangers during the Indian wars
Nature's carnivores	Parasites	The ichneumon wasp and its parasitic hosts
Educational psychology	Psychological testing in schools	The Thematic Apperception Test (TAT) and its present-day adaptations

GENERAL SUBJECT	FIRST NARROWING	FURTHER NARROWING
Banking	Restrictions on banking powers	The role of the Federal Reserve in credit management

The first attempt at narrowing a subject usually is easier than the second, which must yield a specific topic. Use trial and error until you have a topic with which you are comfortable. Further narrowing, if necessary, will suggest itself once you are into the actual research. Note that whatever subject you choose must be approved by your instructor. So before you become too involved in narrowing the subject, be sure that in its basic outline your teacher approves of it. Here is a list of new topics, organized by academic discipline, worth investigating:

HUMANITIES

The evolution of children's literature
The decline of Broadway
Contemporary minimalist fiction
Modern fiction with a political message
Fictional protagonists with psychological problems
Classical mythology in modern literature
Themes in Nobel Prize winners' speeches
Nihilism as a theme in modern literature
Optimism as a theme in modern literature
Early American films
American literature of minority cultures (Black, Indian, Jewish, Chicano)
Slang or dialect in American literature
Social commentary in rock lyrics
Aspects of modern architecture, sculpture, painting, or music
Ballet in today's culture

LIFE SCIENCES

The moral implications of cloning
The creation of matter in the Big Bang (or attacking the Big Bang theory)
Theories about the extinction of the dinosaurs
The greenhouse effect
Plastic pollution
Marine organisms and medical research
Parasites—good and bad
Wildlife management
The latest research in predicting inherited diseases
Plate tectonics and earthquakes
Mechanics of the hurricane

The latest in genetic engineering
Disposal of toxic wastes
The latest crazes in exercise (for example, step aerobics)
PNI Psychoneuroimmunology (how the mind and body interact)
The inheritance link in alcoholism
Modern diseases (for example, AIDS, anorexia nervosa, Tourette
    syndrome, Epstein-Barr, cystic fibrosis)

SOCIAL SCIENCES

Dirty political campaigning
The destiny of Christopher Columbus's ships the *Niña*, the *Pinta*, and the
    Santa Maria
Hitler's medical problems
Adopted children and their real parents
Alcoholism and genetics
Forced military service
Freedom of the press versus gag rules
Nationalized health or car insurance
The psychology of grief
The problem of aging
Alternative life-styles in the last two decades
Hunger and famine in third-world countries
Homelessness in the United States
The latest research in the nature/nurture debate
Labor, property, and status
Immigrant women and their contributions
Unraveling America's Hispanic past
Ethnic minorities and urban politics
Feminism: the value of women in a free market
Satellites and U.S. security
Revolutions in third-world countries
The effect of public opinion polls on politics

BUSINESS

Gold as an investment
Women in management
Women police officers (or fire officers, ministers, and so on)
Insider trading on Wall Street
Free market versus fair market
The role of the Securities and Exchange Commission
The role of the Federal Trade Commission
Loan programs for college costs
Career development strategies
Ecology and business

TECHNOLOGY

Computer viruses
Causes of aircraft stalling
Solving traffic gridlock in major cities
Modern technology for the blind and deaf
The future of microchips in computers
Applications of superconductors

3

THE LIBRARY

3a   Layout of the library

Most of the research for your paper will be done at a library, and the facilities available for retrieving information will naturally vary. Before we discuss what you are likely to find in any given library, we can state from experience that over the years researchers have found the cooperation of a friendly librarian to be indispensable in aiding their research. Not only are librarians thoroughly grounded in research books and references, most know exactly where to find any given item. Try to enlist the aid of your librarian as you begin your research. As we said, basic architectural design will differ from one library to the next, but certain facilities are nevertheless standard.

3a–1 The computer

Without a doubt, the most revolutionary improvement to library research over the last decade is the introduction of the computer. Most college libraries now use computers to catalogue and organize their collections. In fact, many libraries no longer subscribe to book-type indexes or even keep their card catalogs current (see 3a–2) because of the expense involved and the obvious superiority of the computer over manual storage methods. The two most popular computerized systems are *Comcats* and *On-line computer catalogs*. The comcat consists of microforms (very small photographs of printed materials) and microform reader screens conveniently located throughout the library. Comcats display information on all the books and periodicals found in a library collection and usually are updated every three months. On-line computer catalogs—clearly the wave of the future—provide up-to-date cataloguing information instantly on a computer screen. To use an on-line computer, you simply sit or stand in front of a computer terminal and type in key words such as the author, title, or subject into a terminal. In a blink the answer is displayed directly on the screen. Many libraries provide helpful directions beside the terminals explaining how to use their system. Spend a few minutes learning how to input a request for books or periodicals on a certain topic and you will be repaid amply by the blazing speed of the computer.

3a–2 Card catalog

The card catalog is an alphabetical index of all books in the library. It consists of 3×5 cards that are stored in little drawers, usually near the main entrance of the library. The card catalog lists all books under at least three headings: author, subject, and title. The cards are alphabetized by the first important word in the heading. A book that straddles two or more subjects will be listed separately under each subject. If an editor, translator, or illustrator is involved, the book also will be listed under the name of each, in addition to being listed under the name of the author. A jointly authored book is also likely to be listed under the name of each author.

Basic research generally begins with a search of the card catalog or its computerized equivalent, both of which literally put a wealth of information at a researcher's fingertips. On pages 18–20 are examples of index cards that list the same book in different ways.

In combing the card catalog for books and sources on a topic, do not overlook the possibility of finding useful material under separate but related headings. For example, if you are looking for sources on "Pablo Picasso," you should also look under such cross-references as "Modern Art," "French Art," "Abstract Art," and "Cubism."

3a–3 Microform indexes

Many libraries now use microform indexes for periodicals as well as for their permanent book collections. Systems vary from one library to another. Microfilm systems are used by some libraries to index the articles of major periodicals. Most such systems depend on microfilm readers that allow for a fast scan or slow search. A microfiche storage system is also used to catalog articles published in major national newspapers. Either system (or both) may be available in your own library. Large libraries have on-line computerized systems for their permanent collections. Ask the librarian.

3a–4 Stacks

"Stacks" is the name given to the shelves on which the books and periodicals are stored in the library. The stacks may be either *open* or *closed*. If the stacks are open, readers may roam at will among the shelves and handle the books; if the stacks are closed, readers are denied direct access to the shelves and must obtain books from clerks by listing the title of the book, its author, and its call number on a request slip. Closed stacks are more common at larger libraries; in smaller libraries the stacks are usually open. While inconvenient to a reader, closed stacks reduce the chance of pilferage, misfiling, and defacement of books. Open stacks, on the other hand, allow a reader to browse at leisure.

3a–5 Reference room

Encyclopedias, indexes, gazetteers, and other works that ordinarily are consulted for information rather than read from cover to cover are stored in a reference room. Usually large and unwieldy, these volumes generally are confined to use within the reference room; they cannot be checked out and taken home.

Figure 3-1 Author card (also called "Main entry")

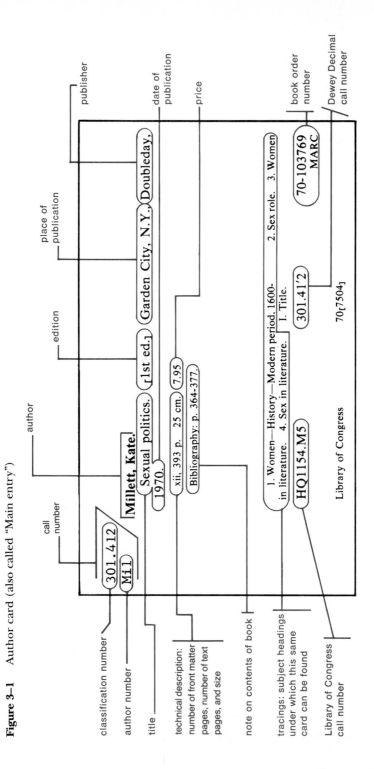

title
(usually
typed in
black ink)

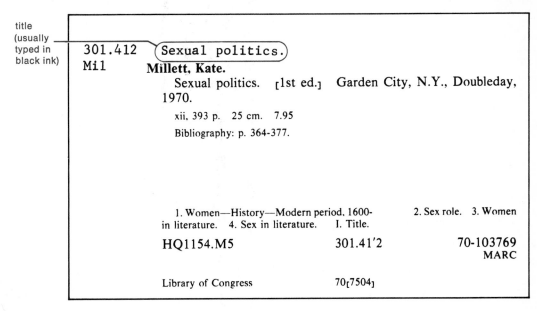

301.412
Mi1

Sexual politics.

Millett, Kate.

Sexual politics. [1st ed.] Garden City, N.Y., Doubleday, 1970.

xii, 393 p. 25 cm. 7.95

Bibliography: p. 364-377.

1. Women—History—Modern period, 1600-in literature. 4. Sex in literature. 2. Sex role. 3. Women I. Title.

HQ1154.M5 301.41'2 70-103769 MARC

Library of Congress 70[7504]

Figure 3–2 Title card

Figure 3–3 Subject card

subject
heading
(usually
typed in
red ink)

301.412
Mi1

WOMEN--HISTORY

Millett, Kate.

Sexual politics. [1st ed.] Garden City, N.Y., Doubleday, 1970.

xii, 393 p. 25 cm. 7.95

Bibliography: p. 364-377.

1. Women—History—Modern period, 1600-in literature. 4. Sex in literature. 2. Sex role. 3. Women I. Title.

HQ1154.M5 301.41'2 70-103769 MARC

Library of Congress 70[7504]

subject heading (usually typed in red ink)

```
301.412    (FEMINISM)
Mil        Millett, Kate.
                Sexual politics.   [1st ed.]   Garden City, N.Y., Doubleday,
           1970.
                xii, 393 p.   25 cm.   7.95
                Bibliography: p. 364-377.




                1. Women—History—Modern period, 1600-      2. Sex role.   3. Women
           in literature.   4. Sex in literature.   I. Title.
           HQ1154.M5                              301.41′2                  70-103769
                                                                                MARC

                Library of Congress                    70[7504]
```

Figure 3–4   Cross-reference card

3a–6 Main desk

The main desk functions as an information center as well as a checkout counter for books. Librarians and clerks stationed here are trained to help the researcher find material or track down difficult sources. Library personnel can be of invaluable assistance; if you are confused and lost, do not be afraid to ask them for help.

3a–7 Reserve desk

Reserve books are kept at the reserve desk. Books on reserve are available for use only in the library and only for a limited time—generally for an hour or two. Teachers will often place on reserve any book or magazine essential to their lectures or courses. When the demand for a book exceeds the supply, the book often will be placed in the reserve collection, which in many libraries is listed in a separate reserve catalog.

3a–8 Audiovisual room

Cassettes, tapes, picture slides, filmstrips, and other nonbook media are stored in an audiovisual room and generally indexed by whatever conventional filing system the library uses (see Dewey Decimal System and Library of Congress System). The audiovisual librarian will help you locate this kind of material. Often the audiovisual supply room adjoins an equipment area where students can listen to tapes or watch a film. Some libraries, replete with extensive new audiovisual hardware, now call themselves media centers rather than libraries.

3a–9 Microform room

Microfilm and microfiche are stored in a microform room. Microfilm is material photographically stored on filmstrips; microfiche is material photographically mounted on frames. For centuries, back issues of journals, magazines, and newspapers were piled up in dusty heaps in the dark, cobwebbed stockrooms of libraries. But with the advent of cameras that can reduce entire pages to a tiny filmstrip, periodical material now is stored economically in this microscopic form and read with magnifying equipment.

3a–10 Newspaper racks

Many libraries subscribe to major national and foreign newspapers. Current issues generally are displayed on long wooden clamps, known as newspaper racks, that hold and store the newspapers. Often the newspaper racks are surrounded by comfortable chairs in which a reader can sit for a leisurely assessment of world events. Typical newspapers found in these racks include the *New York Times*, the *Washington Post*, the *Los Angeles Times*, the *Christian Science Monitor*, the *Wall Street Journal*, the *London Times*, the *Manchester Guardian*, the *Hindustan Times*, and *Die Zeit*.

3a–11 Copy room

Duplicating machines are available in most libraries for photocopying. The charge for this service ranges anywhere from a nickel to a quarter.

3a–12 Typing room

Typewriters are available in many libraries, either at a reasonable rental rate or without charge. The machines usually are kept in a designated typing room which is often soundproof. Many modern libraries also have computers available for word processing.

3a–13 Carrels

Carrels are small enclosed desks equipped with bookshelves and are designed especially to provide students with a quiet, insulated enclosure for reading or research. The carrel section of a library is set aside for students intent on serious scholarship. Some libraries even impose fines on students caught capering in this area. Carrels can generally be reserved by advanced students for either a semester or an entire school year; the remaining carrels are distributed among lower-division students on a first-come, first-served basis.

3a–14 Interlibrary loan

Most libraries are part of an interlibrary loan (ILL) system that makes sources from other libraries available on a loan basis. More and more students are finding ILL to be essential to their research.

3b Organization of the library

Even the great libraries of antiquity, such as the one in Nineveh in the sixth century B.C., or in Alexandria in the third century B.C., searched constantly for more efficient systems of organizing their collections. Clay tablets were grouped by subject and stored on shelves; papyrus rolls were stacked in labeled jars. The Chinese, whose library tradition dates back to the sixth century B.C., grouped their writings under four primary headings: classics, history, philosophy, and belles lettres. And by 1605 the English philosopher Sir Francis Bacon had independently devised a system of classifying all knowledge into three similar categories of history, poetry, and philosophy, which then were subdivided further to yield specific subjects.

Knowledge has grown so enormously, and classification systems have become so complex, that today librarians are trained extensively in classifying books. The two major classification systems now used by libraries are the Dewey Decimal System and the Library of Congress System.

3b–1 The Dewey Decimal System

Devised in 1873 by Melvil Dewey and first put to use in the library of Amherst College, the Dewey Decimal System divides all knowledge (fiction and biography excepted) into ten general categories:

000–099	General Works
100–199	Philosophy and Psychology
200–299	Religion
300–399	Social Sciences
400–499	Language
500–599	Pure Science
600–699	Technology (Applied Sciences)
700–799	The Arts

| 800–899 | Literature |
| 900–999 | History |

Each of these ten general categories is subdivided into ten smaller divisions. For example, the category of Literature (800–899) is divided further into:

800–809	General Works (about Literature)
810–819	American Literature
820–829	English Literature
830–839	German Literature
840–849	French Literature
850–859	Italian Literature
860–869	Spanish Literature
870–879	Latin Literature
880–889	Greek and Classical Literature
890–899	Literature of Other Languages

The specific category of English Literature is divided further into narrower groups:

820	English Literature (General)
821	Poetry
822	Drama
823	Fiction
824	Essays
825	Speeches
826	Letters
827	Satire and Humor
828	Miscellany
829	Minor Related Literature

An endless number of more specific headings is created easily through the addition of decimal places. For instance, from the category of English Literature—820—the more specific heading of Elizabethan Literature is devised: 822.3. The addition of another decimal place creates an even more specific category for the works of Shakespeare: 822.33.

The obvious advantage of the Dewey Decimal System is the ease with which it yields specific categories to accommodate the rapid proliferation of books. Probably for this reason, the system currently is used in more libraries throughout the world than all other systems combined.

3b–2 The Cutter/Sanborn Author Marks

The Dewey Decimal System generally is used in conjunction with the Cutter/Sanborn Author Marks, devised originally by Charles Ammi Cutter and later merged with a similar system independently invented by Kate Sanborn. The Cutter/Sanborn Author Marks distinguish between books filed under an identical Dewey number. In the early days of the Dewey system, books with the same Dewey number simply were shelved alphabetically by author. But as more and more books were published, alphabetical shelving became impossibly difficult, leading eventually to the invention of the Author Marks.

The Author Marks eliminate alphabetical shelving by assigning a number to every conceivable consonant/vowel or vowel/consonant combination that can be used to spell the beginning of an author's surname. These numbers are published in a table that alphabetically lists the various combinations and assigns each a number. For instance, the "G" section of the Cutter/Sanborn Table lists the following combinations and numbers:

Garf	231	Garn	234
Gari	232	Garnet	235
Garl	233	Garni	236

To assign, for example, an Author Mark to the book *Double Taxation: A Treatise on the Subject of Double Taxation Relief* by Charles Edward Garland, a librarian: (1) looks up the combination of letters in the Cutter/Sanborn Table closest to the spelling of the author's surname—in this case, "Garl," with the number 233; (2) places the first letter of the author's surname before the number; and (3) places after the number the first letter or letters of the first important word in the title, giving an Author Mark of G233d. The call number of the book is its Dewey Decimal number plus its Author Mark:

336.294
G233d

Similarly, the book *Religion and the Moral Life* by Arthur Campbell Garnett has a Dewey Decimal number of 170 and an Author Mark of G235r, giving the following call number:

170
G235r

Under this dual system, a book is shelved first by sequence of its Dewey Decimal number and then by sequence of its Author Mark. To find any title, a student must therefore first locate the Dewey Decimal category on the shelf and then identify an individual book by its Author Mark.

Fiction and biography are classified in a special way under the Dewey Decimal System. Fiction is marked with the letter "F" and biography with the letter "B." Fiction is alphabetized by author, biography by subject. For example, F-Pas is the classification of a novel by Boris Pasternak; B-C56 is one of the several biographies about Sir Winston Churchill. If the library has an especially large fiction or biography collection, these books might also be given Author Marks.

3b–3 The Library of Congress System

The Library of Congress System is named for the library that invented it. Founded in 1800, the Library of Congress at first simply shelved its books by size. Its earliest catalog, issued in 1802, showed the United States as the owner of 964 books and nine maps. By 1812 the nation's collection had increased to 3076 books and fifty-three maps. By 1897, when the library finally acquired a building of its own, the collection had grown to half a million items and was increasing at the staggering rate of 100,000 per year. The library had acquired such a vast and expansive collection that a new system was necessary for classifying it. Publishing in 1904, the Library of Congress Classification System has since grown immensely in popularity and is now widely used, especially by larger libraries.

The system represents the main branches of knowledge with twenty-one letters of the alphabet. These branches are further divided by the addition of letters and Arabic numerals up to 9999, allowing for a nearly infinite number of combinations. The system is therefore especially useful for libraries possessing enormous collections. Here is a list of the general categories:

A	General Works—Polygraphy
B	Philosophy—Religion
C	History—Auxiliary Sciences
D	History and Topography (except America)
E–F	America
G	Geography—Anthropology
H	Social Sciences
J	Political Science
K	Law
L	Education
M	Music
N	Fine Arts
P	Language and Literature
Q	Science
R	Medicine
S	Agriculture—Plant and Animal Industry
T	Technology
U	Military Science
V	Naval Science
Z	Bibliography and Library Science

These general categories are narrowed by the addition of letters. Numerous minute subdivisions are possible. The Language and Literature category, designated by "P," is further subdivided thus:

P   Philology and Linguistics: General
PA   Greek and Latin Philology and Literature
PB   Celtic Languages and Literature
PC   Romance Languages (Italian, French, Spanish, and Portuguese)
PD   Germanic (Teutonic) Languages

The addition of numerals makes possible even more minute subdivisions within each letter category. From the general category "P"—Language and Literature—is derived the more specific category of Literary History and Collections, designated by "PN." The call number PN 6511 indicates works dealing with Oriental Proverbs; PN 1993.5 U65, on the other hand, is the call number for a book about the history of motion pictures in Hollywood.

The classification under this system proceeds from the general to the specific, with the longer numbers being assigned to the more specialized books. Like the Dewey Decimal System, the Library of Congress System also uses an author number to differentiate books shelved within a specific category. To locate a book with a Library of Congress classification, the student must first find the subject category on the shelf and then track down the individual title by its author number. Two printed volumes entitled *Library of Congress Subject Headings* (LCSH) are available in most libraries. These books use subject headings to group materials on the same or a similar topic under one term. You may find it helpful to look up your topic in the LCSH.

3b–4 Classification of periodicals

Periodicals and newspapers are classified differently from books. Current issues usually are shelved alphabetically by title and are accessible to the public (some libraries shelve current issues by call number). Back issues either bound in book form or reproduced on microfilm are stored elsewhere—usually in a special section of the library to which the public may or may not be admitted, depending on whether the stacks are open or closed.

3b–5 Classification of nonbooks

Nonbook materials—films, microfilms, recordings, news clippings, sheet music, reproductions of masterpieces, transparencies, slides, programmed books, and other audiovisual material—may be listed either in the general catalog or as a special collection. No hard-and-fast rule exists for classifying this kind of material; ask your librarian how it is catalogued. (See Figure 3–5, p. 27.)

Figure 3–5   Cross-reference sample catalog cards for nonbook materials

Map
974.1
Nat   National Geographic Society
              Maine with the maritime provinces of
close-up Canada. Washington, D.C., 1975.

SOUND
FILMSTRIP
140   Basic systems of philosophy.
Bas   (SOUND FILM- STRIP). Westwood
               Educational Productions,

TAPE RECORDING
290   Conger, George P.
Con   Philosophical basis for world religion.
           Cincinnati, Ohio, Sound Seminars, n.d.

FILM LOOP   SCATTERING--EXPERIMENTS.
531.1133 Diffraction and scattering around obstacles.
Dif   Educational Services, 1964.

KIT
327.73 The Making of American foreign policy. (Kit)
Mak   Newsweek Educational Division.--New York:
            Newsweek, c1977

(SOUND SLIDE)
709.44 Life and arts in the XIII century.
Lif   (SOUND SLIDE). Harrison, N.Y.,
            Cultural History Research, 1960.
            51 col. slides. 2 x 2 in.
            and tape:

kind of material

(RECORDS)
821.08 The London Library of Recorded English
Lon   XTV 23862 (23863, 23864, 23865)
            Britain Agencies Inc.
            4 s.   12"   33 1/3 rpm

            Album 1, Books I and II.

classification
number

title and
description of
material

1. English poetry-collections

cross-references

THE THESIS
AND THE OUTLINE

 4a The thesis: definition and function

4b The outline

4a The thesis: definition and function

The thesis is a statement that summarizes the central idea of the paper. By convenience and custom, this statement is usually the final sentence of the opening paragraph, as in the following example.

```
          The Bilingually Handicapped Child


     There are approximately five million children in

the United States who attend public schools and speak a

language other than English in their homes and neighbor-

hoods.  Many of these children are handicapped in commu-

nication and thought processes, and have to repeat the

first grades in school several times.  The bilingual

child is usually unable to conceptualize in the English

language taught at school, since he is from a different

cultural and language background.  Early compensatory

educational programs would give the bilingual child a

head start and he would be better prepared for handling

school work.
```

The underlined sentence is the thesis—the central idea for which the writer intends to argue. Once readers have gotten through this first paragraph, the aim of the paper is abundantly clear to them; they know what to anticipate.

The thesis serves at least three functions. First, it establishes a boundary around the subject that discourages the writer from wandering aimlessly. Most of us often are tempted to stray from the point when we write. We begin by intending to write a paper about Rasputin's place in history, then stumble onto some fascinating fact about Russian monasteries and become eager to somehow work it in. With a clear thesis before us, however, we are less likely to be seduced by a digression. Formulated before the actual writing of the paper begins, the thesis commits us to argue one point, discuss one subject, clarify one issue. Writers so committed will not leapfrog from topic to topic, nor free-associate erratically from one minor point to another.

Second, the thesis—if worded properly—can chart an orderly course for the paper, making it easier to write. Consider for instance this thesis:

```
Two defects in the design of the Titanic con-

tributed to her sinking: her steering was sluggish and

unresponsive, even for a ship of her immense size; her

traverse bulkheads, which should have made her virtually

unsinkable, did not extend all the way up to her deck.
```

The course before the writer is as plain as day: first, the sluggish steering of the *Titanic* must be discussed and clarified with appropriate facts and details; second, the design of her traverse bulkheads must be dealt with and the defect thoroughly explained. The writer's job is easier because the thesis conveniently has divided the paper into two parts, establishing not only the topics to be discussed, but also their sequence. It is better and easier by far to write about such a thesis than to write randomly about the sinking of the *Titanic*.

Third, the thesis gives the reader an idea of what to expect, making the paper consequently easier to read. Textbooks have elaborate chapter headings and section headnotes just for this purpose. Newspaper stories are captioned and headlined for a similar reason. It is easier to read virtually anything if we have an anticipation that narrows and focuses our attention. A paper without a thesis creates no such anticipation in a reader and is therefore more difficult to follow.

4a–1 Formulating the thesis

There is no chicken-and-egg mystery about which comes first—the notes or the thesis. One cannot formulate a thesis about a subject unless one first knows a great deal about it. Ordinarily, students therefore will be well into the research and notes before they can formulate the thesis.

Basically, you are looking for a central idea that summarizes the information you have gathered on the subject. Consider, for instance, a paper on Rasputin. The student, after much reading and note-taking, discovered that despite his diabolic reputation, Rasputin did do some good. Specifically, she discovered that (1) Rasputin had intense religious feelings; (2) he had a passionate desire for peace in Russia; and (3) he was deeply devoted to his family and friends. She therefore summarized her findings about Rasputin in the following thesis:

```
Thesis: After six decades of being judged a demoniacal

libertine, Rasputin now deserves to be viewed from

another point of view--as a man who was intensely

religious, who passionately desired peace, and who

was deeply devoted to his family and friends.
```

Notice that the thesis, as worded, specifies exactly what the writer has to do and what information she will need to do it. To begin with, she will have to document Rasputin's reputation as a demoniacal libertine. Having done that, she will have to support her three contrary assertions: that Rasputin was intensely religious, that he passionately desired peace, and that he was deeply devoted to his family and friends. The thesis, moreover, suggests exactly the kind of information that the student will need to write the paper. First, she must cite historical opinion that portrays Rasputin as a demoniacal libertine. Second, she will need to produce anecdotal material, eyewitness accounts, biographical opinions, and similar evidence that support her contrary assertions about Rasputin.

4a–2 Rules for wording the thesis

Properly worded, the thesis should: (1) be clear, comprehensible, and direct; (2) predict major divisions in the structure of the paper; and (3) commit the writer to an unmistakable course, argument, or point of view. The thesis on Rasputin is clear, implies a four-part division in the structure of the paper, and obligates the writer to argue a single proposition: that Rasputin was judged harshly by history. Likewise, the thesis on the *Titanic* disaster is clear and direct, divides the paper into two principal parts, and commits the writer to a single argument: that the ocean liner sank because of defects in her steering and bulkheads. Listed below is a series of rules to guide you in properly wording your thesis.

■ *The thesis should commit the writer to a single line of argument.* Consider this example:

```
Poor   The Roman theater was inspired by the Greek

       theater, which it imitated, and eventually

       the Romans produced great plays in their

       theatrons, such as those by Plautus, who was

       the best Roman comic writer because of his

       robustness and inventiveness.
```

This thesis threatens to wrench the paper in two contrary directions: it commits the student to cover both the origins of Roman theater and the theatrical career of Plautus, one of Rome's greatest comic playwrights. This dual thesis came about because the student laboriously had accumulated two sets of notes—one on the origins of Roman theater and another on the career of Plautus—and was determined to devise a thesis that would allow the use of both. The result is this curiously dual thesis that skews the paper in two contrary directions. Persuaded to relinquish the notes on the origins of the Roman theater and to focus the paper entirely on the career of Plautus, the student drafted the following improved thesis:

> *Better*   Because of his robust language and novel
>
> comic plots, Titus Maccicus Plautus can be
>
> considered the best Roman comic playwright;
>
> his plays are still successfully staged
>
> today.

The paper now is committed to a single line of argument and its focus therefore is vastly improved.

■ *The thesis should not be worded in figurative language.* The reasoning behind this rule is obvious: figurative language is too indefinite and oblique to constitute the central idea of a paper. Consider this thesis:

> *Poor*   Henry James is the Frank Lloyd Wright of the
>
> American novel.

No doubt the writer knew exactly what was meant by this allusion, but its significance is murky to a reader. If one cannot understand the central idea of a paper, what hope does one have of understanding the paper? The following plainly expressed thesis is vastly better:

> *Better*   The novels of Henry James have internal con-
>
> sistency because of the way he unifies his
>
> themes, patterns his episodes, and orders his
>
> images.

■ *The thesis should not be worded vaguely.* Vagueness may tantalize but it does not inform. Moreover, a paper with a vague thesis is a paper without direction and all the more difficult to write. Consider this example of a vague thesis:

> *Poor*   Cigarette smoking wreaks havoc on the body.

Doing a paper on such a thesis truly will put a writer to the test. The thesis suggests no direction, provides no structure, proposes no arguments. Contrast it with this improved version:

> *Better*   Cigarette smoking harms the body by con-
>
> stricting the blood vessels, accelerating
>
> the heartbeat, paralyzing the cilia in the
>
> bronchial tubes, and activating excessive
>
> gastric secretions in the stomach.

The writer knows exactly what points to argue and in what order.

■ *The thesis should not be worded as a question.* The thesis worded as a question does not provide the writer with the obligatory direction given by a statement. Here is an example:

> *Poor*   Who makes the key decisions in U.S. cities?

This sort of question makes a good starting point for research. Indeed, most research will begin with an unanswered question in the mind of the researcher. But the eventual thesis should not be your original question; it should be the answer uncovered in your research.

> *Better*   Key decisions in large U.S. cities are made
>
> by a handful of individuals, drawn largely
>
> from business, industrial, and municipal
>
> circles, who occupy the top of the power
>
> hierarchy.

■ *The thesis should be as concise as possible.* If ever a writer should try for conciseness, it is in the drafting of the thesis. A long, cumbersome thesis is likely to muddle the writer and send the paper flying off in different directions. The reader who cannot fathom the thesis of a paper is even less likely to make sense of its contents. Here is a muddled thesis:

Poor   Despite the fact that extensive time consumed by television detracts from homework, competes with schooling more generally, and has contributed to the decline in the Scholastic Aptitude Test score averages, television and related forms of communication give the future of learning its largest promise, the most constructive approach being less dependent on limiting the uses of these processes than on the willingness of the community and the family to exercise the same responsibility for what is taught and learned this way as they have exercised with respect to older forms of education.

This passage is difficult to unravel. A whole paper based on this thesis would be equally unclear. Here is an improved version:

Better   While numerous studies acknowledge that the extensive time spent by students watching television has contributed to the decline in the Scholastic Aptitude Test scores, leading educators are convinced that television holds immense promise for the future of learning, provided that the family and the community will prudently monitor its use.

To paraphrase an old saying, "Like thesis, like paper." A muddled, incoherent thesis will generate an equally muddled and incoherent paper.

4a–3 Placing the thesis

Some variation in placement of the thesis does exist, but most teachers distinctly prefer it as the final sentence of the initial paragraph. Here are three examples of theses introduced in this customary place:

He is a vagabond in aristocratic clothing--
shabby but grand. As he scurries along in
his cutaway and derby hat, aided by a cane,
he is obviously a tramp, but a tramp with the
impeccable manners of a dandy. He is willing
to tackle any job, but seldom does it properly. He often falls in love, but usually
the affair sours in the end. His only ene-
mies are pompous people in places of authority. The general public adores him because

Thesis   he is everyman of all times. <u>Charlie
Chaplin's "Tramp" has remained a favorite
international character because he is a
character with whom the average person
can empathize.</u>

A quarter of a million babies are born each
year with birth defects. Of these defects,
only 20 percent are hereditary. Most of them
could have been prevented because they are

Thesis   the tragic results of poor prenatal care. <u>An
unfavorable fetal environment, such as can be</u>

> caused by malnutrition in the mother or her
> use of drugs, is a primary cause of many
> kinds of birth defects.
>
> Theodor Seuss Geisel wrote and illustrated
> zany children's books, usually in verse,
> under the pseudonym of "Dr. Seuss." He
> wrote twenty-six best-sellers over a period
> of thirty years, and they are all still in
> print. In story after story, this author
> creates a topsy-turvy world where the normal
> becomes aberrant and the aberrant becomes

Thesis normal. The simple vocabulary and rhyming
> lines of Dr. Seuss's books make them easy for
> children to read, but the author's illustra-
> tions are primarily responsible for the imag-
> inative flair in his work.

4a–4 Title of the research paper

No magic formula exists to tell you when to decide on the final wording of your title. Some writers like to work from a title whereas others prefer to word the title after the paper is written. Regardless of when you decide on your title, be sure to make it informative, clear, and specific. For instance, the title "Downward Spiral" gives no clue to the subject of the research. The title "Drugs" is not much better since it is too general. A better title is "Why Women Should Not Take Narcotic Drugs During Their Pregnancies." Usually your thesis statement will provide an excellent springboard for your title.

4b The outline

The outline is an ordered listing of the topics covered in the paper. Varying in complexity and style, outlines are nevertheless useful to both the

writer and the reader. The writer who writes from an outline is less likely
to stray from the point or to commit a structural error such as overdevel-
oping one topic while skimping on another. The reader, on the other
hand, benefits from the outline as a complete and detailed table of contents.

4b–1 Visual conventions of the outline

The conventions of formal outlining require that main ideas be designated by Roman numerals such as I, II, III, IV, V. Subideas branching off
from the main ideas are designated by capital letters A, B, C, D, and so on.
Subdivisions of these subideas are designated by Arabic numerals 1, 2, 3,
4, and so forth. Minor ideas are designated by lower-case letters a, b, c, d,
and so on. Here is an example of the proper form of an outline:

```
I.   Main idea

     A.   Subidea

     B.   Subidea

          1.   Division of a subidea

          2.   Division of a subidea

               a.   Minor idea

               b.   Minor idea

II.  Main idea
```

The presumption behind this sort of arrangement is obvious: namely,
that students will not merely generalize but will support their contentions
and propositions with examples and details. Indeed, that is exactly what
the writer of a research paper is expected to do—to make assertions that
are supported by concrete examples and specific details. If you have done
your research badly and have not been diligent in gathering specific facts
about the topic, this deficiency will now become painfully obvious.

Notice that every category must be subdivided at least once since it is
impossible to divide anything into fewer than two parts. An outline dividing the subject into three or four levels—that is, down to examples or
details—is generally adequate for most college-level research papers. If
further subdivisions are necessary, the format is as follows:

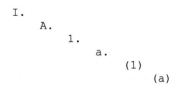

The basic principle remains the same: larger ideas or elements are stacked to the left, with smaller ideas and elements to the right.

4b–2 Equal ranking in outline entries

The logic of an outline requires that each entry be based on the same organizing principle as another entry of equal rank. All capital-letter entries consequently must be equivalent in importance and derived from the same organizing principle. Notice the lack of equal ranking in the following example:

```
I.  Rousseau gave the people a new government to work

    toward.

    A.  It would be a government based on the general

        will.

    B.  The new government would serve the people in-

        stead of the people serving the government.

    C.  The people tore down the Bastille.
```

The C entry is out of place because it is not of equal rank with entries A and B. A and B are subideas that characterize the new government proposed by Rousseau; C is a statement that describes the revolt of the French people against the old government.

4b–3 Parallelism in outline entries

The clarity and readability of an outline are improved immeasurably if its entries are worded in similar grammatical form. Notice the lack of parallelism in the following outline:

```
I.  The uses of the laser in the military

    A.  For range-finding

    B.  For surveillance

    C.  To illuminate the enemy's position
```

Entries A and B consist of a preposition followed by a noun, while entry C is worded as an infinitive phrase. C should therefore be reworded to make it grammatically similar to entries A and B:

```
I.  The uses of the laser in the military

    A.  For range-finding

    B.  For surveillance

    C.  For illuminating an enemy's position
```

The outline now is easier to read because its entries are grammatically parallel.

4b–4 Types of outlines

The three main types of outlines are the topic outline, the sentence outline, and the paragraph outline. The formats of these different outlines cannot be mixed or combined; one type of outline must be used exclusively.

a. The topic outline

The topic outline words each entry as a phrase, breaking down the subject into major subheadings. Topic outlines are particularly useful for outlining relatively simple subjects. Here is a topic outline of the paper on Rasputin:

```
                    Rasputin's Other Side


Thesis: After six decades of being judged a demoniacal

        libertine, Rasputin now deserves to be viewed

        from another point of view--as a man who was

        intensely religious, who passionately desired

        peace, and who was deeply devoted to his family

        and friends.

    I.  The ambiguity of the real Rasputin

        A.  His birth

        B.  Popular historical view

            1.  His supporters

            2.  His detractors
```

```
 II.   Rasputin's religious feelings

       A.  His rich nature and exuberant vitality

       B.  His simple peasant faith

III.   Rasputin's desire for peace in Russia

       A.  His concern for the Russian underdog

           1.  His loyalty to the peasantry

           2.  His opposition to anti-Semitism

       B.  His opposition to all wars

 IV.   Rasputin's gentle, compassionate side

       A.  His kindness to the Romanovs

       B.  His love for family
```

Notice that the thesis of the paper is placed as a separate entry immediately after the title. It is also customary to omit "introduction" and "conclusion" entries.

b. The sentence outline

The sentence outline uses a complete grammatical sentence for each entry. (Some instructors allow the entries to be worded as questions, but most prefer declarative sentences.) Sentence outlines are especially well-suited for complex subjects, the detailed entries giving the writer an excellent overview of the paper. Here is a sentence outline of the paper on Rasputin:

```
                 Rasputin's Other Side



Thesis: After six decades of being judged a demoniacal

        libertine, Rasputin now deserves to be viewed

        from another point of view--as a man who was

        intensely religious, who passionately desired

        peace, and who was deeply devoted to his family

        and friends.
```

I. The real Rasputin is difficult to discover.

    A. The birth of Rasputin coincided with a "shooting star."

    B. The popular historical view of Rasputin portrays him as primarily evil.

        1. Supporters called him a spiritual leader.

        2. Detractors called him a satyr and charged that his depraved faithful were merely in awe of his sexual endowments.

II. Rasputin had intense religious feelings.

    A. He had a rich nature and exuberant vitality.

    B. He had a simple peasant faith in God.

III. Rasputin's passionate desire for peace in Russia revealed itself in several ways.

    A. He was concerned for the Russian underdog.

        1. He wanted a Tsar who would stand mainly for the peasantry.

        2. He spoke out boldly against anti-Semitism.

    B. Because of his humanitarian spirit, he was opposed to all wars.

IV. Rasputin had a gentle, compassionate side.

    A. He showed great kindness to the Romanovs.

    B. Maria Rasputin tells of her father's love for his family.

c. The paragraph outline

The paragraph outline records each entry as a complete paragraph, thus providing a condensed version of the paper. This form is useful mainly for long papers whose individual sections can be summarized in whole paragraphs but is seldom recommended by instructors for ordinary college papers. Here is the Rasputin paper in the form of a paragraph outline:

Rasputin's Other Side

Thesis: After six decades of being judged a demoniacal
        libertine, Rasputin now deserves to be viewed
        from another point of view--as a man who was
        intensely religious, who passionately desired
        peace, and who was deeply devoted to his family
        and friends.

I. Rasputin himself always attached great signifi-
    cance to the fact that at the time of his birth, a
    shooting star was seen streaking across the hori-
    zon. He saw this phenomenon as an omen that he
    was fated to have influence and special powers.
    The popular historical view of Rasputin paints
    him primarily as evil. In his day, however, he
    attracted numerous supporters who viewed him as
    their spiritual leader. But he also had many
    detractors who called him a satyr and accused
    his followers of sexual depravity.

II. Rasputin had intense religious feelings. He was
    so filled with exuberance and vitality that he
    could stay awake until the early hours of the
    morning, dancing and drinking in frenzied reli-
    gious fervor. He did not have the theology of
    a sophisticated church cleric, but rather he

expressed his religion in the simple terms of a
Russian peasant.

III.   Rasputin's passionate desire for peace in Russia
revealed itself in several ways. For instance, he
was concerned for such Russian underdogs as the
peasants and the Jews, always encouraging the Tsar
to protect these unfortunate groups. Also, his
humanitarian and pacifist nature made him a determined opponent of all wars.

IV.   Rasputin had a gentle, compassionate side. He was
completely devoted to the Tsar's family and was
known to have had a calming influence on the hemophiliac son of the Tsar. Maria Rasputin gives a
glowing report of her father's kindness and love.

4b–5   The decimal notation of an outline

Other outline forms exist that use various methods of indenting, labelling,
and spacing. One form that has been gaining favor in business and science
is the decimal outline. Based on the decimal accounting system, this outline form permits an infinite number of possible subdivisions through the
simple addition of another decimal place. Here is the body of the
Rasputin paper notated in the decimal outline form:

```
                    Rasputin's Other Side


    1.   The ambiguity of the real Rasputin
         1.1.  His birth
         1.2.  Popular historical view
               1.2.1.  His supporters
               1.2.2.  His detractors

    2.   Rasputin's religious feelings
         2.1.  His rich nature and exuberant vitality
         2.2.  His simple peasant faith
```

```
3.  Rasputin's desire for peace in Russia
    3.1.  His concern for the Russian underdog
          3.1.1.  His loyalty to the peasantry
          3.1.2.  His opposition to anti-Semitism
    3.2.  His opposition to all wars

4.  Rasputin's gentle, compassionate side
    4.1.  His kindness to the Romanovs
    4.2.  His love for family
```

Notice that though a decimal notation is used, this outline arranges its entries on the same indentation principle used in other outlines, with larger ideas stacked to the left, and smaller ideas to the right.

4b–6 Which kind of outline should you use?

If you have a choice, if you are a beginning writer, and if your research has uncovered much detail on your subject, do not hesitate a minute: use a detailed sentence outline. Develop it at least down to the third level—the level of Arabic numerals. In doing so you actually erect a kind of scaffolding for the essay. To write the rough draft, you merely transcribe from the outline, fill in the blanks, insert transitions and connectives, and you have an essay.

The main entries of this outline should be the topic sentences of various paragraphs. Its details should be exactly the kind you intend to use to support the topic sentence. Here, as an example, is an outlined paragraph from a sentence outline of a paper on Agatha Christie's fictional sleuth, Hercule Poirot:

```
I.  Hercule's unique personality and character set him

    apart from other fictional detectives.

    A.  His physical appearance was unique.

        1.  He was 5'4", had a black handlebar mustache,

            an egg-shaped head, and catlike eyes that

            grew greener as the solution to a crime drew

            near.

        2.  He wore a black coat, pin-striped pants, a

            bow tie, shiny black boots, and, usually, a

            coat and muffler.
```

Here is the paragraph as it appeared in the essay:

```
    Hercule's unique personality and character set him
apart from other fictional detectives.  One of the memo-
rable features of his personality and character was his
physical appearance.  He was "a diminutive five foot
four inches tall and slender."⁷  His hair was an "unre-
pentant" black, neatly groomed with hair tonic.  His
upper lip displayed his pride and joy and his more dis-
tinctive feature, a small black handlebar mustache.⁸  He
had catlike eyes that grew greener as the solution to a
crime drew near and a head the shape of an egg.  Thus
Poirot has been referred to as a "mustachioed Humpty
Dumpty."⁹  This "extraordinary looking little man, who
carried himself with immense dignity," almost always
wore the same outfit, consisting of a black jacket,
striped pants, a bow tie, and, in all but the hottest
weather, an overcoat and muffler.  He also wore patent
leather boots that almost always displayed a dazzling
shine.¹⁰
```

Notice the close correspondence between the outline and the final paragraph. First, the main entry of the outline is exactly the same as the topic sentence of the paragraph. Second, subidea A is fleshed out and used in the paragraph to introduce the details that follow. Third, the details in the outline are used nearly word-for-word in the paragraph. Naturally, there is more material in the paragraph than in the outline, which is not surprising, since the second is a short-hand version of the first.

If you are going to be following an outline as you write, this kind is especially useful. Once drafted, it becomes a condensed version of the essay. Any paragraph is easy to write when you know exactly what its main point must be and what details it should contain. That and more is provided by the detailed sentence outline.

5

DOING
THE RESEARCH

5a What information to look for

Library materials—the sources you actually will cite as supporting references in your paper—typically consist of book chapters or essays, magazine articles, journal articles, treatises, pamphlets, newspaper articles, and tape or disc transcriptions. These materials may be in printed form or on microfilm, microfiche, computer disk, or tape. Exactly what kind of material you will need to look for will depend largely on your topic, thesis, and even the point of view you will use in the paper. Generally speaking, however, all library materials may be usefully grouped into three broad categories: single-fact information, general information, and in-depth information.

5a–1 Single-fact information

Single-fact information answers such specific and factual questions as: In what year was Julius Caesar born? What percentage of students admitted into Harvard Medical School in 1988 were Hispanic? How many cantons does Switzerland have? Answers to these and similar single-fact questions can be found in dictionaries, almanacs, encyclopedias, novels, reports, magazines, or even telephone books. To get the answers to such questions you can always ask your reference librarian, who is specially trained in information management, storage, and retrieval. Some libraries even have a reference librarian available to answer readers' queries over the telephone.

5a–2 General information

General information sources are those that provide an overview of a subject or a particular topic. They can also steer you to important in-depth sources. For example, if you were writing a paper on Zionism, the movement to create a Jewish national state in Palestine, the *Columbia Encyclopedia* would be a good general information source for a summary history. A brief article will answer such general questions as: When did the movement start? What brought it about? Who were its leaders? Where does the movement stand today? Encyclopedias and other general information sources usually are found in a reference room or reference section in most college libraries. (For further guidelines about general information sources, see Section 5e.)

5a–3 In-depth information

In-depth information is derived from sources that provide detailed coverage of a specific topic. For example, *Admiral of the Ocean Sea* by naval historian Samuel Eliot Morrison provides in-depth information about the voyages and life and times of Christopher Columbus. *The Soul of a New Machine* by Tracy Kidder gives an in-depth look at the process of building a new computer system. In-depth information usually is found in books, since many topics are too complex to be detailed in any other form. But essays and articles can also be useful sources of in-depth information, especially about new or particularly focused topics.

Research papers typically will blend all three kinds of information—single-fact, general, and in-depth—the proportion between them varying with the nature and complexity of the particular topic.

5b Where to look for information

Libraries differ markedly in their cataloguing and indexing of available material. Some offer sophisticated computer cataloguing of all available sources. The majority, however, rely heavily on printed lists and card catalogs. We shall have more to say about computer searches in Section 5c and in the General and Specialized Reference Appendix. But for those of you who must use a traditional library, we suggest the following steps:

■ To find the subheadings related to your subject, scanning an encyclopedia article on it is usually a helpful first step. For example, if you were researching ancient Egyptian art, the encyclopedia entry "Egypt" would list "Mesopotamia," "Predynastic Egypt," and "ceramic art" as related subheadings. "Fascism," "Italy," "dictatorship," and "totalitarianism" are related subheadings on the topic of Benito Mussolini. "Abigail Adams," "Mercy Warren," "Elizabeth Stanton," and "Susan B. Anthony" are possible subheadings on the early feminist movement in the United States. In searching the card catalog for sources, look under both the main headings as well as the related subheadings. If your library uses the Library of Congress System, consult the two-volume *Library of Congress Subject Headings* (LCSH) for a list of subject headings.

■ Consult the appendix of this book for an annotated listing of useful reference sources.

■ Check the bibliography at the end of encyclopedia articles.

■ For definitions of technical or controversial terms, check the various standard dictionaries.

■ Check the card catalog under the subject heading as well as under any cross-listings noted on the cards.

■ Check the *Book Review Digest* for summaries of the contents of reviewed books.

■ Check the various *Who's Who* volumes for information about noteworthy people.

■   For information about places and countries, consult gazetteers and atlases.

Aside from the card catalog and general references such as encyclopedias, the various indexes to published information are useful sources to consult at the beginning of your research. Basically, these are classified under two broad headings: general indexes and specialized indexes.

5b–1 General indexes

A general index catalogues information published in magazines, newspapers, and journals. Up-to-date information on a subject can be found in recently published magazines such as *Time, Psychology Today, Ebony*; newspapers such as the *New York Times, Washington Post, Atlanta Constitution*; or journals such as *Kenyon Review, Scientific American, Quarterly Review of Biology*. Magazines and newspapers typically cover topical subjects; journals have a narrower and more specialized focus. Articles in these publications are not indexed in the card catalog but rather in either bound general indexes or computerized data systems. Some of these indexes not only list the published article, but also provide an abstract or summary of it. The *Readers' Guide to Periodical Literature* (1905–present) is the most popular general index, covering more than 180 popular periodicals. It is organized alphabetically by topic, with each relevant article listed below the heading. Figure 5–1 shows a facsimile of a typical page, with our editorial explanations added.

Magazine Index catalogues articles from twice as many magazines as *Readers' Guide* but its listings begin only in 1976. A current reel lists only articles for the last five years. Articles are arranged by both subject and author.

Indexes to newspapers are invaluable for tracking down news articles about a subject. Usually the index will give the exact location of each article, an indication of its length, and even a brief summary of the content. Articles are listed by subject. Figure 5–2 (p. 52) is a sample entry from the *New York Times Index*, with our editorial explanations added.

5b–2 Specialized indexes

Specialized indexes catalogue information on specific subjects. For example, the *Social Sciences Index* is a useful source for articles in the social sciences; for material on the humanities or education, the *Humanities Index* and the *Education Index* should be consulted. Other specialized indexes are listed in our appendix, pp. 301–47. Ask your librarian to direct you to the index most appropriate to your subject and to help you interpret its listings. As an example of a specialized index, we include a facsimile page from the *Art Index*, which alphabetically lists works by both author and subject. If you were researching, say, the political influences on art, you could consult the *Art Index* under the heading of "Art and politics." Figure 5–3

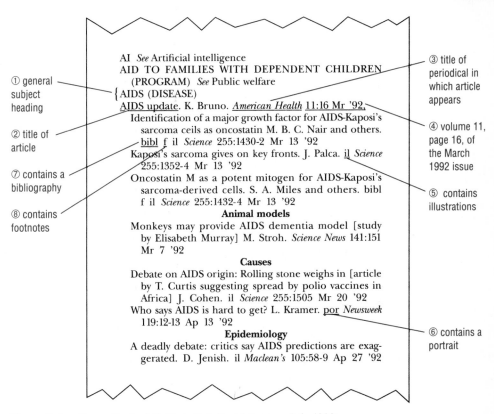

Figure 5–1   From *Readers' Guide to Periodical Literature,* July 1992

(p. 53) shows the page as it would appear in facsimile form, with our editorial explanations added.

For a paper on child abuse, you would investigate an index such as *Psychological Abstracts,* consisting of numbered non-evaluative summaries of periodical literature in psychology. After looking up "Child Abuse" in the brief index following the general category of "Physical and Psychological Disorders," the entry in Figure 5–4 (p. 53) would appear. We have added our editorial explanations.

The *Social Sciences Index* is an excellent source of information on a social science topic such as, say, the Kurd population in Iraq. Figure 5–5 (p. 54) is a reproduced page from the index, with our editorial explanations added.

For a paper on the novel *Gone With the Wind* by Margaret Mitchell, consult the *Book Review Index* (BRI), which catalogues reviews of thousands of books, periodicals, and books-on-tape. Entries are arranged in single alphabetical sequence by author (or by title if there is no primary author). A separate title index also is provided for those readers who have incomplete author information. A reproduced page from the index appears on p. 54 (Figure 5–6), with our editorial explanations added.

main heading

other suggested heading(s)

brief summary of article

{WATER POLLUTION. See also
{Acid Rain

Morocco appeals to Britain, France, Spain and Portugal for aid in cleaning up 37 million gallons of oil from abandoned Iranian tanker Kharg-5 that threatens its coast; France to send experts to assess spill (S), Ja, 1,I,2:3

Casablanca port authority says about 27,000 tons of oil have spilled from abandoned Iranian tanker and that oil still leaks from vessel; oceanographer Jacques-Yves Cousteau warns of ecological disaster (S), Ja 1,I,2:4

Oil cleanup specialists try to patch up crippled Iranian supertanker and protect Moroccan coastline from 37 million gallons of spilled crude oil that has formed 108-square-mile slick in Atlantic Ocean; map (S), Ja 2,A,9:1\

Barge loaded with 350,000 gallons of gasoline hits bridge and ruptures, spilling gasoline into Monongahela River in Pennsylvania (S), Ja 2,A,16:1

Helicopters spray chemical agents on 100-square-mile oil slick and cleanup crews vacuum some of muck from surfaces of Atlantic Ocean in efforts to protect Morocco's coastline; Morocco says about 19 million gallons of crude oil have spewed from crippled Iranian supertanker; map; photo (M), Ja 3,A,3:3

US Coast Guard spokesman says that commanding officer of service's oil-spill response team will visit Morocco to see if US could aid in oil spill containment and cleanup efforts (S), Ja 3,A,3:6

(S) indicates short article [(M) indicates an article of medium length; (L) indicates a long article]

date, section, page, column (January 1, section I, page 2, column 4)

Figure 5–2 From *New York Times Index*, 1990

5c Using the computer in your search

The computer terminal, consisting of a video screen and typewriter keyboard, is the focal point for researchers working in a computerized library. "User-friendly" terminals allow you to call up a subject heading, bibliographic information connected with written works, or, with on-line databases, the actual works themselves. To find all subheadings of a given subject, say *apartheid*, you typically type in the library's own access number, APARTHEID, and then press DISPLAY/RECORD, followed by SEND. A list of all subheadings related to your subject will appear on the screen. Type in the title of a book and its card catalog information will be displayed: call number, author, publisher, publication date, number of pages, as well as related subject headings. A note on the screen will also tell you if the library owns a copy of the book. For a display of all the works written by a certain author, simply type in the author's name.

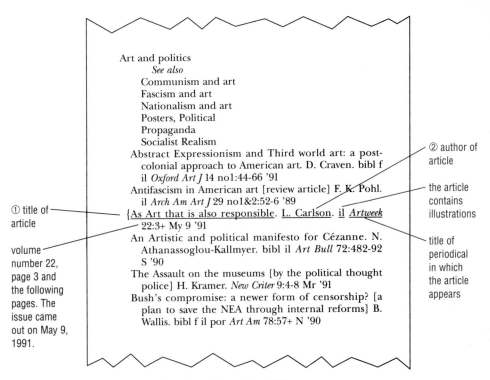

Figure 5–3 From *Art Index*, October–November 1991

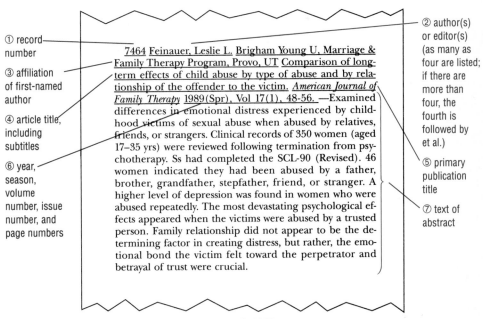

Figure 5–4 From *Psychological Abstracts*, March 1991

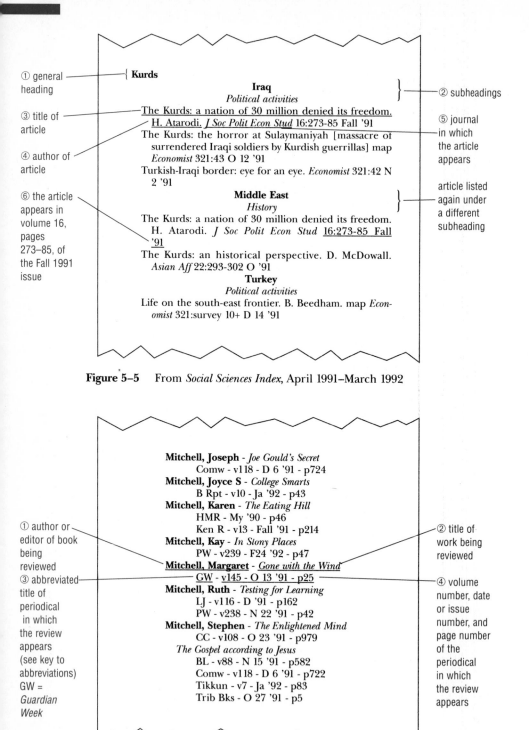

① general heading

② subheadings

③ title of article

⑤ journal in which the article appears

④ author of article

⑥ the article appears in volume 16, pages 273–85, of the Fall 1991 issue

article listed again under a different subheading

Kurds

Iraq
Political activities
The Kurds: a nation of 30 million denied its freedom. H. Atarodi. *J Soc Polit Econ Stud* 16:273-85 Fall '91
The Kurds: the horror at Sulaymaniyah [massacre of surrendered Iraqi soldiers by Kurdish guerrillas] map *Economist* 321:43 O 12 '91
Turkish-Iraqi border: eye for an eye. *Economist* 321:42 N 2 '91

Middle East
History
The Kurds: a nation of 30 million denied its freedom. H. Atarodi. *J Soc Polit Econ Stud* 16:273-85 Fall '91
The Kurds: an historical perspective. D. McDowall. *Asian Aff* 22:293-302 O '91

Turkey
Political activities
Life on the south-east frontier. B. Beedham. map *Economist* 321:survey 10+ D 14 '91

Figure 5–5   From *Social Sciences Index,* April 1991–March 1992

① author or editor of book being reviewed

③ abbreviated title of periodical in which the review appears (see key to abbreviations) GW = *Guardian Week*

② title of work being reviewed

④ volume number, date or issue number, and page number of the periodical in which the review appears

Mitchell, Joseph - *Joe Gould's Secret*
  Comw - v118 - D 6 '91 - p724
Mitchell, Joyce S - *College Smarts*
  B Rpt - v10 - Ja '92 - p43
Mitchell, Karen - *The Eating Hill*
  HMR - My '90 - p46
  Ken R - v13 - Fall '91 - p214
Mitchell, Kay - *In Stony Places*
  PW - v239 - F24 '92 - p47
Mitchell, Margaret - *Gone with the Wind*
  GW - v145 - O 13 '91 - p25
Mitchell, Ruth - *Testing for Learning*
  LJ - v116 - D '91 - p162
  PW - v238 - N 22 '91 - p42
Mitchell, Stephen - *The Enlightened Mind*
  CC - v108 - O 23 '91 - p979
  The Gospel according to Jesus
  BL - v88 - N 15 '91 - p582
  Comw - v118 - D 6 '91 - p722
  Tikkun - v7 - Ja '92 - p83
  Trib Bks - O 27 '91 - p5

Figure 5–6   From *Book Review Index,* January–April 1992

Computerized libraries also can retrieve vast quantities of information stored in a database. Basically, a *database* is a complex program for the computerized storage and management of information. Databases make entire books, magazine articles, or abstracts available to a researcher via a keyboard and terminal. Most databases are menu-driven—that is, the user is prompted by a variety of choices narrowing to the most appropriate selection. Free of charge in most libraries, on-line general indexes are a good first step to begin your search. Most are user-friendly and provide listings of humanities, social science, education, general science, and business journals. For an in-depth listing of print and database indexes, see the General and Specialized Reference Appendix.

Magazine Summary and *Periodical Abstracts* represent the newest trend in on-line computer catalogs. These computerized indexes list the titles of journal articles and book reviews, sometimes summarizing content in an abstract or paragraph, and provide a feature to help a researcher narrow a topic. For example, the MLA International Bibliography lists critical documents on literature, language, linguistics, and folklore; Psychlit index summarizes the literature in psychology and related fields. Help sheets explaining the features and operating procedures of these general indexes usually are provided by libraries.

As you browse through either *Magazine Summary* or *Periodical Abstracts*, you can enter two headings to narrow a subject. For instance, you can type in the words SOLAR ENERGY AND HOUSING, and the index will provide specific references to this topic.

Another general index offered by many libraries is Infotrac, which catalogues articles published over the last six months in newspapers and periodicals such as the *New York Times*. Infotrac does not provide summaries of articles, but its search features can help a researcher narrow a topic. Informative help sheets are also available with this computerized index. Among the many databases that are available on-line to libraries, the following are the most common:

ERIC: ERIC is an acronym for the Educational Research Information Center, a network of clearinghouses that gather and produce unpublished materials such as project reports, dissertations, and research findings. Each of the sixteen ERIC clearinghouses specialize in one of these subjects: career education; counseling and personnel services; early childhood education; educational management; handicapped and gifted children; higher education; information resources; junior colleges; languages and linguistics; reading and communication skills; rural education and small schools; science, mathematics, and environmental education; social studies and social science education; teacher education; tests, measurement, and evaluation; and urban education.

BRS: Bibliographic Retrieval Services offers access to over thirty databases.

Mead Data Control:	Mead distributes and produces LEXIS and NEXIS. The first is an enormous library of legal information, including millions of court opinions and federal and state statutes. NEXIS is a news retrieval service.
New York Times Information Service:	Abstracts from over twenty news services along with many special and general interest publications.
OCLC:	Online Computer Library Center, based in Columbus, Ohio, is a database listing the collections of over 1000 member libraries. OCLC also includes an on-line listing of all Library of Congress materials in English catalogued since 1968. Many member libraries have interlibrary loan arrangements that permit a student to obtain a needed book from the collection of another school.

This list gives you an idea of the kinds of databases available to many libraries. Ask your librarian about the facilities of your own library. Although most of the computerized indexes offered by your library will be free, a few such as DIALOG levy a steep per-minute charge that can be rather costly. You will want to make sure that such an index is essential to your research needs before incurring the expense. DIALOG provides an extensive catalog of useful information, but the persistent researcher can usually ferret out much the same material from one of the free sources. Ask your librarian whether the use of a fee-based index is necessary for your particular topic.

While the actual response to a database search request will naturally vary from one library to another, the following are fairly typical.

5c–1 Sample subject display

You have asked the computer for a list of subject headings on "Chinese literature." Here is the result:

```
T S CHINESE LITERATURE
                              SUMMARY DISPLAY
RESULT:    57 headings.
```

The computer indicates that there are fifty-seven subject headings on Chinese literature. You can ask the computer to display these subjects ten headings at a time:

```
S 1-10
                              AUTHORITY DISPLAY
    2. Chinese literature
    3.     --To 221 B.C.
```

```
     4.       --Chin and Han dynasties, 221
              B.C.--220 A.D.
     5.       --Three kingdoms, 220-265
     6.       --220-589
     7.       --Chin dynasty, 265-419
     8.       --Northern Sung dynasty, 420-479
     9.       --Sui dynasty, 581-618
    10.       --Tang dynasty, 618-907
```

5c–2 Sample bibliographic display

You can also ask the computer to tell you what books are available on the subject heading you identified.

```
F S CHINESE LITERATURE
                         SUMMARY DISPLAY
RESULT:    95 bibliographic items.
```

The computer indicates that ninety-five items are listed under that heading in the bibliographic file. You can now ask the computer to display the full bibliographic record of any of these items. Here is an example:

```
S 1
                    BIBLIOGRAPHIC DISPLAY


     Mao's harvest : voices from China's
new generation / edited by Helen F. Siu and
Zelda Stern. New York : Oxford University
Press, 1983.
         lvi, 231 p. : ill. ; 24 cm.
     ISBN 0195032748 : $$17.95
         1. Chinese literature--20th
century.  2. China--Politics and
government--1949-1976--Addresses, essays,
lectures.  3. China--History--1949-1976--
Literary collections.  I. Siu, Helen F.
II. Stern, Zelda.
     ocm08-763349
```

Notice that the computerized entries are similar to those of the card catalog.

5c–3 Sample database source display

You have initiated a database search on the subject of "education and nuclear war." Here is one printout:

```
DIALOG File 11: PSYCINFO-67-85/NOV (Copr.
Am. Psych. Assn.)
```

```
72-23763
  A decisionmaking approach to nuclear
education. Special Issue, Education and the
threat of nuclear war.
  Snow, Roberta; Goodman, Lisa
  Harvard Medical School, Boston
  Harvard Educational Review, 1984 Aug Vol
54 (3)
321-328 CODEN: HVERAP ISSN: 00178055
  Journal Announcement, 7209
  Language: ENGLISH Document Type: JOURNAL
ARTICLE
  Describes a US senior high school
curriculum that addresses 4 areas: personal
values as a basis for political views,
technological aspects of the nuclear arms
race, the history of the nuclear arms race,
and action for social change. The program's
content, focus, and structure are detailed,
and its effects on student attitudes are
discussed. Excerpts from student essays are
presented, and examples of appropriate class
projects are suggested.
  Descriptors: NUCLEAR WAR .(34567); STUDENT
ATTITUDES .(50300); EDUCATION .(16000);
CURRICULUM .(12810); HIGH SCHOOL STUDENTS .
(22930); ADOLESCENCE .(00920)
  Identifiers: high school curriculum,
decision-making approach to nuclear
education, high school students
  Section Headings, 3530 .(CURRICULUM
PROGRAMS TEACHING METHODS)
```

The computer has given you a summary of the source. Sometimes full articles can be displayed.

5d   Assembling a working bibliography

The bibliography is a list of sources on the research topic. The *working bibliography* is made up of those sources consulted for information; the *final bibliography* is an alphabetical list of those sources actually used in the paper.

The working bibliography is assembled as the researcher scans the references and card catalog for information on the subject. Promising sources are noted down on 3 × 5 bibliography cards (to be distinguished from the 4 × 6 note cards). The bibliography card should contain information about the sources to be consulted, along with a brief note on why they are likely to be useful. (See examples on pp. 59–61.)

Some instructors do not require that students use cards for a working bibliography, merely that they have one, however compiled. Others insist that the cards be used in the form described here.

If you have a choice, use the bibliography cards. Because they are portable and can be easily arranged in alphabetical order, they are generally more useful than a notebook or scraps of paper. Each source actually *used* will be recorded on two kinds of cards: the title will appear on the smaller bibliography card; notes on the source will appear on the larger note card. If the source merely is checked but not used, it will appear only on the working bibliography card. Once the source is eliminated from contention, its card can be placed in an inactive pack.

- Record each source in ink on a separate 3 × 5 card.
- Use the same form on the bibliography cards as will be used later in the final bibliography. This format makes it possible to prepare the final bibliography by simply transcribing from the cards those titles actually used in writing the paper. The following basic information must be listed on the cards:

> Name of author(s)
> Title of work
> Facts of publication
> Page(s) of information

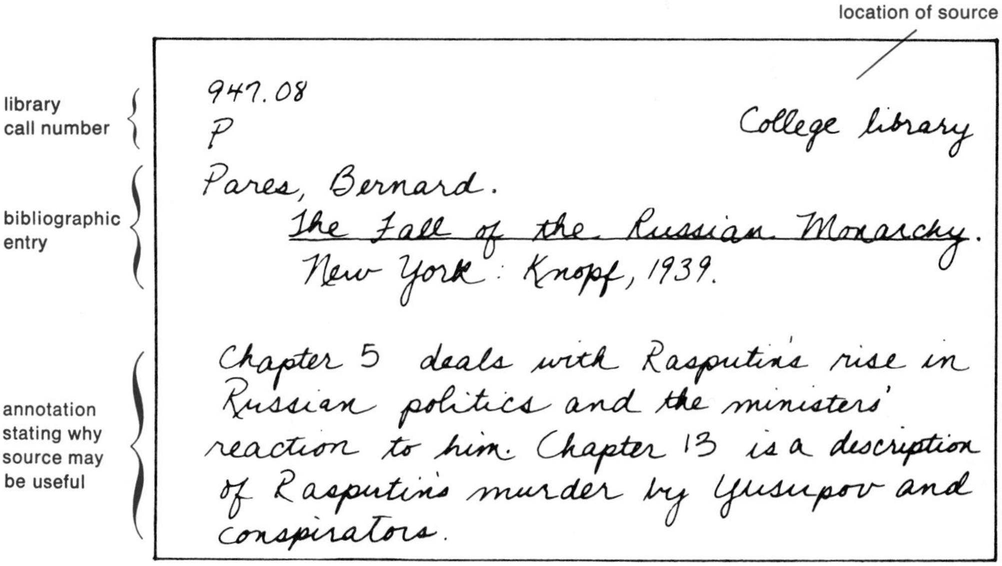

Figure 5–7 Bibliography card for a book

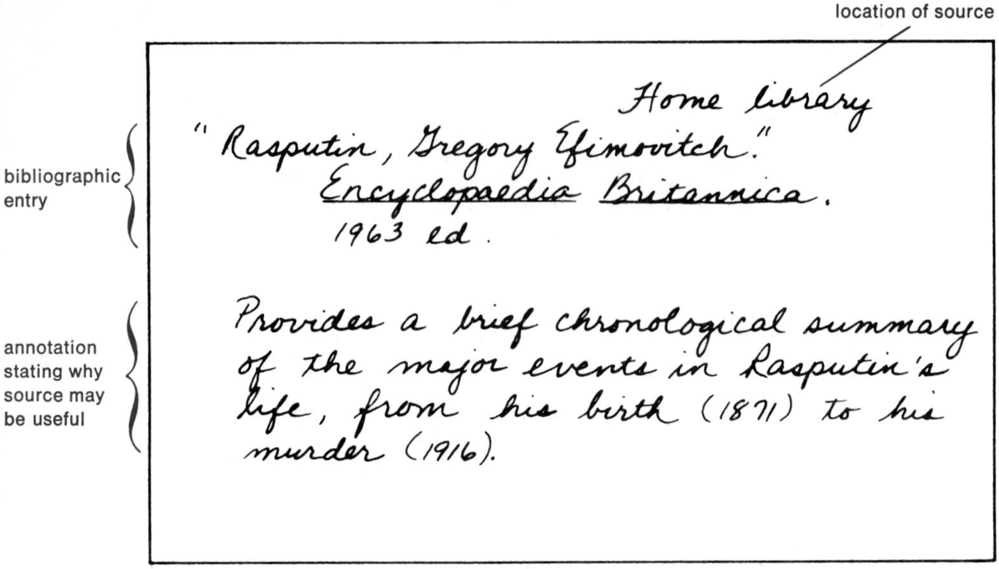

location of source

bibliographic
entry

> "Rasputin, Gregory Efimovitch."
>   *Home library*
>   *Encyclopaedia Britannica.*
>   1963 ed.

annotation
stating why
source may
be useful

> Provides a brief chronological summary
> of the major events in Rasputin's
> life, from his birth (1871) to his
> murder (1916).

Figure 5–8   Bibliography card for an encyclopedia article

Figure 5–9   Bibliography card for a periodical

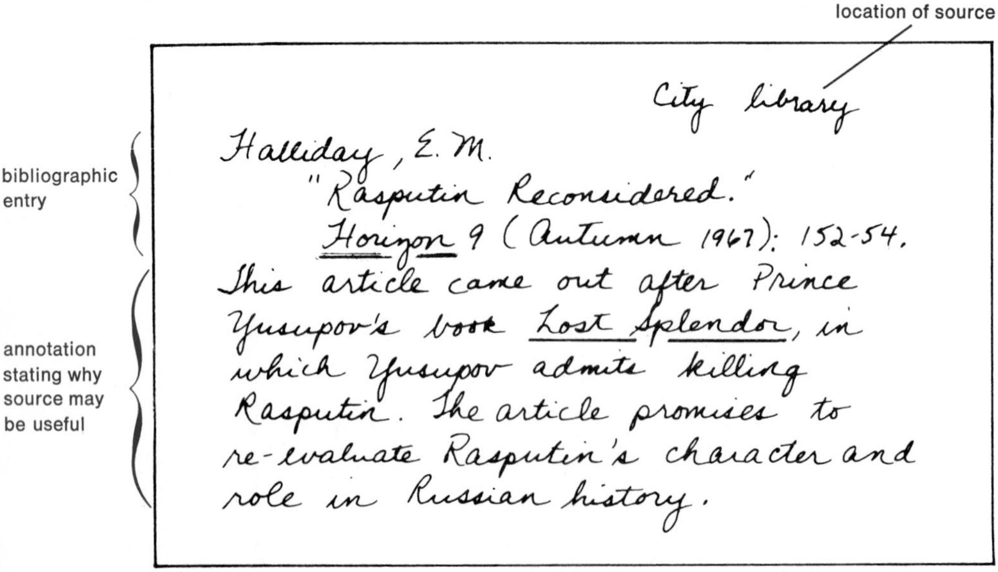

location of source

bibliographic
entry

> Halliday, E. M.
>   "Rasputin Reconsidered."
>   *Horizon* 9 (Autumn 1967): 152-54.
>   *City library*

annotation
stating why
source may
be useful

> This article came out after Prince
> Yusupov's book *Lost Splendor*, in
> which Yusupov admits killing
> Rasputin. The article promises to
> re-evaluate Rasputin's character and
> role in Russian history.

location of source

Microfilm from
L.A. Times

bibliographic
entry

" *Interview with Rasputin's Daughter.*"
Los Angeles Times 9 June 1976,
Sec.1: 1, 10, 11.

annotation
stating why
source may
be useful

Interviewed as a dying old woman,
Maria Rasputin insists that her
father was a gentle, good man, subject
to many temptations.

Figure 5–10   Bibliography card for a newspaper article

- In the upper right-hand corner of the card, name the library or place where the source was found, as for example, "Main City Library."
- In the upper left-hand corner of the card, cite the library call number of the source, so that it can be found easily even if reshelved (see Figure 5–7).

Generally you will end up with many more sources in the working bibliography than are listed in the final bibliography. This is as it should be. Many sources will be consulted, but few chosen. False starts and dead-end trails are to be expected. Books will lure one on with a promising table of contents and title, but once skimmed, will prove to be excessively technical, dated, or beside the point. The researcher must ignore the irrelevant and worthless sources while tracking down those articles, essays, and books that promise to be useful.

5e   Selecting your sources

Researchers seldom have time to faithfully read every book or article written about their subject. Instead, the experienced researcher will initially skim a source to determine its usefulness. In skimming, one searches for major ideas in a piece of writing merely to confirm its appropriateness as a research source. If an initial skimming indicates the source is helpful and to the point, it can be read carefully later. However, if the source appears to be farfetched, ponderous, dated, irrelevant, or otherwise useless, then it should be set aside and more promising leads pursued. Do not, however, destroy the bibliography card of the discarded source since you may wish to return to it later.

Skimming, like most skills, improves with practice. Here are some hints on how to skim a piece of writing for major ideas:

- Glance at the preface of a book. Often an author will state there what the book concerns. Likewise, an afterword often will recount the major ideas of a book.

- Look up the subject in the index of the book. Frequently one can tell from the number of pages devoted to the subject whether or not the book is likely to be useful. For instance, if you are looking in a Russian history book for information on Rasputin, and see from its index that it contains only two pages about him, you should probably move on to some other source.

- Read the chapter headings. Often these will reveal what the chapter regards. Similarly, the major ideas in a chapter are sometimes summarized in headnotes to its various sections.

- Read the first and last two sentences in a paragraph to find out what information it contains. Generally, the main idea of a paragraph is stated in its initial sentences and summed up in its final sentences.

- Glance at the opening paragraph of an article, essay, or book chapter. Often the author's thesis will be stated in the first paragraph or two of an article or essay. Similarly, the thesis of a chapter may be given in its initial paragraph.

- Glance at concluding paragraphs in an article, essay, or book chapter. Often these final paragraphs will sum up the discussion and restate major ideas.

- Run your eye down the page, reading randomly every fourth or fifth sentence. Most readers who do this can get a fair inkling of what the material concerns.

5e–1 Primary and secondary sources of evidence

The judgments or conclusions in your paper must be based on evidence. *Primary* sources of evidence are original writings by an author, documents, artifacts, laboratory experiments, or other data providing firsthand information. A literary paper about an author might quote letters, memoirs, an autobiography, novels, short stories, plays, and personal notes by the author as primary sources of evidence.

Secondary sources of evidence are writings, speeches, and other documents *about* a primary source. The opinions of critics are important and widely used secondary sources. An experiment may be a primary source; commentary on it by others is a secondary source. Making a legalistic distinction between these two is not necessary. It is merely necessary to know that your papers will consist of both kinds of evidence.

5e–2 Evaluating sources of evidence

All sources are not created equal. They vary in quality of scholarship, force of argument, and accuracy of detail. Some sources are useful, scholarly, and accurate; others are worthless, silly, and misleading. For example, a student writing a paper on human evolution would be grievously mistaken in taking the fossil remains of the Piltdown Man to be the "missing link"— no matter how many library sources said so. In a brief burst of glory the Piltdown Man was hailed as the "missing link" in human evolution. Many articles and books in the library still make this claim, though their authors would now dearly love to retract, since the Piltdown Man has been exposed as an elaborate hoax. Anthropologists know all about the Piltdown Man's checkered career, though a student researcher might not. All fields similarly are littered with past errors preserved in the collections of libraries. Yet the researcher, who is often a novice in the subject, must nevertheless discriminate between error and truth in the writings of experts—a tricky thing to do.

Fortunately, there are some common-sense ways of evaluating sources of evidence:

- Verify one opinion against another. No one who conscientiously has researched the literature on human fossils would be duped by the early claims on behalf of the Piltdown Man, for these have been thoroughly discredited in later writings. In any given field, authors often comment on the work of their peers. The diligent researcher soon perceives a consensus of opinion among the experts that can be used to judge the reputation of an author or source.

- Note the date of the evidence. In researching any topic you should attach greatest importance to the most recent data. If two sources are identical except in date, cite the later one as your authority.

- Use common sense. Try to evaluate the logic and probable authenticity of any source you intend to use. For example, if you are doing a paper on the possible existence of UFOs, you can and should analyze carefully the testimony of alleged eyewitnesses. Common sense and keen attention to detail are the chief requirements for evaluating this kind, as well as many other kinds, of evidence.

- Check your evaluations against those of professionals. For example, the opinions of critics can give you an inkling of how experienced readers have viewed a certain novel. The *Book Review Digest* is a good source for critical opinions on books. You can also check the credentials of an author or expert in any of the various biographical dictionaries or *Who's Who* volumes to judge how much weight an expert evaluation should be given.

■   Beware of statistics. Because we tend to believe that figures are more accurate than words, we can easily be duped by statistics. You should question the credibility of a source that uses general and exaggerated numbers such as, "Millions of black youths walk the streets of Atlanta, unemployed." The attentive reader will recognize this assertion as figurative language and strive for impartiality. Admittedly this impartiality is hard to achieve, especially if your position is already biased. Nevertheless, you should try to evaluate all data and statistics with an open mind.

5f   Note-taking

The information uncovered on your topic through research should be transcribed onto 4 × 6 note cards and eventually incorporated into the body of the paper. Bear in mind, as you read and take notes, that a research paper should contain a variety of material taken from different sources. It is not enough to simply write down your own ideas and speculations while ignoring everyone else's opinions on the subject. Your own ideas should be derived from evidence and information uncovered on the subject through research, and the reader should be made aware not only of your conclusions, but also of the substance and reasoning that led you to them.

Students often are puzzled about how much of the paper should consist of their original writing and how much of material drawn from researched sources. No exact rule exists. You should not write a paper consisting of a string of quotations and paraphrases but containing nothing of your own. Nor should you glut the paper entirely with your own notions, with only a token quotation or paraphrase added here and there to give the illusion of research. Ideally, the paper should consist of information from sources blended judiciously with your own commentary and interpretation. Certainly you should say what you think, but you should also say why you think it—what evidence exists to support your opinions; which authorities on the subject agree with you; and why those of a different opinion are probably in error. In sum, the paper demands not merely opinionated conclusions, but conclusions supported by other opinions.

5f–1   Format of the note cards

■   Use 4 × 6 cards for note-taking. Large enough to accommodate fairly long notes, 4 × 6 cards are also unlikely to be confused with the smaller 3 × 5 bibliography cards.

■   Write in ink rather than pencil so that the cards can be shuffled without blurring the notes.

■ Write down only one idea or quotation on each card. Cards with only a single note can be put in any sequence simply by shuffling. If the note is so long that two cards have to be used, staple them together.

■ Identify the source of the note in the upper left-hand corner of the card. Since the bibliography card already lists complete information on the source, use only the author's last name or key words from the title followed by a page number. For example, use "Fülöp-Miller 10," or "Holy Devil 10," to identify a note taken from page 10 of *Rasputin, the Holy Devil* by René Fülöp-Miller.

■ Jot down in the upper right-hand corner of the card a general heading for the information the card contains. These headings make it easy to organize the notes by shuffling the cards. (Write in pencil so that the heading can be changed.)

5f–2 Kinds of notes

The notes gathered from your research must be blended into the body of the paper to provide documentation, proof, and evidence in support of the thesis. These notes are of four kinds: the *summary*, the *paraphrase*, the *quotation*, and the *personal comment*.

a. The summary

A summary is a condensation of significant facts from an original piece of writing. A chapter is condensed into a page, a page into a paragraph, or a paragraph into a sentence, with the condensation in each case retaining the essential facts of the original. Consider the summary of an eight-page description of Rasputin (Figure 5–11).

Common sense should govern your use of the summary. Some facts need to be quoted in detail, but others do not, and can be just as effectively summarized. For instance, the note card shown was for a paper on Rasputin that dealt mainly with the historical truth about the man, not with his physical appearance. It was therefore enough for the student to summarize certain features of Rasputin that made him simultaneously repulsive and attractive. In another context, say in a paper on the physical disfigurement of famous people, it might have been necessary for the student to quote generously from the eight-page description which, in this instance, she needed only to summarize.

b. The paraphrase

To paraphrase means to say in one's own words what someone else has said. The paraphrase—unlike the summary—does not condense but restates a

Fülöp-Miller 3-10.   *Rasputin's appearance*

Rasputin's appearance was a combination of coarse, unkempt peasant burliness and mystical, poetic religiosity. He was at once repulsive and attractive. Strangers who met him were first disgusted by such details as his pock-marked skin and his dirty fingernails, but inevitably they came under the spell of his urgent, probing blue eyes.

Figure 5–11   Sample note card containing a summary

passage in approximately the same number of words as the original, using the syntax and vocabulary of the paraphraser. Ordinarily, the paraphrase is the most frequently used note in the preparation of a research paper.

Paraphrasing achieves two purposes: first, it shows that the student has mastered and assimilated the material to the extent of being able to rephrase it; second, it gives the paper an even, consistent style, since both original and source material are cast in the words of the student writer. Below is a short passage from *The Fall of the Russian Monarchy* by Bernard Pares. An appropriate student paraphrase is given in Figure 5–12.

> Meanwhile Rasputin, as he appears to have done earlier, disappeared into the wilds of Russia. Here too he was true to an historical type. Always, throughout Russian history, there had been *stranniki* or wanderers who, without any ecclesiastical commission, lived in asceticism, depriving themselves of the most elementary of human needs, but gladly entertained by the poor wherever they passed. Some of them went barefoot even throughout the winter and wore chains on their legs. This self-denial gave them a freedom to address as peasant equals even the Tsars themselves, and there are many instances of their bold rebukes scattered over Russian history.

c. The quotation

The quotation reproduces an author's words exactly as they were spoken or written, preserving even peculiarities of spelling, grammar, or punctu-

> Pares 134-35.   Rasputin as nomad, ca. 1902
>
> For some time Rasputin became like the well-known *stranniki*, those wandering ascetics who, without official priestly license, wandered all over Russia depending, wherever they passed, on the poor for food and shelter. Some of the nomads even walked barefoot in the freezing Russian winter with chains clinking around their legs. This kind of self-denial bestowed on them the peculiar right to address even a Tsar as their peasant equal. In this role of half priest half beggar, Rasputin roamed the wilds of Russia.

Figure 5–12   Sample note card containing a paraphrase

ation. Use of an occasional quotation is justified only where the authority of the writer is being evoked or where the original material is so splendidly expressed as to be altogether ruined by summary or paraphrase.

Student papers commonly are flawed by the overuse of quoted material. Moreover, many teachers regard the excessive inclusion of quotations as a sign of padding. A good rule of thumb therefore is to limit quoted material to no more than ten percent of the total paper. Another good rule is to quote only when the authority of the writer is needed, or when the material simply cannot be either paraphrased or summarized.

The rules for placing quotations on note cards are:

- Place quotation marks around the quotation.
- Introduce the quotation or place it in proper context.
- Copy quotations exactly as they are written.

Occasionally, a summary or paraphrase is combined with a quotation on a note card, the key phrases or words from the original source being used to add literary flavor or authenticity to the note. Below is an original passage from *The Fall of the Russian Monarchy* by Bernard Pares, followed by a note card (Figure 5–14) that combines a paraphrase with a quotation from this source.

Nothing is more untrue than the easy explanation that was so often given, that he became the tool of others. He was far too clever to sell himself to anyone. He did not ask for presents and had no need; he had only to accept all that was showered upon him, and that he did briefly and almost casually, in many cases at once passing on the largess to the poor; his position was that of one who plundered the rich for the poor and was glad to do it.

d. The personal comment

Personal-comment notes can be used to record any ideas, conjectures, or conclusions that occur to you during the research. These notes generally are used to explicate a fuzzy statement, stress a particular point, draw a conclusion, clarify an issue, identify an inconsistency, or introduce a new idea. Jot down these ideas as they dawn on you. If the personal-comment note deals with material contained on another card, staple the two cards together. An example of a personal-comment note card is given in Figure 5–15 (p. 70).

5g   Plagiarism: what it is and how to avoid it

Plagiarism is the act of passing off another's words and ideas as one's own. The question of when one has plagiarized and when one simply has asserted a general truth from an unknown source can be sometimes puzzling. In a cosmic sense, the process of learning is made up of countless tiny crimes of plagiarism, since we all borrow freely from one another. No generation speaks a language of its own invention; few people are creators of the proverbs and sayings that they utter daily. The mother who tells her child, "A thing of beauty is a joy forever," is plagiarizing from the poet John Keats; the father who warns his son, "Hell hath no fury like a woman scorned," has plagiarized from the playwright William Congreve. Innumerable other examples can be given to show how we freely and wantonly borrow ideas and expressions from one another.

Blatant plagiarism, however, involves the conscious and deliberate stealing of another's words and ideas, generally with the motive of earning undeserved rewards. The student who copies the paper of a friend is guilty of blatant plagiarism. Likewise, the student who steals an idea from a book, expresses it in his or her own words, and then passes it off as original, has committed an act of plagiarism.

The conventions of writing research papers dictate that students must acknowledge the source of any idea or statement not truly their own. This acknowledgment is made in a note specifying the source and author of the

Fülöp-Miller 366.   The murder of Rasputin

Farewell letter from Empress Alexandra to the murdered Rasputin:

"My dear martyr, grant me your blessing to accompany me on the sorrowful road I have still to tread here below. Remember us in Heaven in your holy prayers. Alexandra."

Figure 5–13   Sample note card containing a quotation

Pares   140, 141.   Rasputin's generosity to the poor

Some critics have accused Rasputin of becoming "the tool of others" in order to acquire expensive personal gifts or other material advantage. Nothing could be further from the truth. Rasputin was too clever "to sell himself to anyone." He did not need to. All he had to do was sit back and accept all the luxuries offered to him by high society. And, in fact, one of his favorite roles was that of a Russian Robin Hood who "plundered the rich for the poor" by taking gifts offered and immediately passing them on to people in need.

Figure 5–14   Sample note card combining paraphrase and quotation

Personal Comment   The Czarina's initial attraction to Rasputin

It becomes clear, from all accounts describing the first meeting between Alexandra and Rasputin, that initially this peasant monk gained entrance to the Czarina's confidence by offering hope for the health of her hemophiliac son, at a time when she was utterly sunk in grief and despair. In the grip of maternal terror, she wanted to believe that God had sent a simple peasant to perform miracles.

Figure 5–15   Sample note card containing a personal comment

borrowed material. All summaries, paraphrases, or quotations must be documented; only personal comments may remain undocumented. In sum, to avoid plagiarism students must:

- Provide a note for any idea borrowed from another.
- Place quoted material within quotation marks.
- Provide a bibliography entry at the end of the book for every source used in the text or in a note.

Not every assertion is documentable, nor is it necessary for students to document matters of general and common knowledge. For instance, it is commonly known that the early settlers of America fought wars with the Indians—an assertion a student could safely make without documentation. Similarly, a student could write, "Russia was in turmoil during the years preceding the Bolshevik Revolution," without documenting this statement, since the turmoil of prerevolutionary Russia is common knowledge. As a rule of thumb, a piece of information that occurs in five or more sources may be considered general knowledge. Proverbs and sayings of unknown origins are also considered general knowledge and do not have to be documented.

The following, however, must be accompanied by a citation specifying author and source:

- Any idea derived from any known source.
- Any fact or data borrowed from the work of another.
- Any especially clever or apt expression, whether or not it says something new, that is taken from someone else.
- Any material lifted verbatim from the work of another.
- Any information that is paraphrased or summarized and used in the paper.

To illustrate plagiarism in different degrees, we have reproduced a passage from a book, followed by three student samples, two of which are plagiarisms.

Original passage   Alexander III died on 20 October, 1894, and was succeeded by his son Nicholas. The new emperor was more intelligent and more sensitive than his father. Both those who knew him well, and those who had brief and superficial contact with him, testify to his exceptional personal charm. The charm was, however, apparently associated with weakness and irresolution. Nicholas appeared to agree with the last person he had talked to, and no one could tell what he would do next.

Student Version A (plagiarized)   When Alexander III died on October 20, 1894, he was succeeded by his son Nicholas, who was more intelligent and more sensitive than his father. People who knew him well and also some who knew him only superficially testify that he was exceptionally charming as a person. This charm, however, was associated with weakness and an inability to make decisions. Nicholas always seemed to agree with the last person he had talked to, and no one could predict what he would do next.

This is an example of outright plagiarism. No documentation of any sort is given. The student simply repeats the passage almost verbatim, as though he or she had written it.

Student Version B (plagiarized)   When Alexander III died on October 20, 1894, he was succeeded by his son Nicholas, who was

more intelligent and more sensitive than his
father. People who knew him well, and also
some who knew him only superficially, testify
that he was exceptionally charming as a person. This charm, however, was associated
with weakness and an inability to make decisions. Nicholas always seemed to agree with
the last person he had talked to, and no one
could predict what he would do next.[3]

[3] Hugh Seton-Watson, The Russian Empire, 1801-1917,
vol. 3 of The Oxford History of Modern Europe (Oxford:
Oxford UP, 1967) 547.

Though documented with a footnote, the passage is still a plagiarism
because the student has merely changed a word or two of the original,
without doing a proper paraphrase.

*Student
Version C
(not plagiarized)*

Emperor Nicholas II, who came to the throne
of Russia following the death of his father,
Alexander III, was apparently a man of exceptional personal charm and deep sensitivity.
Ample testimony has come to us from both intimate as well as casual acquaintances, indi-
cating that indeed he possessed a magnetic
personality. However, the general consensus
is also that he was a man who lacked the
ability to make hard decisions, preferring to
agree with the last person he had seen, and
thus making it impossible to predict what he
would do next.[3]

³ Hugh Seton-Watson, <u>The Russian Empire, 1801-1917</u>, vol. 3 of <u>The Oxford History of Modern Europe</u> (Oxford: Oxford UP, 1967) 547.

This is an acceptable use of the material. The original is paraphrased properly and its source documented with a footnote.

6

TRANSFORMING THE NOTES INTO A ROUGH DRAFT

6a   Preparing to write the rough draft: a checklist

The following is a practical checklist of things you should do before beginning to write the rough draft:

- You should formulate a thesis. The research paper is the sort of writing that requires considerable premeditation from a writer. Information sifted from the sources and assembled on the note cards has to be carefully grafted into the main body of the paper. Arguments have to be thought out in advance and checked against the opinions of experts. In sum, no matter how spontaneous a writer you may be, you should nevertheless have a definite thesis in mind before you begin to write the rough draft.
- You should go over the note cards, picking out those cards relevant to the thesis, and setting aside all others. Bear in mind, moreover, that you are very likely to have more notes than you can use. To attempt to cram every single note into the paper is to be misled by an impulse that has ruined thousands of papers. You must exercise selectivity over the note cards, based upon the wording of the thesis, or the paper will end up an incoherent muddle of unrelated notes.
- You should arrange and rearrange the cards until they are organized in the order in which they will be used. This order should be dictated by the wording of the thesis and the nature of the information entered on the individual cards.
- You should sketch an outline or abstract of the paper, breaking down the thesis into an ordered listing of topics. This stage is where you should experiment with different approaches to your research subject. Juggle the topics until they are arranged in the most logical and emphatic order. If necessary, rephrase the thesis until it generates a more definite structure for the paper.

Once you have formulated the thesis, sorted the cards in their proper sequence, and drafted the outline or abstract, you are ready to begin writing the rough draft. Work from the outline and note cards. Triple space the rough draft to allow room for penciling in afterthoughts or corrections. Use a separate sheet for each paragraph so that additional ideas, words, or phrases that occur to you can be tacked on to the paragraphs without creating an unreadable jumble. Keep a dictionary and thesaurus handy, using the first to avoid misspelled or incorrect words, and the second to insure word precision and variety, even in your first draft. If you are writing with a word processor, be sure to run the draft through a spelling checker.

6b Using a word processor

Much of the information given in this text assumes that the paper will be written with a typewriter. So, for example, our instructions on centering the title on the title page specify in detail exactly how this task should be done. However, if you were writing your paper with a word processor, centering would be automatically done for you by the program, as would footnotes and even endnotes with some programs. Many word processors automatically hyphenate words at the end of a line and others even have built-in outliners which, after minimal input by the writer, will generate an outline of the paper, eliminating the drudgery of that thankless chore. We cannot stress enough how invaluable the word processor can be to the harried student who must write many papers over the course of a term. Nor, for that matter, can we adapt this book to any single word processor since there is a bewildering array of choices available to any writer. We can, however, suggest this elementary caution: If your paper requires footnotes or endnotes and your word processor has a routine for automatically handling them, be sure that the printed output conforms to the style your teacher requires. For example, be sure that footnotes are single-spaced within notes and double-spaced between notes. With many programs it is possible to specify exactly how you wish the automatically generated note to look. Read the manual. Be assured that whatever pains you might take to adapt the program to any particular documentation style will be more than repaid in increased speed and reduced drudgery. For those students lucky enough to have a word processor, writing a research paper will not be the chore it was for their parents or grandparents who had to labor over a manual or electric typewriter.

6c Incorporating note-taking into the flow of the paper

The notes you have taken must be blended smoothly into the natural flow of the paper—this is the prime rule for writing the rough draft. Documentation should add clarity, not clutter. Paraphrases, summaries, indirect quotations, and allusions must be edited for smoothness. Quotations, of course, have to be used verbatim and must not be altered in any way. Transitions between ideas should be made logically and smoothly. The paper should not seem a cut-and-paste hodgepodge bristling with numerous unrelated quotations. In sum, you must observe the rhetorical principles of unity, coherence, and emphasis (see Section 6d).

6c–1 Using summaries and paraphrases

The sources of summaries and paraphrases must be given within the text or in parentheses. Below is an example of a paraphrase used without mention of its source in the text:

> When the court life of Russia died out at the imperial palace of Tsarskoe Selo, all kinds of political salons suddenly made their appearance in various sections of St. Petersburg. While these new salons became the breeding ground for the same kinds of intrigues, plots, counterplots, and rivalries that had taken place at the imperial palace, somehow their activities seemed dwarfed and their politics lacked the grandeur and dazzle that had accompanied the political style at the palace (Fülöp-Miller 101).

In this case, parenthetical documentation of the paraphrase is sufficient. However, the writer who wishes to state a paraphrase more emphatically, or to throw the weight of an expert or authority behind the summary, should mention the source in the text, as in the following example:

> As Hugh Seton-Watson points out in the preface to his book on the Russian empire, most people tend to forget that the Russian empire was multinational and therefore peopled with many non-Russian citizens, most important of which were the Polish (ix).

The summary here is more emphatic because it is coupled with the name of the authority whose work is being summarized.

Sometimes students are so dazzled by the writing style of a source that they unwittingly adopt its flavor and language in their summaries; the result is a discordant mixture of styles within a single paragraph. Here is an example:

> The hull of the <u>Titanic</u> was traversed by watertight bulkheads, capable of withstanding enormous pressure.

The engineering notion was that if the ship sprang a leak, water would seep into individual compartments and be harmlessly trapped. At worst, the liner would list, and her passengers be slightly uncomfortable as she limped her way back to port. <u>Metallurgical fabrication techniques employed in the construction and deployment of each bulkhead were consonant with the best engineering and metallurgical knowledge extant at the time of the Titanic's construction.</u> In short, the <u>Titanic</u>, though considered "unsinkable," was neither better nor worse built than any of her other sisters then at sea.

The underscored sentence is a summary of information found in a book on marine engineering. Notice how stylistically different the summary seems from the rest of the paragraph. Having pored over the book, the student then unconsciously mimicked its wooden flavor when writing the summary. Before using it, she should have edited the summary to blend it in with the style of the paragraph. Here is an improved version:

The hull of the <u>Titanic</u> was traversed by watertight bulkheads, capable of withstanding enormous pressure. The engineering notion was that if the ship sprang a leak, water would seep into individual compartments and be harmlessly trapped. At worst, the liner would list, and her passengers be slightly uncomfortable as she limped her way back to port. These bulkheads were built according to the best metallurgical techniques known at the time of the <u>Titanic</u>'s construction. In short, the <u>Titanic</u>, though considered "unsinkable," was neither better nor worse built than any of her other sisters then at sea.

6c–2 Using direct quotations

Quotations must be reproduced in the exact phrasing, spelling, capitalization, and punctuation of the original. Staple or paste the quotation note card to the rough draft rather than copy the quotation. Later, when you write the final draft, you will have to transcribe the quotation from the note card onto the paper. By stapling the note card to the rough draft, you avoid having to transcribe quotations twice, thus reducing the chance of error.

Any modification made in a quotation—no matter how minor—must be indicated either in a note placed in square brackets within the quotation or in parentheses at the end of the quotation.

```
Milton was advocating freedom of speech when he said,

"Give me the liberty to know, to think, to believe, and

to utter freely [emphasis added] according to con-

science, above all other liberties" (120).
```

Quotations must fit logically into the syntax of surrounding sentences, so as not to produce an illogical or mixed construction. The following quotation is integrated poorly:

```
Chung-Tzu describes a sage as "suppose there is one who

insists on morality in all things, and who places love

of truth above all other values" (58).
```

Here is the same quotation properly integrated into the sentence:

```
Chung-Tzu describes a sage as "one who insists on moral-

ity in all things, and who places love of truth above

all other values" (58).
```

Here is another example of a badly integrated quotation:

```
The poet showed his belief in self-criticism by writing

that "I am a man driven to scold myself over every triv-

ial error" (15).
```

Here is the quotation properly handled:

```
The poet showed his belief in self-criticism when he
wrote this about himself: "I am a man driven to scold
myself over every trivial error" (15).
```

a. Overuse of quotations

No passage in the paper should consist of an interminable string of quotations. A mixture of summaries, paraphrases, and quotations is smoother
and easier to read; moreover, such a mixture gives the impression that students have done more than patch together bits and pieces from books and
articles they have read. Here is an example of a paragraph littered with
too many quotations:

```
According to McCullough, "the groundswell of public
opinion against the Japanese started in the early 1900s"
(191). This is when the United States Industrial Com-
mission issued a report stating that the Japanese "are
more servile than the Chinese, but less obedient and far
less desirable" (Conrat 18). At about the same time,
the slogan of politician and labor leader Dennis Kearney
was "the Japs must go!" (10). The mayor of San Fran-
cisco wrote that "the Japanese cannot be taken into the
American culture because they are not the stuff of which
American citizens are made" (Daniels 9-10). In 1905,
writes McCullough, "the Japanese and Korean Expulsion
League held its first meeting and spawned many other
such similar organizations" (102).
```

Here is an improved version, which deftly turns many of the quotations
into summaries and paraphrases, resulting in a cleaner, less cluttered
paragraph:

```
The anti-Japanese movement in America goes back to the
turn of the century, when the United States Industrial
```

Commission claimed that the Japanese "are more servile than the Chinese, but less obedient and far less desirable" (Conrat 18). At about the same time, the slogan of politician and labor leader Dennis Kearney was "The Japs must go!" while the mayor of San Francisco insisted that it was impossible for the Japanese to assimilate into American culture and that they were "not the stuff of which American citizens are made" (Daniels 9-10). In this xenophobic atmosphere, the Japanese and Korean Expulsion League was formed in 1905 and a number of other anti-Japanese societies followed (McCullough 102).

Notice, by the way, that the improved version contains fewer references than the original. In the first version, the student was forced to document every quotation, even though successive quotations sometimes came from the same source. The blend of summaries, paraphrases, and quotations not only reduced clutter, but also cut down on the number of notes by combining references from the same source into a single sentence and under a single note.

b. Using brief quotations

Brief quotations (four lines or less) may be introduced with a simple phrase:

Betty Friedan <u>admits</u> that it will be quite a while before women know "how much of the difference between women and men is culturally determined and how much of it is real."

"God is the perfect poet," <u>said</u> Browning in "Paracelsus."

Hardin Craig <u>suggests</u> that "in order fully to understand and appreciate Shakespeare, it is necessary to see him as a whole."

In Shakespeare's <u>Antony and Cleopatra</u>, Cleopatra <u>prefers</u> "a ditch in Egypt" as her grave to being hoisted up and shown to the "shouting varletry of censuring Rome."

<u>According to</u> David Halberstam, when McNamara began to take over the Vietnam problem, "there was a growing split between the civilians and the military over the assessment of Vietnam."

In contrast to Eichmann's concept of justice, Thoreau <u>believed</u> that "a true patriot would resist a tyrannical majority."

Note that if the quotation is grammatically part of the sentence in which it occurs, the first word of the quotation does not need to be capitalized, even if it is capitalized in the original.

*Original
quotation*   "Some infinitives deserve to be split."

Bruce Thompson

*Quotation used
as part of a
sentence*   Bruce Thompson affirms what writers have always suspected, namely that "some infinitives deserve to be split."

Moreover, if the quotation is used at the end of a declarative sentence, it will be followed by a period whether or not a period is used in the original.

*Original
quotation*   "Love is a smoke rais'd with the fume of sighs; . . ."

Shakespeare

Quotation used in a declarative sentence   In Act I Romeo describes love as "a smoke rais'd with the fume of sighs."

Finally, you should strive for variety in the introduction of quotations, rather than ploddingly serving them up with the same words and phrases. If you introduce one quotation with, "So-and-so says," try something different for the next, such as, "In the opinion of at least one critic," or "A view widely shared by many in the field affirms that," and so on.

c. Using long quotations

Unlike quotations of four lines or less, longer quotations need to be introduced by a formal sentence, placed in context, and properly explained. Moreover, long quotations must be set off from the text by double spacing, indented ten spaces from the left margin, and typed with double spacing but without quotation marks (unless the quotation itself contains quotation marks). If two or more paragraphs are quoted, then the sentence beginning each paragraph should be indented five spaces. Each long quotation should be preceded by a colon. (See Figure 6–1, p. 85.) If the quotation consists of only a single paragraph, or if the opening sentence of the quotation is not the start of a paragraph, then the first line of the quotation need not be indented five spaces:

In his novel <u>Lady Chatterley's Lover</u>, D. H. Lawrence creates a mesmeric and ritualistic effect as he describes the love scene between Mellors and Connie:

> But he drew away at last, and kissed her and covered her over, and began to cover himself. She lay looking up to the boughs of the tree, unable as yet to move. He stood and fastened up his breeches, looking round. All was dense and silent, save for the awed dog that lay with its paws against its nose. He sat down again on the brushwood and took Connie's hand in silence. (150)

Lawrence has created a trancelike mood that conveys the symbolic importance of this scene.

Figure 6–1   A long quotation of two paragraphs

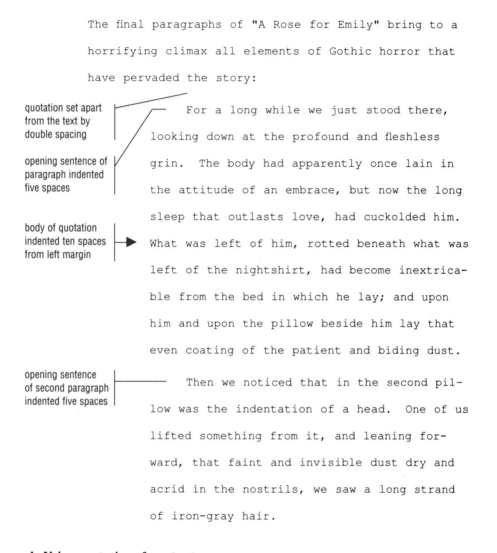

The final paragraphs of "A Rose for Emily" bring to a horrifying climax all elements of Gothic horror that have pervaded the story:

quotation set apart from the text by double spacing

opening sentence of paragraph indented five spaces

body of quotation indented ten spaces from left margin

For a long while we just stood there, looking down at the profound and fleshless grin. The body had apparently once lain in the attitude of an embrace, but now the long sleep that outlasts love, had cuckolded him. What was left of him, rotted beneath what was left of the nightshirt, had become inextricable from the bed in which he lay; and upon him and upon the pillow beside him lay that even coating of the patient and biding dust.

opening sentence of second paragraph indented five spaces

Then we noticed that in the second pillow was the indentation of a head. One of us lifted something from it, and leaning forward, that faint and invisible dust dry and acrid in the nostrils, we saw a long strand of iron-gray hair.

d. Using quotations from poetry

Unless the stanzaic line needs to be preserved for stylistic emphasis, short passages of verse should be enclosed by quotation marks and incorporated into the text. Quotations of two or three lines may also be part of the text, but with the lines separated by a slash (/) with a space on each side of the slash:

The line "I have been half in love with easeful Death" expresses a recurrent theme in Keats's poetry--the

```
desire for permanent residence in a world free from pain

and anguish.

"The raven's croak, the low wind choked and drear, / The

baffled stream, the gray wolf's doleful cry" are typical

Romantic images used by William Morris to create a mood

of idle despair.
```

Verse quotations that exceed three lines should be separated from the text by triple spacing, indented ten spaces from the left margin (or less, if the line is so long that it would cause the page to look unbalanced), double-spaced without quotation marks (unless the poem itself contains quotation marks), and introduced with a colon. The spatial arrangement of the original poem (indentation and spacing within and between lines) should be reproduced with accuracy:

```
In the following lines from "You Ask Me Why, Tho' Ill at

Ease," Tennyson expresses the poet's desire for freedom

to speak out:

          It is the land that freemen till,

              That sober-suited Freedom chose,

              The land, where girt with friends or foes

          A man may speak the thing he will.
```

The quotation beginning in the middle of a line of verse should be reproduced exactly that way and not shifted to the left margin:

```
As Cordelia leaves her home, exiled by Lear's folly, she

reveals full insight into her sisters' evil characters:

                  I know you what you are;

          And like a sister am most loath to call

          Your faults as they are nam'd.  Love well

              our father:
```

```
To your professed bosoms I commit him:

But yet, alas, stood I within his grace.

I would prefer him to a better place.

(Lr. 1.1.272-77)
```

e. Using a quotation within another quotation

Use single quotation marks to enclose a quotation within another brief quotation:

```
Rollo May is further exploring the daimonic personality

when he states that "in his essays, Yeats goes so far

as to specifically define the daimonic as the 'Other

Will.'"
```

For quotations within long, indented quotations, use double quotation marks:

```
In his essay "Disease As a Way of Life," Eric J. Cassell

makes the following observation:

          As the term "diarrhea-pneumonia complex" sug-

          gests, infants in the Navajo environment com-

          monly suffered or died from a combination of

          respiratory and intestinal complaints that are

          not caused by any single bacterium or virus.
```

f. Punctuating quotations

The rules for punctuating quotations are few and simple:

- Place commas and periods inside the quotation marks:

```
"Three times today," Lord Hastings declares in Act 3,

"my foot-cloth horse did stumble, and started, when
```

```
he look'd upon the Tower, as loath to bear me to the

slaughter-house."
```

■ Place colons and semicolons outside the quotation marks:

```
Brutus reassures Portia, "You are my true and hon-

ourable wife, as dear to me as are the ruddy drops

that visit any sad heart"; consequently, she insists

that he reveal his secrets to her.
```

■ Place question marks and exclamation marks inside the quotation marks if they are part of the quotation, but outside if they are not:

```
King Henry asks, "What rein can hold licentious

wickedness when down the hill he holds his fierce

career?"
```

But:

```
Which Shakespearean character said, "Fortune is

painted blind, with a muffler afore her eyes"?
```

g. Interpolations in quoted material

Personal comments or explanations within a quotation must be placed in square brackets (not parentheses), which may be handwritten if no such key exists on your typewriter. The word "sic" within square brackets means that the quotation—including any errors—has been copied exactly.

```
The critical review was entitled "A Cassual [sic] Analy-

sis of Incest and Other Passions."
```

The "sic" indicates that "cassual" is reproduced exactly as it is spelled in the quotation.

Here is an explanatory interpolation, also set off in square brackets:

```
Desdemona answers Emilia with childlike innocence:

"Beshrew me if I would do such a wrong [cuckold her

husband] for all the whole world."
```

h. The ellipsis

The ellipsis—three dots (. . .) with a space before and after each dot—is used to indicate the omission of material from a quotation. Such omissions are necessary when only a part of the quotation is relevant to the point you are making. Use of the ellipsis, however, does not free a researcher from an obligation of remaining faithful to the intent of the author's original text. The following example illustrates the misuse of the ellipsis to distort an author's meaning:

Original   Faulkner's novels have the quality of being lived, absorbed, remembered rather than merely observed.

Malcolm Cowley

Quotation   ```
Malcolm Cowley further suggests that "Faulk-
ner's novels have the quality of being . . .
merely observed."
```

If you are quoting no more than a fragment and it is clear that something has been left out, no ellipsis is necessary:

```
Malcolm Cowley refers to Faulkner's "mythical kingdom."
```

But when it is not clear that an omission has been made, the ellipsis must be used.

■   *Omissions within a sentence* are indicated by three spaced dots:

Original   Mammals were in existence as early as the latest Triassic, 190 million years ago, yet for the first one hundred and twenty million years of their history, from the end of the Triassic to the late Cretaceous, they were a suppressed race, unable throughout that span of time to produce any carnivore larger than cat-size or herbivore larger than rat-size.

<div align="right">Adrian Desmond</div>

Quotation   ```
Adrian Desmond, arguing that the dinosaurs
were once dominant over mammals, points out
that "mammals were in existence as early as
the latest Triassic . . . yet for the first
one hundred and twenty million years of their
history . . . they were a suppressed race,
```

```
unable throughout that span of time to pro-

duce any carnivore larger than cat-size or

herbivore larger than rat-size."
```

Two omissions are made in the quotation and both are indicated by an ellipsis of three spaced dots.

- *Omissions at the end of a sentence* use a period followed by three spaced dots:

```
Adrian Desmond, arguing that the dinosaurs were once

dominant over mammals, points out that the mammals

were, for millions of years, "a suppressed race, un-

able throughout that span of time to produce any car-

nivore larger than cat-size. . . ."
```

Notice that the first dot is a period and is placed immediately after the last word without an intervening space.

   If the ellipsis is followed by parenthetical material at the end of a sentence, use three spaced dots and place the sentence period after the final parenthesis:

```
Another justice made the following, more restrictive,

statement: "You have the right to disagree with those

in authority . . . but you have no right to break the

law . . ." (Martin 42).
```

- *Omissions of a sentence or more* are also indicated by four dots, but with this proviso: that a complete sentence must both precede and follow the four dots. Here is an example:

Original   *Manuscript Troana* and other documents of the Mayas describe a cosmic catastrophe during which the ocean fell on the continent, and a terrible hurricane swept the earth. The hurricane broke up and carried away all towns and forests. Exploding volcanoes, tides sweeping over mountains, and impetuous winds threatened to annihilate humankind, and actually did annihilate many species of animals. The face of the earth changed,

> mountains collapsed, other mountains grew and rose over the
> onrushing cataract of water driven from oceanic spaces, num-
> berless rivers lost their beds, and a wild tornado moved through
> the debris descending from the sky.
>
> Immanuel Velikovsky

*Unacceptable
use of four
dots to mark
an omission*

```
That species of animals may have been made

extinct by some worldwide catastrophe is not

unthinkable.  Immanuel Velikovsky states that

according to "Manuscript Troana and other

documents. . . . The face of the earth

changed, mountains collapsed, other mountains

grew and rose over the onrushing cataract of

water driven from oceanic spaces, numberless

rivers lost their beds, and a wild tornado

moved through the debris. . . ."
```

   The quotation is unacceptably reproduced because the fragment "*Manuscript Troana* and other documents," rather than an entire sentence, is
placed before the four dots. Here is an acceptable use of this material:

```
That species of animals may have been made extinct

by some worldwide catastrophe is not unthinkable.

Immanuel Velikovsky states that "Manuscript Troana and

other documents of the Mayas describe a cosmic catas-

trophe. . . . The face of the earth changed, mountains

collapsed, other mountains grew and rose over the on-

rushing cataract of water driven from oceanic spaces,

numberless rivers lost their beds, and a wild tornado

moved through the debris. . . ."
```

Complete sentences are reproduced before and after the four periods,
which satisfies the convention.

■   *Omissions of long passages,* such as several stanzas, paragraphs, or pages, are marked by a single typed line of spaced dots:

```
Speaking through the prophet Amos, the God of the

Israelites warns sternly:

            For you alone have I cared

            among all the nations of the world;

            therefore will I punish you

            for all your iniquities.

            . . . . . . . .

            An enemy shall surround the land;

            your stronghold shall be thrown down

            and your palaces sacked.
```

■   *Omissions that immediately follow an introductory statement* require no ellipsis:

```
Acceptable   In Booth's fantastic mind, his act was to be

             "the perfect crime of the ages and he the

             most heroic assassin of all times."


Unacceptable In Booth's fantastic mind, his act was to be

             ". . . the perfect crime of the ages and he

             the most heroic assassin of all times."
```

Although an omission has been made in the beginning of the quotation, the use of an ellipsis following the introductory remark is unnecessary.

6c–3 Using indirect quotations

There are times when you will want to quote an author indirectly. An indirect quotation reports what someone said or wrote but not in the exact words of the original passage. Indirect quotations should not appear in quotation marks. Study the following examples:

Direct quotation J. K. Galbraith makes the following statement: "In the Affluent Society no useful distinction can be made between luxuries and necessaries."

Indirect quotation J. K. Galbraith suggests that in an affluent society rich people don't make any useful distinction between luxuries and necessities.

Direct quotation After defining the qasida as a "pre-Islamic ode," Katharine Slater Gittes comments: "These wholly secular odes glorify the Bedouin life, the life of the wanderer."

Indirect quotation According to Katharine Slater Gittes, the main purpose of the qasida, a pre-Islamic ode, is to glorify the life of the Bedouin wanderer.

The purpose of using indirect quotations is to avoid a choppy style that evolves when one uses a string of direct quotations. Indirect quotations maintain the continuity of the writer's own style, giving the text a smoother flow.

NOTE: Whether using a short, long, or indirect quotation, be sure to avoid vague pronoun references in your introductory phrasing:

Poor In one article <u>it</u> stated, "Numerous victims. . . ."

Better In his article "Anorexia Nervosa," Petersen states, "Numerous victims. . . ."

Poor   In the introduction <u>they</u> point out that the

vote was 59 to 38 against the bill.

Better   The Introduction points out that the vote was

59 to 38 against the bill.

6c–4 How to place and punctuate the page reference parentheses

This section applies only if your paper is documented in the parenthetical style used by the Modern Language Association (MLA) and the American Psychological Association (APA) (see Sections 8d and 8e).

a. Short quotations

When using a quotation of one sentence or less in your running text, place the page reference parentheses *after* the closing quotation mark but *before* the end punctuation, thus including the parentheses within your own sentence:

Noyes, for example, insisted that "there is a language

in the Canticles which I could not apply to the Supreme

Being . . . without feeling guilty of blasphemy" (125).

b. Long quotations

When using a *long, indented quotation*, omit quotation marks and place the page reference parentheses *after* the final period with no period following the parentheses:

Gail Sheehy characterizes certain successful males as

<u>wunderkinder</u>:

The <u>wunderkind</u> often seems to possess a bound-

less capacity to bounce back from career fail-

ures. Business losses, power struggles, lost

elections, even criminal charges are viewed as

```
temporary setbacks; they merely stiffen his resolve to

come out a winner. (191)
```

c. Quotations ending in an ellipsis

If the quotation (long or short) ends in an ellipsis, place the final period after the parentheses (see Section 6c–2*h*).

6c–5 Use quotations to explore and discover

The writer's role in the research paper is not simply to cite a parade of authority opinions; rather, it is also to react to them according to the writer's personal theories and views as reflected in the paper. Authority opinion should be used to support or confirm your own viewpoint, not to displace it. If you agree with an opinion, say so and why. On the other hand, if you disagree, state the case for your disagreement. In writing the research paper, you must claim your seat at the banquet table of opinion as an intellectual equal. The thesis should reflect your own original views or speculations on the topic, and the authorities you cite should never be allowed to overawe your personal judgment.

What we have described is, of course, an ideal that often is undone by the timidity of research paper writers. Many students feel that they cannot or should not doubt authority, much less debate its views. That, however, is exactly what you must do if your research paper is to be original. You must assert your opinion; you must react to the uncovered research; you must say why you think it right or wrong. Here is an example from a student paper on the politics of the Philippines. The writer came across this quotation by Bob Drogin, the *Times*' Manila bureau chief, written for an essay in the April 26, 1992, *Los Angeles Times Magazine*:

> More than half the [Filipino] population of 64.2 million live in appalling poverty. The economy is stagnant, mired in $29 billion in debt. There's runaway population growth—at 2.8%, the rate is higher than in Bangladesh. Rotting garbage and countless squatters continue to clog Manila's squalid streets. Provincial warlords have returned in force. So have many of Marcos' closest cronies. No wonder the national ambition is to leave: More than 600,000 Filipinos have applied to immigrate to the United States.

This statistical report led the student to a personal conclusion, which she forcefully expressed:

```
Obviously the Aquino chapter of Philippine politics

was just a farce.  The tear-jerker idea that the

saintly widow, whose husband was murdered by a ruthless
```

dictator, would devote her life to reestablishing jus-

tice for the downtrodden poor of the Philippines was

nothing more than sentimental reverie. The hard fact is

that the Philippines is run by a dynasty of feudal fami-

lies who have never relinquished their hold on the land,

money, and citizens who, long after Marcos's forced ex-

ile and death in Hawaii, continue to be oppressed.

Here is another example from a paper arguing that boxing should be banned because its only objective is to cause injury in an opponent. Early on in his paper the student cited Joyce Carol Oates's famous essay "On Boxing":

> To turn from an ordinary preliminary match to a "Fight of the Century" like those between Joe Louis and Billy Conn, Joe Frazier and Muhammad Ali, Marvin Hagler and Thomas Hearns is to turn from listening or half-listening to a guitar being idly plucked to hearing Bach's *Well-Tempered Clavier* perfectly executed, and that too is part of the story's mystery: so much happens so swiftly and with such heart-stopping subtlety you cannot absorb it except to know that something profound is happening and it is happening in a place beyond words.

So angered was the writer by the quotation that he followed it with this satirical commentary:

One can only imagine the deviant mind that can draw a

parallel between the divine music of Bach and the bes-

tial antics of professional boxers. How can one compare

hands that break skulls, detach retinas, crush spleens,

and cause fatal injuries to hands that create musical

chords to soothe human souls and transport people away

from pain to a sphere of peace and pleasure?

No particular formula exists for judging ideas; the process will always be idiosyncratic and grounded in personal values. Quintilian, a first-century Roman rhetoric teacher, suggests we evaluate ideas by asking three questions: (1) Did it happen?; (2) What is it?; and (3) Is it good or bad? The first two questions can be answered by factual research; the third depends entirely on the writer's values. For example, if we apply these questions to the sore topic of animal experimentation, we have to admit that it does happen and that it entails the use of living animals in experiments that often cause injury and death. But as to whether animal experimentation is viewed as good or bad depends entirely on one's values. It could be argued that the discomfort to animals is more than offset by the resulting good to humans. Insulin, for example, which has saved the lives of millions of human diabetics, was discovered through experiments conducted primarily on dogs. The contrary point of view, voiced in the credo of the ALF (Animal Liberation Front), contends that animal research "is an ethical travesty that justifies extraordinary cruelty and immoral regulations against the innate rights of animals." Research should inform our best decisions and influence our values, but there will always be issues over which sincere people will disagree significantly. And as a research paper writer, you should neither be afraid to defend what you believe nor to disagree with those with whom you differ.

6c–6 Interpret quotations with personal commentary

The personal comment is used primarily to supply the reader with information otherwise unobtainable from the stark research data. Personal comments serve to interpret material, mark transitions from one idea to another, and draw conclusions. In a manner of speaking, the thesis statement also can be regarded as an elaborate personal comment in which the student enunciates a general design and focus for the entire paper.

   The example below illustrates the use of the personal comment to interpret material. The student's paper is on the career of Pope Innocent III; the discussion in the preceding paragraph centered on a crusade for which Innocent III had just called. Interjecting a personal comment, the student interprets the motive of Innocent III in launching this crusade:

```
Innocent III's call for this crusade shows that he was

trying to establish that the Papacy was the temporal

authority on earth.  As the head of Christendom, he

couldn't tolerate any philosophy that would divert at-

tention away from the teaching of the Catholic church.
```

   Personal comments also are used to establish smooth transitions as the discussion moves from one idea to another. Here is an example taken from this same student paper. The preceding paragraph summarized the reaction of Innocent III to the heresy of the Cathars.

```
The heresy of the Cathars was not the only anti-Catholic

philosophy that Innocent III endeavored to crush.  He

desired to crush the heresy of the Moslems as well.
```

The paper then moves on to a discussion of the efforts of Pope Innocent III to crush the Moslems.

Finally, the personal comment is widely used to make summations and draw conclusions. The paper on Innocent III ends with this summation of the Pontiff's career:

```
Innocent III's pontificate was the zenith of the me-

dieval papacy. He involved himself in world affairs by

endeavoring to stop heresy and by exerting his authority

over kings.  He crushed the Cathar heresy and brought

the Greek church under his control.  He used the kings

of Europe like pawns on a chessboard.  Therefore one can

conclude that Innocent III made the theory of papal

theocracy into a reality.
```

6d Writing the paper with unity, coherence, and emphasis

6d-1 Unity

The rhetorical principle of unity dictates that a paper should stick to its chosen thesis without rambling or digressing. If the thesis states that Japanese art influenced French Impressionism, the paper should cover exactly that subject and nothing more. If the thesis proposes to contrast the life-styles of inner city residents and suburban dwellers, the paper should concisely pursue such a contrast, ignoring all side issues, no matter how personally fascinating to the writer.

To observe the principle of unity, a writer merely has to follow the lead of the thesis. Properly drafted, the thesis will predict the content of a paper, control its direction, and obligate the writer to a single purpose. The writer introduces only material relevant to the thesis, suppressing the urge to dabble in side issues or to stray from the point. Such admirable single-mindedness will produce a paper written according to the principle of unity and consequently be easier for a reader to follow.

The principle of unity should govern the progression of ideas within an individual paragraph as well as throughout the entire structure of an essay. Paragraphs should be written to scrupulously deliver exactly what the topic sentence promises, for the content of a paragraph is controlled by its topic sentence much as the structure and direction of an essay are determined by its thesis.

6d–2 Coherence

If unity means sticking to the point, coherence means "sticking together." A paragraph is said to be coherent if its sentences stick together in some obvious logical pattern that readers can follow. When writing is incoherent, on the other hand, a reader will have trouble following what a writer means and what the paragraph really says. Consider the following example:

```
     In the past year it's been through times of extreme

highs and lows in my emotional outlook on life.  The

trend of any life seems to follow this general pattern.

Some of the high moments were meeting new people that

turned out to be much more than mere acquaintances, hav-

ing the newly-met person turn into a friend a person

could know for the rest of one's life.  Competing in

sports and in the area of track and field and baseball

was exhilarating.  Meeting and going out with a few

girls, which in our relationship between each other

bloomed into a special kind of affection for ourselves.
```

This paragraph is incoherent because its sentences are devoted to separate and unrelated ideas instead of adhering to some common overall purpose. To avoid incoherent writing, you must think of the paragraph as a single unit of expression to which individual sentences contribute increments of meaning. Here are four suggestions to help you achieve paragraph coherence:

■ *Be precise about word reference.* Either repeat key words or make certain that the pronouns you use clearly hark back to them. In the passage that follows, notice how the key word *villain* is either repeated or replaced by a pronoun clearly referring to it:

> The <u>villain</u> in science fiction movies is always the
> personification of evil. One way this concentration
> of evil is achieved is by surrounding the <u>villain</u> with
> numerous henchmen. Without henchmen, the <u>villain</u>
> would appear much less powerful. To accentuate his
> <u>villainy, he</u> surrounds <u>himself</u> by ruthless storm
> troopers, evil robots, slime monsters, or whatever.
> With these associates by <u>his</u> side, the eventual tri-
> umph of the hero over the <u>villain</u> takes place against
> a backdrop of overwhelming odds.

Repetition of the word *villain,* and of the pronouns *he* or *his* that refer to *villain,* provides a common thread connecting all five sentences.

■ *Use parallel structures.* Deliberate repetition of certain words, phrases, or clauses in a paragraph also can provide sentences with a cohering rhythm and harmony, as repetition of *can* and a verb does in the following example:

> Fleas of various species <u>can jump</u> 150 times their own
> length, <u>can survive</u> months without feeding, <u>can accel-</u>
> <u>erate</u> 50 times faster than the space shuttle, <u>can</u>
> <u>withstand</u> enormous pressure, and <u>can remain</u> frozen for
> a year and then revive.

■ *Use transitional markers.* Transitional markers are words or phrases used to assert the relationships between the sentences of a paragraph. Common among these markers are the conjunctions *and, or, not, but,* and *for.* But other, lengthier connectives also are used to ensure coherence. Consider the underlined words in this passage:

> The type A person is forever nervous and uptight about
> coming events--always desiring success, but fearing
> failure. Type A's feel perpetually insecure and vul-
> nerable because they suspect that they are flawed. <u>As</u>

an illustration, consider Howard Hughes, the brilliant entrepreneur. He started a highly feasible car industry, but shut it down overnight when he reasoned that he had failed since his automobile was not perfect. Such reasoning is typical of type A personalities, who often set themselves up for failure because their best efforts never seem good enough. In constrast to type A persons, type B's pride themselves on their optimism and relaxed attitude. Type B's are the kinds of people who may study hours for an exam and do poorly; yet, they will still feel good about themselves because they did all that was possible. For instance, Doug Moe, former coach of the Denver Nuggets, outlasted the average basketball coach tenure because he did not place unrealistic demands on his players, who in turn responded by performing to their highest potential.

The underlined transitional markers add to the coherent and smooth development of the ideas in a paragraph. Here are some of the most common transitional markers and how they are used:

Adding: furthermore, in addition, moreover, similarly, also
Opposing: however, though, nevertheless, on the other hand, unlike
Concluding: therefore, as a result, consequently
Exemplifying: for example, for instance, to illustrate, that is
Intensifying: in fact, indeed, even, as a matter of fact
Sequencing: first, second, finally, in conclusion, to sum up, in short

- *Avoid mixed constructions.* Mixed constructions are sentences that begin in one kind of grammatical pattern but lurch unexpectedly into another. Here are some examples, followed by a corrected version:

Mixed   Whereas he was poor growing up caused him to be bitter in middle age.

Improved   Because he was poor growing up, he became bitter in middle age.

Mixed   With every new service on the part of government suggests that our taxes are going to be raised.

Improved   Every new service on the part of government suggests that our taxes are going to be raised.

Mixed   Meeting and going out with a few girls, which in our relationship between each other bloomed into a special kind of affection for ourselves.

Improved   Meeting a few girls and going out with them fostered relationships that bloomed into special affections between us.

6d–3 Emphasis

The rhetorical principle of emphasis requires the expression of more important ideas in main or independent clauses, and of less important ideas in dependent or subordinate clauses. In sum, properly emphatic writing will attempt to rank ideas through grammatical structure. Here is an example of an unemphatic piece of writing:

Poor   The gifted child is a high achiever on a spe-
emphasis   cific test, either the Otis or Binet I.Q. test. These tests are usually administered

```
          at the end of the second grade.  They deter-

          mine the placement of the child in third

          grade.  These tests are characterized by

          written as well as verbal questions, so that

          the child has the opportunity to express him-

          self creatively.
```

The grammatical treatment of ideas is altogether too egalitarian. A reader simply cannot distinguish between the important and the unimportant ideas, because they are all expressed in a similar grammatical structure. Here is the same passage made emphatic:

Improved   A child is considered gifted if he has
emphasis
```
          achieved a high score on a specific test such

          as the Otis or Binet I.Q. test.  Character-

          ized by written as well as verbal questions

          so that the child has the opportunity to

          express himself creatively, these tests are

          administered at the end of the second grade

          in order to determine the proper placement of

          the child in third grade.
```

By placing subordinate ideas in subordinate clauses, the writer achieves a purposeful focus missing from the unemphatic version.

6e   Using the proper tense

6e–1 Maintain the present tense except when reporting an event that happened in the past

In the following passage, note the appropriate shift from past to present.

```
     In the 1950s there was among the medical profession a

     sudden enthusiasm for the surgical removal of infected
```

lung tissue, and expensive plans <u>were</u> made to build new

surgical wards in many hospitals. But when streptomycin

<u>came</u> along, much of this surgery <u>became</u> unnecessary.

Thus huge amounts of money <u>had been</u> wasted. The truth

<u>is</u> that a much higher priority needs to be given to

basic research in biologic science. This <u>is</u> the best

way of saving health care expenses in the long run.

Beginning with the sentence "The truth . . . ," the shift from past to present is smoothly accomplished.

6e–2 Keep your tense or mood consistent

Wrong   The wildlife of the beaches <u>would be</u> contami-

nated in the event of an oil spill. The sand

and water <u>becomes</u> covered with oil sludge and

residue.

Right   The wildlife of the beaches <u>would be</u> contami-

nated in the event of an oil spill. The sand

and water <u>would become</u> covered with oil

sludge and residue.

The writer began the idea in the conditional and must complete it in that mood.

6e–3 Use the present tense for most comments by authorities because they usually continue to be true and in print

Thomas Jefferson <u>supports</u> the idea of . . .

Gilbert Highet <u>criticizes</u> . . .

Milton and Shakespeare, like Homer, <u>acknowledge</u> the

desire . . .

```
"Art rediscovers . . . what is necessary to humanness,"

declares John Gardner.
```

But use the past tense for actions or events completed in the past.

```
When Horace wrote the Ars Poetica, . . .


The nationwide founding of the Brewers Association was a

factor contributing . . .


In the 17th century, Seventh-Day Baptists were among the

followers of Oliver Cromwell.
```

6f Writing the abstract

An abstract, a summary of the major ideas contained in your research paper, is usually required for papers written in the natural or social sciences, but not in the humanities. While the abstract replaces an outline, we still suggest for the sake of logical progression and balance in the paper that you write an outline, even if you are not required to submit one.

In writing the abstract, use no more than one page. Center the title "Abstract" (without quotation marks) one inch from the top of the page. (Remember that the whole point of abstracting is to condense.) The page containing the abstract must follow the title page but precede the actual body of the paper. It should have a running head and page number. Writing the abstract in coherent paragraphs will be relatively easy if you have outlined your paper. To produce a smooth abstract you need only link and condense the main ideas of the outline with appropriate commentary. See the sample student paper abstract on pp. 268–269 for an example.

STYLE

7a   Aim for a readable style

A clear and readable style is of utmost importance in any writing, but especially so in English research papers where the focus is often on interpreting the ideas of different disciplines. At the least, you should strive for a research writing style that allows you to make your points with economy and directness. For an example of the kind of style to avoid, consider this paragraph from a research paper dealing with the problems faced by minorities attempting a college education:

> What is matriculation? It is a plan. Moreover, it is a collaborative, personal, representational effort reflecting the best and highest quality of the talents, skills, abilities, and processes needed and required to effectively operate in the changes of education in our highly technical information age. Now, these efforts include affiliations, relationships, courtesy, and cooperation with an eye on the end product of achieving goals, objectives, and effective results to meet the changing needs in today's underrepresented student population at a time when the great ship of education is drifting on shifting waters.

The wrongs of this paragraph are many and varied. First, the paragraph is cluttered with repetitions or imprecise words that are either unnecessary or wholly unrelated. For example, in the third sentence "personal" is at odds with "collaborative" and "representative." "Affiliations," "relationships," and "cooperation" in the fourth sentence are all words that mean "working together"; "courtesy" does not belong among them. The fifth sentence lumps together "goals," "objectives," and "results" in tiresome repetition. "Best" and "highest" as well as "needed" and "required" are redundant. In addition to being glutted with unnecessary words, the paragraph ends lamely on a hopelessly mixed metaphor, "great ship of education is drifting on shifting waters." After reading the paragraph, we are left with the impression that the writer only dimly understands the meaning of "matriculation."

The cardinal principle for cultivating a good research paper writing style and avoiding a bad one comes neither from grammar nor rhetoric, but from common sense: know and understand the researched topic. If you are unclear about the meaning of your research, you cannot possibly explain it to a reader. For example, here is a revision of the above paragraph written after the student had returned to the library and finally mastered the concept of matriculation. Notice the directness and vigor of the new style:

```
     What is matriculation?  It is the process of creat-

ing a working partnership between the university and the

student for the purpose of identifying and achieving

the student's educational goals.  In this partnership,

the university will provide the instructional and sup-

port services needed, and the student will make use of

these services in pursuit of his or her goals.
```

The increased clarity of the second paragraph over the first is due largely to the writer's improved mastery of the subject. A good style cannot wholly compensate for a weak grasp of content. Nor can a strong grasp of content completely overcome the defects of a bad style. In a writing project as complex as the research paper, style and mastery of content contribute equally to a successful outcome. To help you master a blend of good style and solid content in your own paper, we offer the following practical suggestions.

7a–1 Understand your sources

Reread all difficult passages until you completely understand them. Do not pretend an understanding you do not really have and do not quote a passage whose meaning you have not grasped fully. Paraphrasing an author's ideas is a useful way of testing your understanding of them.

7a–2 Be scrupulously accurate

Be scrupulously accurate in transcribing the information you gather from your sources. One student began a research paper in political science with this blunder: "Benjamin Franklin's 'Declaration of Independence' is a perfect causal analysis, stating exactly why a young nation rebelled and overthrew a colonial master it considered tyrannical." The confusion of Benjamin Franklin with Thomas Jefferson not only got this paper off to a bad start, but also cast doubt on its overall validity. Accuracy is especially important in the use of names, dates, and statistics. To write that China must feed 500 million when its population exceeds a billion is to commit an inaccuracy that cannot be overcome by stylistic elegance.

7a–3 Be precise

Precision is essential in any discussion of technical material, mainly for the sake of your reader's understanding. Notice the difference in precision between the following two paragraphs, taken from the first and second drafts of a student paper on the origin of Indian castes:

Imprecise   The occupations of the four major castes were spelled out in the <u>Laws of Manu</u>: The Brahmin were the highest, the Kshatriyas came second, the Vaishyas followed, and the Sudras were at the bottom of the pile.

The vagueness of this passage resulted from the writer's false assumption that readers already would be familiar with the general divisions of Indian castes. When the instructor pointed out that more information was needed, the student produced this revision:

More precise   The occupations of the four major castes were spelled out in the <u>Laws of Manu</u>: The Brahmin were to teach, interpret the Vedas (holy scriptures), and perform the required ritual sacrifices. The Kshatriyas were to be the warriors and social governors (even kings). The Vaishyas were to tend the livestock and to engage in commerce in order to create wealth for the country. As for the Sudras, they were to become the servants of the three higher castes--doing their bidding without malice or resentment.

This greater precision adds immeasurably to the writer's style, making it seem less superficial and empty.

7a–4 Be concise

Conciseness means using the least number of words necessary for clarity. Indeed, conciseness generally adds to clarity by ridding explanations of jargon and verbiage. The goal of concise writing is to delete any word that does not add significantly to meaning.

Not concise   In the early years of 1970 the National Aeronautics and Space Administration conducted an investigation to find funds from Congress for this new concept of a reusable space vehicle. The Administration decided that the establishment of a careful approach on its part was an important necessity since some members of Congress would doubtless show a strong opposition to the replacement of the expendable Saturn rockets that had carried the Apollo astronauts to the moon. There was tremendous precision and careful documentation in the preparation and submission of the request to Congress.

Concise   In the early 1970s the National Aeronautics and Space Administration (NASA) decided to see if Congress would fund its new concept of a reusable space vehicle. The Administration approached the problem carefully because some Congressional members had already opposed replacing the expendable Saturn rockets that

```
had carried the Apollo astronauts to the

moon.  A precise and well-documented request

was submitted to Congress.
```

The fuzziness of the first version comes from main ideas being couched in verb nominalizations: "conducted an investigation of" instead of "to see"; "the establishment of a careful approach was a necessity" instead of "The Administration approached the problem carefully"; and "the replacement of" instead of "replacing." It is always cleaner and clearer to express the action of a sentence in a verb rather than in a noun or a noun preceded by a preposition.

Three other common sources of wordiness are the use of redundant expressions, meaningless words or phrases, and snobbish diction.

- *Redundant expressions* occur when unnecessary words are used to repeat what has already been said. Here is an example:

```
During that time period the park area was popu-

lated with Indians who were sullen in appearance and

made a living by working with silver metal.
```

That "time" is a "period," "park" an "area," "sullen" an "appearance," and "silver" a "metal," is already clear from the context of the sentence. It is enough to write:

```
During that time the park was populated with In-

dians who looked sullen and made a living by working

with silver.
```

- *Meaningless words and phrases*, used incessantly, add murkiness to one's style. Consider the italicized words in the following passage:

```
The problem of world hunger is by and large a

matter of business and politics.  Basically, the two

become virtually entwined until for all intents and

purposes they cannot be addressed separately in any

given city or country.
```

Getting rid of the useless modifiers produces a clearer idea:

> The problem of world hunger is a matter of busi-
> ness and politics. The two become entwined until they
> cannot be addressed separately in any city or country.

■   *Snobbish diction* consists of words used not to clarify but to impress.
One writer submitted this purple patch:

> A person <u>desirous of</u> an interview must be <u>cog-</u>
> <u>nizant of</u> the fact that the interviewer may have
> dozens of other candidates to evaluate. A smart can-
> didate will <u>endeavor to utilize</u> the time wisely and
> will <u>facilitate</u> the interviewer in <u>ascertaining</u> the
> candidate's qualifications.

Replacing the italicized words with their more common equivalents results
in a sharper and less pompous style:

> A person wanting an interview must be aware that
> the interviewer may have dozens of other candidates to
> evaluate. A smart candidate will try to use the time
> wisely and will help the interviewer find out the can-
> didate's qualifications.

7a–5 Use the active voice

Because the passive voice is erroneously associated with objectivity and detachment, many writers are tempted to use it in their research papers. But
one may be objective and detached without sounding either textbookish
or stilted. Consider the following excerpt from a student paper on the
Great Pyramid at Giza:

> Who built the Great Pyramid? When? How? Through-
> out history students of archaeology have been baffled by
> these questions. All sorts of mystical theories have

been propounded by Egyptologists, but it has been concluded by most experts today that the Great Pyramid was
built by Egyptian citizens using the simplest of tools
and technology.

Notice the greater directness and vigor when the passage is recast in the active voice:

Who built the Great Pyramid? When? How? Throughout history these questions have baffled students of
archaeology. Egyptologists have propounded all sorts of
mystical theories, but most experts today have concluded
that the Great Pyramid was built by Egyptian citizens
using the simplest of tools and technology.

There are only two exceptions that call for the passive voice: one, for an occasional change of pace—to add an inviting pleat in an otherwise seamless bolt of writing; two, for the sake of maintaining a certain focus, especially when the action is more important than the actor. An example of this second exception occurs in the last sentence of the excerpt. Since the Great Pyramid is the focus both of the research and the passage, it deserves the emphasis it receives from this passive construction. Compare the last passage, for example, with the following:

Who built the Great Pyramid? When? How? Throughout history these questions have baffled students of
archaeology. Egyptologists have propounded all sorts of
mystical theories, but most experts today have concluded
that Egyptian citizens using the simplest of tools and
technology built the Great Pyramid.

Recasting the final sentence in the active voice removes the pyramid from center stage and replaces it with "Egyptian citizens." But the focus of the paragraph is on the Great Pyramid, not on "Egyptian citizens." The passive voice in this instance is therefore more emphatic.

7a–6 Take an objective stance

Research papers consist mainly of information found in books, periodicals, and other sources on which the writer must pass personal judgments or offer clarification. In the past, most instructors insisted that students write such papers only from the third-person point of view, which was thought to stress the objectivity of the writer. Here are examples of the two points of view that are generally used:

First-person point of view

In my research I found that the most extreme negative criticism of Jefferson Davis places the full weight of the Southern defeat on his head.

Third-person point of view

Research indicates that the most extreme negative criticism of Jefferson Davis places the full weight of the Southern defeat on his head.

Lately, however, many prestigious journals have relaxed their rules. Authors now are allowed to use the "I" or "we" point of view when reporting research data or when drawing attention to their findings, as the following examples show:

> In this essay I do not assert that all Mexican-American houses display the traits that I describe.
> —Daniel D. Arreola, *Geographical Review*, July 1988

> A complicating feature of marriage transactions in complex societies is that there may be variability by social status, wealth, region, or ethnic group. Where this problem has arisen in coding for this study, we selected the preferred form of the dominant stratum or ethnic group within the society.
> —Alice Schlegel and Rohn Eloul, *American Anthropologist*, June 1988

Should you ever use the first-person point of view ("I" or "we") in your research papers, and if so, when? If your instructor enforces an absolute ban on any but the objective third-person point of view, that, of course, is the rule you will have to follow. Otherwise, a safe rule of thumb is this: Use the first-person point of view only for expressing your own personal comments or judgments. Here are some examples:

I have tested these assumptions on a body of data gathered from three anthropologists.

To produce a better fit with reality, I have made the following adjustments in my interpretations of the findings.

Thus I theorized that. . . .

My findings indicated the exact opposite.

Our advice to the beginning research writer is this: Use the third-person point of view, but try not to sound stuffy.

7a–7 Avoid sexist language

Over the last decades feminists have complained about elements in our language that reflect the values and biases of a male-dominated society. Publishers have reacted to this criticism by encouraging the use of sex-neutral generic pronouns and sex-neutral nouns in place of those that automatically, and perhaps even inaccurately, specify the male sex. We urge you to do likewise. For example, the statement "Every anthropologist involved in the dig agreed that his job was made easier . . ." can be replaced easily with "All anthropologists involved in the dig agreed that their jobs were made easier. . . . " If the subject cannot be made plural, identify the specific anthropologist by name: "In her fieldwork Margaret Meade found that she. . . . " Avoid the use of gender-biased words such as "mankind," "chairman," "congressman," "poetess," "woman surgeon," or "actress." These can be changed to inoffensive equivalents of "humankind," "chair," "member of congress," "poet," "surgeon," "actor." Certainly sexist language is entirely inappropriate in a research paper.

7b   Use a clear introduction

No part of your research paper is more important than its introduction, for here you either rivet the reader's attention or lose it. The first requirement of a good introduction is to specify with clarity what your paper proposes to argue, assert, or do. Here is an example of a muddled introduction:

Most women think that they will be victimized by men and that this is a normal state of affairs; therefore it is important that women fight back by standing up for themselves. They must refuse to play second fiddle to men. On the other hand, given the present distribution of power and privilege, women are bound to be tinged by the historical leftovers of inequality. In order to get along in the world, they will have to show a certain amount of admiration for men and a willingness to service them. My paper is an attempt to demonstrate this point.

This introduction is muddled with too many themes: women are victimized by men; women should stand up to men; women's roles are still affected by the inequality in their past; to get along in the world, women must show a willingness to service men. The student was advised to focus her research on one point and develop that in a rewritten paper. Here is her rewritten introduction:

Today our society enforces femininity by certain unspoken threats, and if a woman tests the limits of her gender beyond a certain point, she will lose the approval of women as well as men. For example, if she is viewed as pushy, assertive, aggressive, and selfish, she may lose her job, her boyfriend, and alienate her family. Moreover, a woman who dares to oppose this patriarchal system risks being perceived as both unfeminine and undesirable. That is why many women have resigned themselves to playing a narrowly prescribed role in this male-dominated drama. Indeed, an implicit definition of femininity in our culture is based on this unacknowledged principle of surrender to masculinity.

With the thesis now plainly stated in the final sentence, the introduction is both provocative and clear.

7b–1 Strategies for lively introductions

Common among the well-known strategies for beginning a paper are these three: use a quotation, ask a question, or present an enlightening illustration.

a. Use a quotation

Beginning the paper with an apt quotation that your opening remarks can either support or refute has the advantage of plunging the discussion immediately into the topic. The quotation may be a well-known saying or any especially apt comment. A dictionary of familiar quotations is available in the reference section of all libraries, with quotations listed by subject headings. Be sure that the quotation you use is so applicable to your topic that it will lead naturally to your thesis. Here is an example of an aptly used quotation in a paper suggesting that civil servants should be trained professionals:

```
"There are some things we can no longer afford--above

all we can no longer afford to do without highly trained

government officials."  These words are found in the

diary of Felix Frankfurter, Chief Justice of the United

States under Franklin Delano Roosevelt.  Frankfurter's

warning that government jobs cannot be left to amateurs

appointed because they gave money to a President's elec-

tion campaign or otherwise curried special favor with

the candidate, is even more true today than it was fifty

years ago.
```

b. Ask a question

Any question you ask should draw your reader into your topic. Here is an example from a paper advocating expanded welfare assistance to single mothers with children to support:

Would you really want to exchange places with a mother

on welfare because she gets for free money others earn?

Before you say "yes," consider the case of Joan Smith.

She washes her clothes in a bathtub. She travels every-

where by bus or foot. She lives with rickety furniture

in an apartment that rattles every time trucks drive by.

Shootings that endanger her children's daily lives are

common in her neighborhood. She feels disgraced because

she is poor and dependent ·on the public dole. The irony

of her situation is that she is bright and filled with

intellectual curiosity. She could go to college if only

someone would pay her way. I believe in a welfare sys-

tem that helps single mothers with dependent children

improve their lives by offering them a free education so

they can pursue a career that will eventually help them

get off welfare and live with independent dignity.

Using a question has the advantage of allowing you to steer the discussion in exactly the direction you want it to go.

c. Present an illustration

Anecdotes or examples that illustrate a point are popular openings in both sermons and papers. Open your paper with a riveting illustration, and your reader will willingly follow you the rest of the way. Here is an example from a paper arguing that the original versions of fairy tales, although more macabre than the modern ones, were also harmless and more appealing:

When Cinderella's wicked stepsisters saw the prince

holding up the glass slipper during the ball and looking

eagerly for the girl who could wear it, they sliced off

their heels and toes in an effort to make that slipper

```
fit.  This scene appears in the original version of Cin-

derella.  It is rather grisly but typical of many fairy

tales before they were sanitized to omit the more grue-

some details for fear they might scare children or

harden them to torture, torment, and mayhem.  But modern

research by a number of leading psychiatrists and psy-

chologists reveals that coping with imaginary evil,

including violence, is healthy for children and does

not turn them into neurotic or cold-blooded adults.
```

Aptly chosen, the right anecdote or example can be an effective introduction for your research paper.

7c   Write an effective conclusion

An effective conclusion will briefly summarize the content of the paper, suggest what a reader should do, and end rather than stop. It will not fade out or simply sputter to a lame or inconclusive ending.

7c–1 Summarize your main points

To summarize your main points means to identify and concisely review the major ideas in your paper. Avoid further explanation, tangential comment, or detailed analysis. Here is what we mean, from a paper on Josef Mengele, a Nazi physician accused of committing atrocities on the inmates of Auschwitz:

```
Josef Mengele was not the charismatic superhuman Satan

lawyers and writers have described.  Rather, he was sim-

ply a pathetic schizoid man who had a demented vision of

"purifying" the gene pool of Germany by studying twins

to assess which personality traits were caused by bio-

logical heredity and which by cultural influence.  He

tried to achieve this sick goal by exercising total
```

```
control over his scientific experiments at Auschwitz.

Acts of murder and sadism came naturally to him if they

promoted his scientific protocol.  In other words, his

ambition, backed by his psychic numbness, justified in

his deranged mind all acts of cruelty.
```

7c–2 Suggest what the reader should do

Especially in an argumentative paper, a good conclusion demands something from the reader—if only a change in attitude. Notice how the following conclusion from a paper about handicapped people in the work force demands a response from the reader:

```
We must stop promoting the myth that if a company hires

a handicapped person to do a job for which he or she

is qualified insurance rates will skyrocket, job perfor-

mance decline, safety records be ruined, and work areas

have to be redesigned to accommodate the outrageous

demands of the handicapped.  Statistics clearly prove

that handicapped job-seekers deserve to be hired and

that little difference exists in workplace performance

between handicapped and non-handicapped workers.
```

7c–3 End rather than stop

To stop is simply to place a period at the end of your paper regardless of whether or not you have penned an effective conclusion. Here is an example from a paper arguing that television coverage of the Vietnam War was unrealistic:

```
So, as you have read in this paper, the television

footage of combat was simply inadequate.
```

This conclusion is too abrupt, as if the writer has merely grown weary of writing. When the conclusion's weakness was pointed out, the student came up with this improved version:

Because time constraints allowed only a tiny part of the
action associated with combat in Vietnam to be aired on
television; because the mechanics of television reporting (need for camera, sound equipment, film) handicapped
field reporting; and because Americans refused to watch
scenes depicting battlefield suffering, what Americans
saw on television during the Vietnam war was cinema, not
reality.

The rewritten ending sums up the main points of the paper, tries to elicit
agreement from the reader, and concludes smoothly yet forcefully.

8

SYSTEMS OF DOCUMENTATION

8a   When to provide documentation

General knowledge, common sayings, self-evident opinions, and conclusions do not need to be documented. The rule of thumb is simply this: If the idea, opinion, or conclusion is of the kind that any well-read person is likely to know, then no documentation is necessary. For instance, the assertion that the Nazi regime under Hitler committed atrocities against the Jews is common knowledge and therefore requires no documentation. However, if you quote from eyewitness accounts of these atrocities, acknowledgment must be given in either a footnote, an endnote, or in parentheses. In sum, any idea, conclusion, information, or data specifically derived from the work of someone else must be acknowledged. (See also Section 5g, pp. 68–73—Plagiarism: what it is and how to avoid it.)

8b   Types of documentation

Documentation is the process by which you give credit to the appropriate sources for every borrowed idea used in your paper. Borrowed ideas may be incorporated into the paper either as direct quotations, summaries, or paraphrases. But no matter what form you use to incorporate the idea of another into your paper, you must give appropriate credit in a specific and conventional style that allows a reader to trace your sources and, if necessary, to investigate their accuracy or applicability. (See also Section 5f–2, pp. 65–68.)

Two basic styles of documentation are used now in research: (1) note citations and (2) parenthetical citations. The older style, note citations, calls for footnotes or endnotes. This style is preferred by two major fields, the humanities (but *not* language and literature) and the fine arts (music, art, and dance). Footnotes and endnotes both require superscript numbers within the text and corresponding documentary notes either at the bottom of the page (footnotes) or at the end of the paper (endnotes). For example, a paper on Salvador Dali's religious paintings might include the following passage:

```
One of Dali's most popular paintings, Christ of Saint

John of the Cross, pictures the crucified Christ sus-

pended over Iligat Bay, a port on the east coast of

Spain.  Christ is symbolized as the nucleus of the atom,

that is, the unity of the universe.[3]
```

In the footnote style, the superscript *3* would have the following corresponding footnote at the bottom of the same page on which the superscript *3* appeared:

> [3] Salvador Dali, <u>Dali</u>, trans. Eleanor R. Morse (New York: Abrams, 1970) 33.

The endnote style requires the same reference note (only double-spaced within and between notes) in numerical order according to the superscripts, in a separate section entitled "Notes" at the end of the paper. (See p. 142.)

The note citation style also requires a separate bibliography at the end of the paper in which all sources used are listed alphabetically by the surnames of the authors or, in cases where there is no author, by the first significant word of the title of the work:

> Dali, Salvador. <u>Dali</u>. Trans. Eleanor R. Morse. New
>
> York: Abrams, 1970.

Each source will therefore be documented at least twice: in a footnote or endnote and in a bibliography entry. Slight differences exist in the format of each kind of documentation—differences which must be observed. Footnotes or endnotes cannot simply be transferred to the bibliography page of the paper; nor can a bibliography entry serve as a note.

Parenthetical citations, a second style of documentation, now dominate in the sciences as well as in language and literature. Here references are placed not in endnotes or footnotes but in parentheses within the text itself. The parenthetical note refers the reader to a bibliography entry, which includes complete publication details on the source. Let us assume, for instance, that a paper on the history of passive resistance alludes to a work by Ralph Templin. In the parenthetical documentation style, all of the important documenting information would appear in the text, with only a short reference in parentheses:

> As Ralph Templin notes (253), nonviolence does not sim-
>
> ply ignore evil so that peace can be maintained.

or

> Nonviolence does not simply ignore evil so that peace
>
> can be maintained (Templin 253).

The full Templin reference is in the bibliography section at the end of the paper—labeled "Works Cited" or "Reference List." Simplicity is the main virtue of this style. In the past, beleaguered students had to perform double labor in documenting their papers. First, they had to laboriously type out footnotes on the bottoms of their pages, often ruining otherwise good pages because they had miscounted the number of lines a note required. Next, they had to repeat the nearly identical information in a bibliography citation. The use of endnotes required the same double labor. Nowadays, however, computerized word processors make the job easy. Even so, the parenthetical style calls for only one complete citation—the bibliography entry. Within the text itself the parenthetical reference consists of author and page (or, in the case of scientific papers, author and date). This text favors parenthetical documentation, and that is the style it explains in detail. However, for those students whose teachers still prefer the traditional note style, summary guidelines to it, with examples, are provided as well.

8c Guide to systems of documentation

The following list can help you decide which type of documentation your paper requires. Disciplines are listed alphabetically within each group.

GUIDE TO SYSTEMS OF DOCUMENTATION

Author/Work (MLA) (See Section 8d.)	Language Literature	
Author/Year (APA) (See Section 8e.)	Agriculture Anthropology Archaeology Astronomy Biology Botany Business Education	Geology Home Economics Linguistics Physical Education Political Science Psychology Sociology
Traditional (Footnote/Endnote) (See Section 8g.)	Art Dance History Music	Philosophy Religion Theater
Numbers (See Section 8f.)	Chemistry Computer Science Health	Mathematics Medicine Nursing

8d Parenthetical documentation: author and work (MLA style)

College research papers in the field of language and literature have long followed the style laid down by the Modern Language Association (MLA), which, since 1983, has used parenthetical documentation. The MLA style dictates the following conventions:

- Use of Arabic numerals for everything except titles (*Henry IV*) or preliminary pages of a text traditionally numbered with Roman numerals (i, ii, iv, x, and so on).
- Omission of "p." or "pp." for page numbers.
- Omission of "l." or "ll." in favor or "line" or "lines" until lineation is established in the paper.
- A simplified form for journal entries, as follows:

```
Sherry, James J.  "Tennyson and the Paradox of the

     Sign."  Victorian Poetry 17 (1979): 204-16.
```

Note the omission of the comma after the journal title, the order of entries, and the colon following the year to separate the volume and page.

- The bibliography section is headed "Works Cited."

8d–1 Reference citations in the text

The MLA style simplifies the reader's job by suggesting the following rules for in-text citations.

a. Introducing the authority

Introduce paraphrases or quotations by giving the authority's name. Use both the first name and the surname the first time the authority is used:

```
Robert M. Jordan suggests that Chaucer's tales are held

together by seams that are similar to the exposed beams

supporting a Gothic cathedral (237-38).
```

Subsequent citations will refer simply to the authority's surname:

```
Jordan further suggests:
```

b. Identifying the source

Whenever possible, identify what makes the source important:

```
Noam Flinker, Lecturer in English at the Ben-Gurion Uni-

versity of the Negev in Israel, an authority on Biblical

literature, repeatedly suggests . . .
```

c. Documenting without mention of authority

When the authority is not mentioned in the introduction to a paraphrase or quotation, place in parentheses the authority's name, followed by a page reference:

```
Democracy is deemed preferable to monarchy because it

protects the individual's rights rather than his prop-

erty (Emerson 372).
```

d. Material by two or three authors

When referring to material written by two or three authors, mention the names of all authors:

```
Christine E. Wharton and James S. Leonard take the posi-

tion that the mythical figure of Amphion represents a

triumph of the spiritual over the physical (163).
```

Subsequent references would refer simply to Wharton and Leonard.

e. Material by more than three authors

For a work with more than three authors or editors, use the first name followed by "et al." or "and others" (without a comma following the name):

```
G. B. Harrison et al. (Major British Writers) provide an

excellent overview of the best in English literature.
```

f. Mentioning both author and work

When it can be accomplished smoothly, mention both the author and the work in your introduction:

```
In his essay "Criticism and Sociology," David Daiches

insists that "sociological criticism can help to

increase literary perception as well as to explain

origins" (17).
```

g. Anonymous author

When a work is listed as anonymous, mention that fact in the text and place the title of the work from which the piece was taken, or an abbreviated version if the title is very long, in parentheses:

```
Another anonymous poem, "Driftwood" (Driftwood 130-31),

also damns the city for its thoughtless pollution of the

environment.
```

h. No author

When a work has no author, cite the first two or three significant words from the title:

```
Spokane's The Spokesman Review ("Faulkner Dies") gets at

the heart of America's greatest fiction writer when it

states that . . .
```

i. More than one work by the same author

When more than one work by the same author is referred to in the paper, provide a shortened version of the title in each citation. Citing only author and page may confuse the reader since "Works Cited" will contain two or more references to the same author. The following passage is an example of how to handle two works by the same author:

```
Feodor Dostoevsky declares that the "underground" rebel

is representative of our society (Underground 3). He

seems to confirm this view in Raskolnikov's superman

speech (Crime 383-84), where he identifies . . .
```

j. Work in a collection

When citing a work in a collection, state the name of the person who wrote the opinion which you are citing:

```
Lionel Trilling's "Reality in America" does not consider

V. L. Parrington a great intellect.
```

"Works Cited" would then contain the following entry:

```
Trilling, Lionel.  "Reality in America."  Twentieth Cen-

     tury American Writing.  Ed. William T. Stafford.

     New York: Odyssey, 1965. 564-77.
```

k. Multivolume works

When referring to a specific passage in a multivolume work, give the author, the volume number followed by a colon and a space, and the page reference:

```
Other historians disagree (Durant 2: 25) . . . .
```

When referring to an entire volume, give the name of the author, followed by a comma, and the abbreviation "vol.," followed by the volume number: (Durant, vol. 2).

l. Double reference—a quotation within a cited work

```
As Bernard Baruch pointed out, "Mankind has always

thought to substitute energy for reason" (qtd. in

Ringer 274).
```

"Works Cited" would then contain the following entry:

```
Ringer, Robert J.  Restoring the American Dream.  New

     York: Harper, 1979.
```

m. Short passages of poetry

When short passages of poetry are incorporated into your text, observe these rules:

- Set off the quotation with quotation marks.
- Use a slash (with a space before and after the slash) to indicate separate lines of poetry.
- Place the proper documentation in parentheses immediately following the quotation and inside the period, because the reference is part of your basic sentence. The reference will be to the lines of the poem.

Study the following example:

```
Byron's profound sense of alienation is echoed in

Canto 3 of Childe Harold's Pilgrimage: "I have not loved

the World, nor the World me: / I have not flattered its

rank breath, nor bowed / To its idolatries a patient

knee" (190-91).
```

n. Using Arabic numerals

Use Arabic numerals for books, parts, volumes, and chapters of works; for acts, scenes, and lines of plays; for cantos, stanzas, and lines of poetry.

IN-TEXT CITATIONS
Volume 2 of *Civilization Past and Present*
Book 3 of *Paradise Lost*
Part 2 of *Crime and Punishment*
Act 3 of *Hamlet*
Chapter 1 of *The Great Gatsby*

PARENTHETICAL DOCUMENTATION

(*Tmp.* 2.2.45–50)	for act 2, scene 2, lines 45–50 of Shakespeare's *Tempest* (See Section 10g-2*b* for abbreviating titles of Shakespeare's plays.)
(*GT* 2.1.3)	for part 2, chapter 1, page 3 of *Gulliver's Travels* by Swift
(*Jude* 15)	for page 15 of the novel *Jude the Obscure* by Hardy
(*PL* 7.5–10)	for book 7, lines 5–10 of *Paradise Lost* by Milton
(*FQ* 1.2.28.1–4)	for book 1, canto 2, stanza 28, lines 1–4 of *The Faerie Queene* by Spenser

8d–2 Varying your introductions

Vary your introductions to the in-text citations. As you write the paper, you will find a variety of ways to introduce authors and their works. Some possibilities are listed here, but you can create many more:

```
Lionel Trilling, the noted critic and editor, has cham-

pioned this idea (108).
```

```
In The Coming of Age, Simone de Beauvoir contends that

the decrepitude accompanying old age is "in complete
```

conflict with the manly or womanly ideal cherished by
the young and fully grown" (25).

William York Tindall describes this segment as "the
densest part of the Wake" (171).

This attitude is central to the archetypal approach of
interpreting poetry (Fiedler 519).

Richard Chase argues that Billy Budd is a sort of Adam
"as yet untainted by the 'urbane serpent'" (745).

In his eloquent guidebook Style, F. L. Lucas points out
that revision in writing is "a means not only of polish-
ing, but also of compressing" (261).

Others, like Booth (51) and Warren (33), take the opposite point of view.

8e   Parenthetical documentation: author and date (APA style)

Established by the American Psychological Association (APA), this style is
used by the social sciences, business, anthropology, and some of the life
sciences (see Section 8c for a list of the disciplines using it). The APA style
favors a system of parenthetical citations within the text much like the
style recommended by the MLA. But there is a significant difference between the two. An in-text citation done in the APA style mentions only the
author and date of the cited publication, not the author and work.

8e–1 Reference citations in the text

On the whole, scientific papers favor a parenthetical style of documentation that briefly identifies the source of a quotation or a piece of information so that the reader can find it in the alphabetical list of references

at the end of the paper. Because in scientific research the date of publication is often crucial, the APA emphasizes the date by placing it in parentheses following the name of the author. All notes are so treated except for content notes (see Section 8h). This style, like the one used by the MLA, simplifies the job of documentation by eliminating all reference notes at the bottom of the paper or at the end of the paper, requiring instead only a final "Reference List."

The APA distinguishes between a *reference list*, a list of works specifically used in the research and preparation of your paper, and a *bibliography*, a list of works used for background reading or for further reading on the subject. A paper in the sciences, therefore, will end with a reference list, not with a bibliography.

a. One work by a single author

The APA style sheet uses an author-date method of citation; that is, the surname of the author and the year of publication are inserted in the text of the paper at the appropriate point:

```
Johnson (1983) discovered that children were more

susceptible. . . .
```

or

```
In a more recent study (Johnson, 1983), children were

found to be more susceptible. . . .
```

or

```
In 1983 Johnson did another study that indicated chil-

dren were more susceptible. . . .
```

If the name of the author appears as an integral part of your sentence, then cite only the year of publication in parentheses, as in the first example. Otherwise, show both the author and the date of publication in parentheses, as in the second example. If, however, both the year and the author are cited in the textual discussion, then nothing need appear within parentheses, as in the third example.

b. Subsequent references

If you continue to refer to the same study *within* a paragraph, subsequent references do not need to include the year as long as the study cannot be confused with other studies in your paper:

```
In a more recent study, Johnson (1983) found that chil-

dren were more susceptible. . . .    Johnson also found

that. . . .
```

c. One work by two authors

When a work has two authors, always mention both names each time the reference occurs in your text:

```
In a previous study of caged rats (Grant & Change, 1958)

the surprising element was . . .
```

or

```
Much earlier, Grant and Change (1958) had discovered . . .
```

Notice that each time you refer to a work by two authors, you must name both authors.

d. One work by up to five authors

For works with up to five authors, mention all authors the first time the reference occurs; however, in subsequent citations, include only the surname of the first author followed by "et al." (not underlined and without a period after "et") and the year of publication:

First citation:

```
Holland, Holt, Levi, and Beckett (1983) indicate

that . . .
```

Subsequent citation:

```
Holland et al. (1983) also found . . .
```

An exception occurs when two separate references have the same first author and same date and would thus shorten to the same reference. For example, Drake, Brighouse, and High (1983) and Drake, High, and Guilmette (1983) would both shorten to Drake et al. (1983). In such a case always cite both references in full to avoid confusion. Also, multiple-author citations in footnotes, tables, and figures should include the surnames of all authors every time the citations occur.

e. Work by six or more authors

When a work has six or more authors, name only the surname of the first author followed by "et al." (not underlined and without a period after "et") and the year, in the first as well as in subsequent citations. In the final reference list, the names of all authors will appear in full. An exception occurs if two separate references would shorten to the same form. In such a case, list as many authors as are necessary to distinguish the two references, followed by "et al." For instance,

```
Cotton, Maloney, Brauer, Martin, Rodiles, and Tscharner

(1970)
```

and

```
Cotton, Maloney, Jenkins, Martin, Rodiles, and Tscharner

(1970)
```

would be cited as follows in the text:

```
Cotton, Maloney, Brauer, et al. (1970)
```

and

```
Cotton, Maloney, Jenkins, et al. (1970)
```

NOTE: In your running text, join the names of multiple-author citations by the word *and*; however, in parenthetical material, in tables, and in the final reference list, join the names by an ampersand (&), as follows:

```
Anderson and Raoul (1984) demonstrated clearly

that . . .
```

but

```
As was clearly demonstrated earlier (Anderson & Raoul,

1984), certain factors remain . . .
```

f. Corporate authors

Sometimes a scientific work is authored by a committee, an institution, a corporation, or a governmental agency. The names of most such corporate authors should be spelled out each time they appear as a reference source in your text. Occasionally, however, the name is spelled out in the first citation only and is abbreviated in subsequent citations. The rule of thumb for abbreviating is that you must supply enough information in the text for the reader to track down this source in your final reference list. In the case of long and cumbersome corporate names, abbreviations are acceptable in subsequent citations as long as the name is recognized and understood.

First citation in the text:

    (National Institutes of Mental Health [NIMH], 1984)

Subsequent citations:

    (NIMH, 1984)

First citation in the text:

    (Santa Barbara Museum of Natural History [SBMNH], 1984)

Subsequent citations:

    (SBMNH, 1984)

If the name is short or its abbreviation would not be understood easily, spell out the name each time the reference occurs:

    (Harvard University, 1984)

    (Russell Sage Foundation, 1984)

    (Bendix Corporation, 1984)

The names of all of these corporate authors are simple enough to be written out each time they are cited.

g. Works by an anonymous author or no author

When the author of a work is listed as "Anonymous," show the word "Anonymous" in parentheses in the text, followed by a comma and the date:

    (Anonymous, 1984)

In your final reference list, the work will be alphabetized under "A" for "Anonymous."

When a work has no author, simply show, in parentheses, the first two or three words from the title of the book or article, followed by a comma and the year:

```
. . . as seen in most cases ("Time graphs," 1983)
```

```
The study shows that 55% of seniors (College bound

seniors, 1979) have serious difficulty with . . .
```

In the final reference list, works without authors are alphabetized according to the first significant word in the title. Articles (*the, a, an*), prepositions (*from, between, behind,* and so on), and pronouns (*this, those, that,* and so on) do not count. References to statutes and other legal materials are treated like references to works without authors; that is, you will cite the first few words of the reference and the year. Note that court cases cited in the text must be underlined.

```
(Baker v. Carr, 1962)
```

```
(National Environmental Protection Act, 1970)
```

```
(Civil Rights Act, 1964)
```

h. Authors with the same surname

If your paper includes two or more authors with the same surname, include the authors' initials in all text citations even if the date differs. In this way you will be sure to avoid confusion:

```
D. L. Spencer (1965) and F. G. Spencer (1983) studied

both aspects of . . .
```

i. Two or more works within the same parentheses

Sometimes your paper may require that you cite within parentheses two or more works supporting the same point. In such a case, you will list the citations in the same order in which they appear in the reference list and according to reference list guidelines (see Section 9a–1). The following rules will be helpful:

■ *Two or more works by the same author(s)* are arranged in the same order by year of publication. If one work is in the process of being published, cite it last:

```
Research of the past two years (Jessup & Quincy, 1983,

1984) has revealed many potential . . .
```

or

```
Past studies (Eberhard, 1980, 1981, in press)

reveal . . .
```

Different works by the same author that have the same publication date must be identified by "a," "b," "c," and so on:

```
According to these studies (Rodney & Campbell, 1980a,

1980b, in press) the prevalent attitude is . . .
```

■ *Two or more works by different authors* cited within the same parentheses should be listed alphabetically according to the first authors' surnames. Use semicolons to separate the studies:

```
Three separate studies (Delaney & Rice, 1980; Rodney &

Hollander, 1980; Zunz, 1981) tried to build on the

same theory, but . . .
```

j. References to specific parts of a source

Anytime you refer to a specific quotation, figure, or table, you must supply the appropriate page, figure number, or table number:

```
(Spetch & Wilkie, 1983, pp. 15-25)

(Halpern, 1982, Fig. 2)
```

Note that the words *pages* and *Figure* are abbreviated.

k. Personal communications

Personal communications include such items as letters, memos, and telephone conversations. Since they do not represent recoverable data, such

¹² Eudora Welty, "The Wide Net," <u>Story: An Introduction to Prose Fiction</u>, ed. Arthur Foff and Daniel Knaff (Belmont: Wadsworth, 1966) 166.

g. Double reference—a quotation within a cited work

Use the following form for referring to a quotation within a cited work:

¹³ Lin Piao as quoted in Jean Daubier, <u>A History of the Chinese Cultural Revolution</u>, trans. Richard Seaver (New York: Random, 1974) 83.

h. Reference work

For signed articles in well-known encyclopedias, supply name of author, title of entry, name of encyclopedia, and year of edition:

¹⁴ Albert George Ballert, "Saint Lawrence River," <u>Encyclopaedia Britannica</u>, 1963 ed.

The authors of articles in reference works usually are identified by initials that are decoded in a special index volume. If the article is unsigned, begin with the title entry:

¹⁵ "House of David," <u>Encyclopedia Americana</u>, 1974 ed.

¹⁶ "Telegony," <u>Dictionary of Philosophy and Psychology</u>, 1902 ed.

i. Work in a series

¹⁷ Louis Auchincloss, <u>Edith Wharton</u>, University of Minnesota Pamphlets on American Writers 12 (Minneapolis: U of Minnesota P, 1961) 17.

j. Edition

The word *edition* can be understood in three different ways; it can mean: (1) a revised printing of a work; (2) a collection of items edited by one or several authors; or (3) the edited version of one or more works by an editor or editors. The proper forms to use in each of these cases are as follows:

(I) FOR A REVISED EDITION:

> [18] Porter G. Perrin and Jim W. Corder, <u>Handbook of Current English</u>, 4th ed. (Glenview: Scott, 1975) 304-05.

(II) FOR AN EDITED COLLECTION:

> [19] Charles Clerc, "Goodbye to All That: Theme, Character and Symbol in <u>Goodbye, Columbus</u>," <u>Seven Contemporary Short Novels</u>, ed. Charles Clerc and Louis Leiter (Glenview: Scott, 1969) 107.

The reference here is to an editorial critique on one of the novels in the collection.

(III) FOR THE WORK OF AN EDITOR:

> [20] Hardin Craig and David Bevington, eds., <u>The Complete Works of Shakespeare</u>, rev. ed. (Glenview: Scott, 1973) 31-38.

Because the reference is to the editorial work of Craig and Bevington, the names of these editors are listed in place of the author's. But when the paper deals with the work of the original author, rather than with the work of an editor or translator, the author's name must then be listed first:

> [21] Sylvia Plath, <u>Letters Home</u>, ed. Aurelia Schober Plath (New York: Harper, 1975) 153-54.

k. Translation

> [22] Benvenuto Cellini, <u>Autobiography of Benvenuto Cellini</u>, trans. John Addington Symons (New York: Washington Square, 1963) 75-79.

l. Pamphlet

Citations of pamphlets should conform as nearly as possible to the format used for citations of books. Give as much information about the pamphlet as is necessary to help a reader find it:

> [23] Calplans Agricultural Fund, <u>An Investment in California Agricultural Real Estate</u> (Oakland: Calplans Securities, n.d.) 3.

m. *Government publication or legal reference*

Because of their complicated origins, government publications can be difficult to document. Generally, the citation of a government publication should list first the author or agency, then the title of the publication (underlined), followed by the publication facts (place, publisher, date) and the page reference. Although no standard format exists for all such publications, we have tried to supply samples for the kinds of government sources most often cited in undergraduate papers.

(I) *CONGRESSIONAL RECORD*

A citation to the *Congressional Record* requires only title, date, and page(s):

> [24] Cong. Rec., 15 Dec. 1977: 19740.

(II) *CONGRESSIONAL PUBLICATIONS*

The authors are listed either as "U.S. Cong., Senate," "U.S. Cong., House," or "U.S. Cong., Joint":

> [25] U.S. Cong., Senate, Permanent Subcommittee on Investigations of the Committee on Government Operations, Organized Crime--Stolen Securities, 93rd Cong., 1st sess. (Washington: GPO, 1973) 1-4.

"GPO" is the accepted abbreviation for "U.S. Government Printing Office."

> [26] U.S. Cong., House, Committee on Foreign Relations, Hearings on S. 2793, Supplemental Foreign Assistance Fiscal Year 1966--Vietnam, 89th Cong., 2nd sess. (Washington: GPO, 1966) 9.

The titles of government publications, although long and cumbersome, must nevertheless be cited accurately.

(III) *LEGAL PUBLICATIONS*

> [27] Office of the Federal Register, "The Supreme Court of the United States," United States Government Manual (Washington: GPO, 1976) 67.

Names of laws, acts, and the like generally are neither underlined nor placed within quotation marks: Constitution of the United States,

Declaration of Independence, Bill of Rights, Humphrey-Hawkins Bill, Sherman Anti-Trust Act. Citations of legal sources usually refer to sections rather than to pages. Certain conventional abbreviations also are used in such citations:

   [28] U.S. Const., art. I, sec. 2.

   [29] 15 U.S. Code, sec. 78j(b) (1964).

   [30] U.C.C., art. IX, pt. 2, par. 9-28.

Names of law cases are abbreviated and the first important word of each party is spelled out: Brown v. Board of Ed. stands for Oliver Brown versus the Board of Education of Topeka, Kansas. Cases, unlike laws, are italicized in the text but not in the notes. Text: *Miranda v. Arizona.* Note: Miranda v. Arizona. The following information must be supplied in a citation of a law case: (1) the name of the first plaintiff and the first defendant; (2) the volume, name, and page (in that order) of the law report cited; (3) the name of the court that decided the case; and (4) the year in which the case was decided:

   [31] Richardson v. J. C. Flood Co., 190 A. 2d 259 (D.C. App. 1963).

Interpreted, this footnote means that the Richardson v. J. C. Flood Co. case can be found on page 259 of volume 190 of the Second Series of the *Atlantic Reporter.* The case was settled in the District of Columbia Court of Appeals during the year 1963. For further information on the form for legal references, consult *A Uniform System of Citation,* 12th ed. (Cambridge: Harvard Law Review Association, 1976).

n. Classical works

In citing a classical work that is subdivided into books, parts, cantos, verses, or lines, specify the appropriate subdivisions so that a reader using a different edition of the work can easily locate the reference:

   [32] Homer, The Iliad, trans. Richmond Lattimore (Chicago: U of Chicago P, 1937) 101 (3.15-20).

   [33] Dante Alighieri, The Inferno, trans. John Ciardi (New York: NAL, 1954) 37 (2.75-90).

Books or parts have traditionally been indicated by large Roman numerals, cantos or verses by small Roman numerals, and lines by Arabic numerals.

However, the modern trend is toward Arabic numerals for everything (see Section 8d–1*k*).

o. The Bible

Because the King James Bible is such a familiar document, only the appropriate book and verse need be cited. Translations other than the King James must be indicated within parentheses.

King James Bible:

   ³⁴ Isaiah 12:15.   or   ³⁴ Isaiah 12.15.

Other translation:

   ³⁵ 2 Corinthians 2:10 (Revised Standard Version).

or

   ³⁵ 2 Corinthians 2.10 (Revised Standard Version).

8g–6 Sample footnotes for periodicals

a. Anonymous author

   ¹ "Elegance Is Out," Fortune 13 Mar. 1978: 18.

Most periodical articles are written by unidentified correspondents.

b. Single author

   ² Hugh Sidey, "In Defense of the Martini," Time 24 Oct. 1977: 38.

c. More than one author

   ³ Clyde Ferguson and William R. Cotter, "South Africa—What Is to Be Done?" Foreign Affairs 56 (1978): 254.

The format of a citation to a multiple-authored magazine article is the same as for a multiple-authored book. For three authors, list the names of the authors exactly as they appear in the article. Separate the first and second name by a comma, and the second and third by a comma followed by the word "and." For more than three authors, list the name of the first author followed by "et al." with no comma in between.

d. Journal with continuous pagination throughout the annual volume

⁴ Anne Paolucci, "Comedy and Paradox in Pirandello's Plays," <u>Modern Drama</u> 20 (1977): 322.

Since there is only one page 322 throughout volume 20 of 1977, it is unnecessary to add the month.

e. Journal with separate pagination for each issue

⁵ Claude T. Mangrum, "Toward More Effective Justice," <u>Crime Prevention Review</u> 5 (Jan. 1978): 7.

⁶ Janet Stevenson, "Before the Colors Fade: The Return of the Exiles," <u>American Heritage</u> 20.4 (1969): 24.

Since each issue of these journals is paged anew, page 7, for example, will occur in all issues of volume 5; therefore, the addition of the month is necessary. Some journals use numbers to distinguish different issues. Footnote 6, for example, refers the reader to issue 4 of volume 20. Follow the style of the individual journal:

⁷ Robert Brown, "Physical Illness and Mental Health," <u>Philosophy and Public Affairs</u> 7 (Fall 1977): 18-19.

Since this journal is published quarterly and in volumes that do not coincide with the year, adding the season of publication makes the source easier to locate.

f. Monthly magazine

⁸ Flora Davis and Julia Orange, "The Strange Case of the Children Who Invented Their Own Language," <u>Redbook</u> Mar. 1978: 113, 165.

Note the split page reference to the article, which began on one page and was continued at the back of the magazine.

g. Weekly magazine

[9] Suzy Eban, "Our Far-Flung Correspondents," <u>The New Yorker</u> 6 Mar. 1978: 70-72.

h. Newspaper

[10] James Tanner, "Disenchantment Grows in OPEC Group with Use of U.S. Dollar for Oil Pricing," <u>Wall Street Journal</u> 9 Mar. 1978: 3, cols. 3-4.

See also footnote 13.

Listing the columns as well as the page makes the article easier to locate; however, listing the column(s) is optional.

NOTE: If the first word of a newspaper's title is an article, the article is deleted. For example, *The Wall Street Journal* becomes *Wall Street Journal.*

[11] Daniel Southerland, "Carter Plans Firm Stand with Begin," <u>Christian Science Monitor</u> 9 Mar. 1978, western ed.: 1, 9.

Supply the edition or section when available.

i. Editorial

Signed:

[12] William Futrell, "The Inner City Frontier," editorial, <u>Sierra</u> 63.2 (1978): 5.

Unsigned:

[13] "Criminals in Uniform," editorial, <u>Los Angeles Times</u> 7 Apr. 1978, pt. 2: 6.

Listing the part as well as the page makes this newspaper article easier to locate.

j. Letter to the editor

[14] Donna Korcyzk, letter, <u>Time</u> 20 Mar. 1978: 4.

k. Critical review

> ^{15} Peter Andrews, rev. of <u>The Strange Ride of Rud-</u>
> <u>yard Kipling: His Life and Works</u>, by Angus Wilson, <u>Sat-</u>
> <u>urday Review</u> 4 Mar. 1978: 24.

8g–7 Sample footnotes for special items

Citation samples of other sources commonly used in research papers are
given below. For citation forms on sources not covered here, consult your
instructor. Bear in mind that the prime rule of documentation is to provide the information necessary for a reader to trace any cited source.

a. Lecture

As minimum information cite the speaker's name, the title of the lecture
in quotation marks, the sponsoring organization, the location, and the
date. If the presentation has no title, use an appropriate label, such as lecture, speech, or address:

> ^{1} Gene L. Schwilck, "The Core and the Community,"
> Danforth Foundation, St. Louis, 16 Mar. 1978.

> ^{2} Jesse Jackson, address, Democratic National Con-
> vention, San Francisco, 17 July 1984.

b. Film

Film citations should include the title of the film (underlined), the director's name, the distributor, and the year of release. Information on the
producer, writer, performers, and size or length of the film may also be
supplied, if necessary to your study:

> ^{3} <u>The Turning Point</u>, dir. Herbert Ross, with Anne
> Bancroft, Shirley MacLaine, Mikhail Baryshnikov, and
> Leslie Brown, Twentieth Century-Fox, 1978.

c. Radio or television program

Citations should include the title of the program (underlined), the network or local station, and the city and date of broadcast. If appropriate,
the title of the episode is listed in quotation marks before the title of the
program, while the title of the series, neither underlined nor in quotation

marks, comes after the title of the program. The name of the writer, director, narrator, or producer may also be supplied, if significant to your paper:

> [4] "Diving for Roman Plunder," narr. and dir. Jacques Cousteau, <u>The Cousteau Odyssey</u>, KCET, Los Angeles, 14 Mar. 1978.

> [5] <u>World of Survival</u>, narr. John Forsythe, CBS Special, Los Angeles, 29 Oct. 1972.

d. Recording (disc or tape)

For commercially available recordings, cite the following: composer or performer, title of recording or of work(s) on the recording, artist(s), manufacturer, catalog number, and date of issue (if not known, state "n.d."):

> [6] The Beatles, "I Should Have Known Better," <u>The Beatles Again</u>, Apple Records, SO-385, n.d.

(This is a reference to one of several songs on a disc.) A citation of a recording of classical music may omit the title of the recording and instead list the works recorded. Musical compositions identified by form, key, and number are neither underlined nor placed within quotation marks:

> [7] Johann Sebastian Bach, Toccata and Fugue in D Minor, Toccata, Adagio, and Fugue in C Major, Passacaglia and Fugue in C Minor; Johann Christian Bach, Sinfonia for Double Orchestra, Op. 18, No. 1, cond. Eugene Ormandy, The Philadelphia Orchestra, Columbia, MS 6180, n.d.

(When two or more composers and their works are involved, a semicolon separates each grouping.) Citations of recordings of the spoken word list the speaker first:

> [8] Swift Eagle, <u>The Pueblo Indians</u>, Caedmon TC 1327, n.d.

For a recording of a play, use the following form (the participating actors are listed):

> [9] <u>Shakespeare's Othello</u>, with Paul Robeson, José Ferrer, Uta Hagen, and Edith King, Columbia, SL-153, n.d.

In addition to the speaker and title, a citation to a noncommercial recording should state when the recording was made, for whom, and where. The title of the recording is not underlined:

> [10] Michael Dwyer, Readings from Mark Twain, rec. 15 Apr. 1968, Humorist Society, San Bernardino, CA.

e. Personal letter

Published letters are treated as titles within a book. Add the date of the letter, if available:

> [11] Oscar Wilde, "To Mrs. Alfred Hunt," 25 Aug. 1880, <u>The Letters of Oscar Wilde</u>, ed. Rupert Hart-Davis (New York: Harcourt, 1962) 67-68.

For letters personally received, use the following form:

> [12] Gilbert Highet, letter to the author, 15 Mar. 1972.

f. Interview

Citations of interviews should specify the kind of interview, the name (and, if pertinent, the title) of the interviewed person, and the date of the interview:

> [13] Dr. Charles Witt, personal interview, 23 Mar. 1976.

> [14] Telephone interview with Edward Carpenter, librarian at Huntington Library, 2 Mar. 1978.

8g–8 Subsequent references to footnotes/endnotes

Subsequent citations to an already identified source are given in abbreviated form. The rule is to make subsequent citations brief but not cryptic. Ordinarily the author's last name or a key word from the title, followed by a page number, will do. Latin terms such as "op. cit." ("in the work cited"), "loc. cit." ("in the place cited"), and "ibid." ("in the same place") are no longer used.

First reference:

> [1] John W. Gardner, <u>Excellence</u> (New York: Harper, 1961) 47.

Subsequent reference:

> [2] Gardner 52.

If two or more subsequent references cite the same work, simply repeat the name of the author and supply the appropriate page numbers. Do not use "ibid.":

> [3] Gardner 83.

> [4] Gardner 198.

If, however, your paper also contains references to Gardner's other book, *Self-Renewal,* the two books should be distinguished by title in subsequent references:

> [5] Gardner, Excellence 61.

> [6] Gardner, Self-Renewal 62.

If two of the cited authors share the same last name, subsequent references should supply the full name of each author:

> [7] Henry James 10.

> [8] William James 23-24.

For a subsequent reference to an anonymous article in a periodical, use a shortened version of the title.

First reference:

> [9] "The Wooing of Senator Zorinsky," Time 27 Mar. 1978: 12.

Subsequent reference:

> [10] "Zorinsky" 13.

For subsequent references to unconventional or special sources, you may need to improvise.

8h   Content notes

Content notes consist of material that is relevant to your research but that does not need to interrupt the flow of your text. Such notes may consist of an explanation, additional information, reference to other sources, information about procedures used to gain information, or acknowledgment of special assistance. The format of content notes is the same no matter which style of documentation is used in the paper. Some instructors insist that all content notes be gathered together on a page entitled "Notes," placed after the text of the paper but before the "Works Cited" page. Other instructors prefer to have them placed at the foot of the appropriate page so that the reader can look down and read them as they occur. The following rules should be observed when typing content notes:

- Indent the first line of each note five spaces.
- Double-space content notes gathered at the end of the paper (see sample student paper, p. 263), but single-space those shown at the foot of a page. In the latter case be sure to allow for enough space for the entire note. Begin the note four lines below the text. Do *not* type a solid line between the text and the note since this would indicate a note continued from the previous page when space ran out. Single-space the note but double-space between notes if there is more than one note.
- In your text, roll up a half space at the relevant place and strike your note number, as in the following example:

```
The centaur, being half horse and half man, symbolized

both the wild and benign aspect of nature.  Thus the

coexistence of nature and culture was expressed.12
```

The note at the foot of the page then adds the following comment without interrupting the flow of the text:

```
    12 It should be noted that the horse part is the
lower and more animalistic area whereas the human por-
tion is the upper, including the heart and head.
```

- Provide complete documentation to content footnote sources in "Works Cited" or in "Reference List," but do *not* provide complete documentation in the note itself. For instance, the following content footnote might appear in a biology paper:

```
    10 Harvey (1980) disagrees with this aspect of

Johnson's interpretation of handwriting.
```

The following full reference would then appear in "Reference List":

Harvey, O. L. (1980). The measurement of handwriting

considered as a form of expressive movement.

Quarterly Review of Biology, 55, 231-249.

NOTE: An exception is the traditional footnote or endnote style, which provides full documentation in the note as well as in "Works Cited."

Study the following sample content notes gathered at the end of a paper.

8h–1 Content note explaining a term

[1] The "Rebellion of 1837" refers to December of

1837, when William Lyon Mackenzie, a newspaper editor

and former mayor of Toronto, led a rebellion intended

to establish government by elected officials rather than

appointees of the British Crown.

8h–2 Content note expanding on an idea

[2] This pattern of development was also reflected in

their system of allocation: only a small percentage of

tax money was used for agriculture, whereas great chunks

were apportioned to industry.

8h–3 Content note referring the reader to another source

[3] For further information on this point, see King

and Chang (124-35).

NOTE: The "Works Cited" or "Reference List" must provide full documentation for this source:

King, Gilbert W., and Hsien Wu Chang. "Machine Transla-

tion of Chinese," Scientific American 208.6 (1963):

124-35.

8h–4 Content note explaining procedures

[4] Subjects were classed according to their smoking history as never smokers, cigar and/or pipe smokers exclusively, ex-cigarette smokers (smoked cigarettes regularly in the past but not within the year prior to the time of interview), and current cigarette smokers (smoked cigarettes regularly at the time of the inter-view for at least one year).

8h–5 Content note acknowledging assistance

[5] The authors wish to acknowledge the assistance of the Montreal Children's Hospital in providing access to its Hewlett-Packard 3000 computer.

8i Consolidation of references

If a substantial part of your paper is based on several sources that deal with the same idea, consolidating the references into a single note may save space and prevent repetition. The format for handling consolidation of references differs according to the documentation style being used.

8i–1 Footnote using author-work style (MLA)

[1] For this idea I am indebted to Holland (32), Folsom (136-144), and Edgar (15-17).

NOTE: A "Works Cited" or "Reference List" at the end of the paper must provide full documentation for these sources.

8i–2 Footnote using author-date style (APA)

[2] On this point see Hirsbrunner (1981), Florin (1981), and Frey (1981).

NOTE: A "Works Cited" or "Reference List" at the end of the paper must provide full documentation for these sources.

8i–3 Footnote using numbers style

 [3] This section reflects the conclusions reached by Kuller (3), Thompson (4), Copley (7), Eisenberg (8), and Weaver (17).

NOTE: A "Works Cited" or "Reference List" at the end of the paper must provide full documentation for these sources.

8i–4 Footnote using traditional style

 [4] For this idea I am indebted to Laurence Bedwell Holland, <u>The Expense of Wisdom</u> (Princeton: Princeton UP, 1964) 32; James K. Folsom, "Archimago's Well: An Interpretation of <u>The Sacred Fount</u>," <u>Modern Fiction Studies</u> 7 (1961): 136-44; and Pelham Edgar, <u>Henry James: Man and Author</u> (1927; New York: Russell, 1964) 15-17.

NOTE: Separate the individual citations with a semicolon. The "Works Cited" list must repeat the documentation for these sources.

THE BIBLIOGRAPHY

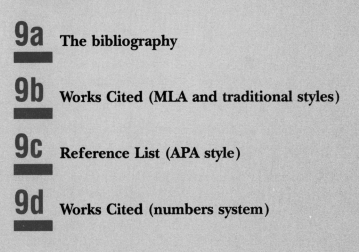

9a　The bibliography

The last part of the research paper is the bibliography—a list in alphabetical order of the sources actually used in the paper. The purpose of this list is to allow the reader to identify and retrieve any source used. Every reference cited in the text must therefore appear in the bibliography; conversely, every work appearing in the bibliography must have been used in the text.

Differences in the format of the bibliography are minor among the various documentation styles. Under the MLA and traditional footnote/endnote styles, the bibliography is titled "Works Cited." The APA style labels it a "Reference List." This chapter concentrates on the formats required in these bibliographies; it also gives examples of the format used in the numbers system.

9a–1 Alphabetizing bibliographic entries

Arrange the entries in your "Works Cited" or "Reference List" in alphabetical order according to the surname of the first author, keeping in mind the following rules:

- Alphabetize letter by letter. Notice, however, that nothing always precedes something. For instance, Rich, Herman B. precedes Richmond, D. L.
- The prefixes *M'*, *Mc*, and *Mac* must be alphabetized literally, not as if they were all spelled *Mac*. Disregard the apostrophe: MacKinsey precedes McCuen and MacIntosh precedes M'Naughton. If the name of an author includes an article or preposition such as *de, la, du, von, van*, the rule is that when the prefix is part of the surname, then alphabetize according to the prefix (Von Bismarck precedes Vonnegut). If the prefix is not part of the name, treat it as part of the first and middle names (Bruy, Cornelis J. de). When in doubt, consult the biographical section of *Webster's New Collegiate Dictionary* (1981).
- Single-author entries precede multiple-author entries beginning with the same surname:

```
Hirsch, E. D.

Hirsch, E. D., and O. B. Wright.
```

Entries by the same author or authors in the same order are arranged alphabetically by the title, excluding *A* or *The*.

■ A row of three hyphens followed by a period replaces the name of the repeated author(s):

Kissinger, Henry Alfred. <u>The Necessity for Choice</u>.

---. <u>Nuclear Weapons and Foreign Policy</u>.

■ Works by authors with the same surname are alphabetized according to the first letter of the first name:

Butler, Alban

Butler, Samuel

■ Corporate authors—associations, government agencies, institutions—are alphabetized according to the first significant word of the name. Use the full name, not an abbreviation:

Brandeis University (not B.U.)

Southern Asian Institute (not SAI)

■ A parent body precedes a subdivision:

Glendale Community College, Fine Arts Department

■ When a work is anonymous, its title moves into the author's place and is alphabetized according to the first significant word in the title.
■ Alphabetize legal references by the first significant word:

Marbury v. Madison

National Labor Relations Act

9a–2 Sample bibliography page

For a sample bibliography page, see Figure 9–1 on p. 166. (See also the sample student papers, pp. 264, 289, and 298.) For details on the form for various bibliographic entries, see Sections 9b and 9c. For rules on alphabetizing the entries, see Section 9a–1.

9b Works Cited (MLA and traditional styles)

If you were careful in copying your sources accurately on the bibliography cards, preparing the bibliography will be mainly a matter of transcribing information. But you must still observe the following:

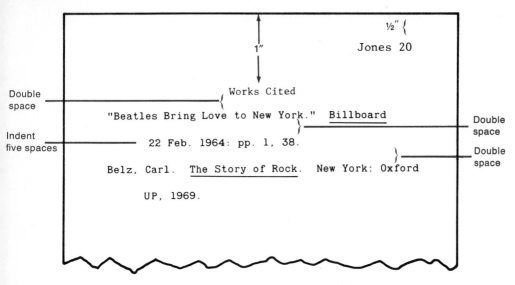

Figure 9–1 Sample bibliography page (MLA style)

- The bibliography must occupy a separate page.
- Center the title "Works Cited" one inch from the top of the page. Leave two spaces between the title and the first entry (see Figure 9–1).
- List all entries in alphabetical order by first author (see Section 9a–1). Anonymous works are listed alphabetically according to the first word of the title, disregarding *a, an,* or *the* if such a word begins the title.
- Place the author's last name first. In case of two or more authors, all authors' names except the first retain their normal order.
- Second and subsequent entries by the same author(s) are listed with three hyphens followed by a period:

```
Lewis, Sinclair.  Babbitt.  New York: Harcourt, 1922.

---.  Main Street.  New York: Harcourt, 1920.
```

- Indent the second line of each entry five spaces.
- Double-space throughout the "Works Cited" list.

Study "Works Cited" at the end of two sample student papers (pp. 264 and 298). Note, however, that for a paper for a course in a field other than the modern languages or literature, your instructor may want you to use a documentation style that differs in some ways from the examples shown in this chapter and in the sample student papers in Chapter 12. To avoid extra work, consult your instructor before the final draft of your paper is typed.

9b–1 General order for bibliographic references to books in "Works Cited"

Bibliographic references to books list items in the following order.

a. Author

The name of the author comes first, alphabetized by surname. If more than one author is involved, invert the name of *only* the first and follow it by a comma:

    Brown, Jim, and John Smith

For more than three authors, use the name of the first followed by "et al.":

    Foreman, Charles, et al.

In some cases the name of an editor, translator, or compiler will be cited before the name of an author, especially if the actual editing, translating, or compiling is the subject of discussion (see Section 9b–1*c*).

b. Title

Cite the title in its entirety, including any subtitle, exactly as it appears on the title page. A period follows the title unless the title ends in some other mark, such as a question mark or an exclamation mark. Book titles are underlined; titles of chapters are set off in quotation marks. The initial word and all subsequent words (except for articles and short prepositions) in the title are capitalized. Ignore any unusual typographical style, such as all capital letters, or any peculiar arrangement of capitals and lower-case letters, unless the author is known specifically to insist on such a typography. Separate a subtitle from the title by a colon:

    D. H. Lawrence: His Life and Work.

c. Name of editor, compiler, or translator

The name(s) of the editor(s), compiler(s), or translator(s) is given in normal order, preceded by "Ed(s).," "Comp(s).," or Trans.":

    Homer.   The Iliad.   Trans. Richmond Lattimore.

However, if the editor, translator, or compiler was listed in your textual citation, then his name should appear first, followed by "ed.," "trans.," or "comp." and a period:

Textual citation:

> Gordon's <u>Literature in Critical Pespective</u> offers
>
> some . . .

"Works Cited" entry:

> Gordon, Walter K., ed.   <u>Literature in Critical</u>
>
> <u>Perspective</u>.   New York: Appleton, 1968.

If you are drawing attention to the translator, use the following format:

Textual citation:

> The colloquial English of certain passages is due to
>
> Ciardi's translation.

"Works Cited" entry:

> Ciardi, John, trans.   <u>The Inferno</u>.   By Dante Alighieri.
>
> New York: NAL, 1961.

d. Edition (if other than first)

The edition being used is cited if it is other than the first. Cite the edition in Arabic numerals (3rd ed.) without further punctuation. Always use the latest edition of a work, unless you have some specific reason of scholarship for using another:

> Holman, C. Hugh.   <u>A Handbook to Literature</u>.   3rd ed.
>
> Indianapolis: Odyssey, 1972.

e. Series name and number

Give the name of the series, without quotation marks and not underlined, followed by a comma, the number of the work in the series in Arabic numerals, and a period:

Unger, Leonard. <u>T. S. Eliot</u>. University of Minnesota

    Pamphlets on American Writers 8. Minneapolis: U of

    Minnesota P, 1961.

f. Volume numbers

An entry referring to all the volumes of a multivolume work cites the number of volumes *before* the publication facts:

Durant, Will, and Ariel Durant. <u>The Story of Civiliza-</u>

    <u>tion</u>. 10 vols. New York: Simon, 1968.

An entry for only selected volumes still cites the total number of volumes after the title. The volumes actually used are listed *after* the publication facts:

Durant, Will, and Ariel Durant. <u>The Story of Civiliza-</u>

    <u>tion</u>. 10 vols. New York: Simon, 1968. Vols. 2

    and 3.

For multivolume works published over a number of years, show the total number of volumes, the range of years, and specific volumes if not all of them actually were used:

Froom, LeRoy Edwin. <u>The Prophetic Faith of Our Fathers</u>.

    4 vols. Washington: Review and Herald, 1950-54.

    Vol. 1.

g. Publication facts

Indicate the place, publisher, and date of publication for the work you are citing. A colon follows the place, a comma the publisher, and a period the date unless a page is cited.

You may use a shortened form of the publisher's name as long as it is clear: Doubleday (for Doubleday & Company), McGraw (for McGraw-Hill), Little (for Little, Brown), Scott (for Scott, Foresman), Putnam's (for G. Putnam's Sons), Scarecrow (for Scarecrow Press), Simon (for Simon and Schuster), Wiley (for John Wiley & Sons), Holt (for Holt, Rinehart & Winston), Penguin (for Penguin Books), Harper (for Harper & Row). For example:

```
Robb, David M., and Jessie J. Garrison.  Art in the

    Western World.  4th ed.  New York: Harper, 1963.
```

But list university presses in full (except for abbreviating "University" and "Press") so as not to confuse the press with the university itself: Oxford UP, Harvard UP, Johns Hopkins UP.

```
Gohdes, Clarence.  Bibliographical Guides to the Study

    of Literature of the U.S.A.  3rd ed.  Durham: Duke

    UP, 1970.
```

If more than one place of publication appears, give the city shown first on the book's title page.

If more than one copyright date is given, use the latest unless your study specifically is concerned with an earlier edition. (A new printing does not constitute a new edition. For instance, if the title page bears a 1975 copyright date but a 1978 fourth printing, use 1975.) If no place, publisher, date, or page numbering is provided, insert "N.p.," "N.p.," "n.d.," or "N. pag.," respectively. "N. pag." will explain to the reader why no page numbers were provided in the text citation. If the source contains neither author, title, nor publication information, supply in brackets whatever information you have been able to obtain:

```
Photographs of Historic Castles.  [St. Albans, England]:

    N.p., n.d.  N. pag.


Farquart, Genevieve.  They Gave Us Flowers.  N.p.: N.p.,

    1886.


Dickens, Charles.  Master Humphrey's Clock.  London:

    Bradbury and Evans, n.d.
```

h. Page numbers

Bibliographical entries for books rarely include a page number; however, entries for shorter pieces appearing within a longer work—articles, poems, short stories, and so on, in a collection—should include a page reference. In such a case, supply page numbers for the entire piece, not just for the specific page or pages cited in the text:

Daiches, David. "Criticism and Sociology." <u>Literature</u>

    <u>in Critical Perspective</u>. Ed. Walter K. Gordon.

    New York: Appleton, 1968. 7-18.

i. Differences between endnotes and bibliographic entries

Endnotes and bibliography entries contain the same information, with the exception of page numbers, but differ considerably in form, as the following examples make clear:

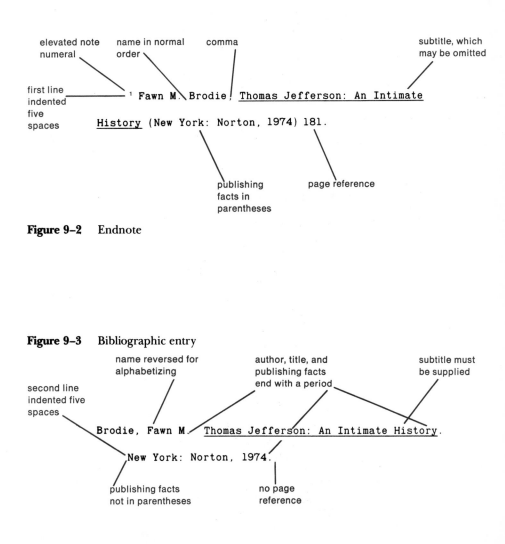

Figure 9–2   Endnote

Figure 9–3   Bibliographic entry

9b–2 Sample bibliographic references to books

a. Book by a single author

Brodie, Fawn M. <u>Thomas Jefferson: An Intimate History</u>.

New York: Norton, 1974.

b. Book by two or more authors

Bollens, John C., and Grand B. Geyer. <u>Yorty: Politics</u>

<u>of a Constant Candidate</u>. Pacific Palisades: Pal-

isades Publ., 1973.

Allport, Gordon W., Philip E. Vernon, and Gardner

Lindzey. <u>Study of Values</u>. New York: Houghton,

1951.

Brown, Ruth, et al. <u>Agricultural Education in a Techni-</u>

<u>cal Society: An Annotated Bibliography of</u>

<u>Resources</u>. Chicago: American Library Assn., 1973.

c. Book by a corporate author

American Institute of Physics. <u>Handbook</u>. 3rd ed. New

York: McGraw, 1972.

NOTE: If the publisher is the same as the author, repeat the information, as shown here:

Defense Language Institute. <u>Academic Policy Standards</u>.

Monterey: Defense Language Institute, 1982.

d. Book by an anonymous or pseudonymous author

No author listed:

<u>Current Biography</u>. New York: Wilson, 1976.

If you are able to research the author's name, supply it in brackets:

[Stauffer, Adlai]. <u>Cloudburst</u>. Knoxville: Review and

Courier Publishing Assn., 1950.

The name of an author who writes under a pseudonym (or *nom de plume*) also may be given in brackets:

Eliot, George [Mary Ann Evans]. <u>Daniel Deronda</u>. Lon-

don, 1876.

e. Work in several volumes or parts

When citing the whole multivolume work:

Wallbank, T. Walter, and Alastair M. Taylor. <u>Civiliza-

tion Past and Present</u>. 2 vols. New York: Scott,

1949.

When citing a specific volume of a multivolume work:

Wallbank, T. Walter, and Alastair M. Taylor. <u>Civiliza-

tion Past and Present</u>. 2 vols. New York: Scott,

1949. Vol. 2.

When citing a multivolume work whose volumes were published over a range of years:

Froom, LeRoy Edwin. <u>The Prophetic Faith of Our Fathers</u>.

4 vols. Washington: Review and Herald, 1950-54.

When citing a multivolume work with separate titles:

Jacobs, Paul, Saul Landen, and Eve Pell. <u>Colonials and</u>

    <u>Sojourners</u>. Vol. 2 of <u>To Serve the Devil</u>. 4 vols.

    New York: Random, 1971.

f. Work within a collection of pieces, all by the same author

Johnson, Edgar. "The Keel of the New Lugger." <u>The</u>

    <u>Great Unknown</u>. Vol. 2 of <u>Sir Walter Scott</u>. 3

    vols. New York: Macmillan, 1970. 763-76.

Selzer, Richard. "Liver." <u>Mortal Lessons</u>. New York:

    Simon, 1976. 62-77.

NOTE: The MLA does not require the use of the word "In" preceding the title of the collection or anthology.

g. Chapter or titled section in a book

Goodrich, Norma Lorre. "Gilgamesh the Wrestler." <u>Myths</u>

    <u>of the Hero</u>. New York: Orion, 1960.

NOTE: List the chapter or titled section in a book only when it demands special attention.

h. Collections: anthologies, casebooks, and readers

Welty, Eudora. "The Wide Net." <u>Story: An Introduction</u>

    <u>to Prose Fiction</u>. Ed. Arthur Foff and Daniel

    Knapp. Belmont: Wadsworth, 1966. 159-77.

Cowley, Malcolm. "Sociological Habit Patterns in Lin-

    guistic Transmogrification." <u>The Reporter</u> 20 Sept.

    1956: 257-61. Rpt. in <u>Readings for Writers</u>. Ed.

    Jo Ray McCuen and Anthony C. Winkler. 2nd ed. New

    York: Harcourt, 1977. 489-93.

i. Double reference—a quotation within a cited work

Daubier, Jean. <u>A History of the Chinese Cultural Revo-</u>

<u>lution</u>. Trans. Richard Seaver. New York: Random,

1974.

Only the secondary source is listed in "Works Cited." See Section 8d-1*l*, p. 130, for an example of how the source of such an entry would appear in text.

j. Reference works

(I) ENCYCLOPEDIAS

Ballert, Albert George. "Saint Lawrence River." <u>Ency-</u>

<u>clopaedia Britannica</u>. 1963 ed.

"House of David." <u>Encyclopedia Americana</u>. 1974 ed.

Berger, Morroe, and Dorothy Willner. "Near Eastern So-

ciety." <u>International Encyclopedia of the Social</u>

<u>Sciences</u>. 1968 ed.

(II) DICTIONARIES AND ANNUALS

"Barsabbas, Joseph." <u>Who's Who in the New Testament</u>

(1971).

"Telegony." <u>Dictionary of Philosophy and Psychology</u>

(1902).

k. Work in a series

(I) A NUMBERED SERIES

Auchincloss, Louis. <u>Edith Wharton</u>. University of Min-
     nesota Pamphlets on American Writers 12. Minneapo-
     lis: U of Minnesota P, 1961.

(II) AN UNNUMBERED SERIES

Miller, Sally. <u>The Radical Immigrant</u>. The Immigrant
     Heritage of America Series. New York: Twayne,
     1974.

l. Reprint

Babson, John J. <u>History of the Town of Gloucester, Cape
     Ann, Including the Town of Rockport</u>. 1860. New
     York: Peter Smith, 1972.

Thackeray, William Makepeace. <u>Vanity Fair</u>. London,
     1847-48. New York: Harper, 1968.

m. Edition

Perrin, Porter G., and Jim W. Corder. <u>Handbook of Cur-
     rent English</u>. 4th ed. Glenview: Scott, 1975.

Rowland, Beryl, ed. <u>Companion to Chaucer: Studies</u>. New
     York: Oxford UP, 1979.

n. *Edited work*

If the work of the editor(s) rather than that of the author(s) is being discussed, place the name of the editor(s) first, followed by a comma, then by "ed." or "eds.":

Craig, Hardin, and David Bevington, eds. <u>The Complete
    Works of Shakespeare</u>. Rev. ed. Glenview: Scott,
    1973.

If you are stressing the text of the author(s), place the author(s) first:

Clerc, Charles. "Goodbye to All That: Theme, Character
    and Symbol in <u>Goodbye, Columbus</u>." <u>Seven Contempo-
    rary Short Novels</u>. Ed. Charles Clerc and Louis
    Leiter. Glenview: Scott, 1969. 106-33.

o. *Book published in a foreign country*

Vialleton, Louis. <u>L'Origine des êtres vivants</u>. Paris:
    Plon, 1929.

Ransford, Oliver. <u>Livingston's Lake: The Drama of
    Nyasa</u>. London: Camelot, 1966.

p. *Introduction, preface, foreword, or afterword*

Davidson, Marshall B. Introduction. <u>The Age of
    Napoleon</u>. By J. Christopher Herold. New York:
    American Heritage, 1963.

q. *Translation*

Symons, John Addington, trans. <u>Autobiography of Ben-
    venuto Cellini</u>. By Benvenuto Cellini. New York:
    Washington Square, 1963.

r. Book of illustrations

```
Janson, H. W.   History of Art: A Survey of the Major

     Visual Arts from the Dawn of History to the

     Present.  With 928 illustrations, including 80

     color plates.  Englewood Cliffs: Prentice and

     Abrams, 1962.
```

s. Foreign title

Use lower-case lettering for foreign titles except for the first word and proper names:

```
Vischer, Lukas.   Basilius der Grosse.  Basel: Reinhard,

     1953.
```

Supply a translation of the title or city if it seems necessary. Place the English version in brackets immediately following the original, not underlined:

```
Bruckberger, R. L.   Dieu et la politique [God and Poli-

     tics].  Paris: Plon, 1971.
```

9b–3 General order for bibliographic references to periodicals in "Works Cited"

Bibliographic references to periodicals list items in the following order:

a. Author

List the author's surname first, followed by a comma, then by the first name or initials. If there is more than one author, follow the same format as for books (see Section 9b–2*b*).

b. Title of the article

List the title in quotation marks, followed by a period inside the quotation marks unless the title itself ends in a question mark or exclamation mark.

c. Publication information

List the name of the periodical, underlined, with any introductory article omitted, followed by a space and a volume number, then by a space and the year of publication within parentheses, then by a colon, a space, and page numbers for the entire article, not just for the specific pages cited:

```
Smith, Irwin.   "Ariel and the Masque in The Tempest."

    Shakespeare Quarterly 21  (1970):  213-22.
```

Journals paginated anew in each issue require the issue number following the volume number, separated by a period:

```
Beets, Nicholas.   "Historical Actuality and Bodily Expe-

    rience."  Humanitas 2.1  (1966):  15-28.
```

Some journals may use a month or season designation in place of an issue number:

```
2  (Spring 1966):  15-28.
```

Magazines that are published weekly or monthly require only the date, without a volume number:

```
Isaacson, Walter.   "After Williamsburg."  Time 13 June

    1983:  12-14.
```

Newspapers require the section or part number, followed by the page:

```
Rumberger, L.   "Our Work, Not Education, Needs Restruc-

    turing."  Los Angeles Times, 24 May 1984, pt. 2: 5.
```

d. Pages

If the pages of the article are scattered throughout the issue (for example, pages 30, 36, 51, and 52), the following formats can be used:

30, 36, 51, 52	(This is the most precise method and should be used when only three or four pages are involved.)
30 and passim	(page 30 and here and there throughout the work)
30ff.	(page 30 and the following pages)
30+	(beginning on page 30)

9b–4 Sample bibliographic references to periodicals

a. Anonymous author

```
"Elegance Is Out." Fortune 13 Mar. 1978: 18.
```

b. Single author

```
Sidey, Hugh.  "In Defense of the Martini." Time 24 Oct.

     1977: 38.
```

c. More than one author

```
Ferguson, Clyde, and William R. Cotter.  "South Africa--

     What Is to Be Done?" Foreign Affairs 56 (1978):

     254-74.
```

If three authors have written the article, place a comma after the second author, followed by "and" and the name of the third author. If more than three authors have collaborated, list the first author's name, inverted, followed by a comma and "et al."

```
Enright, Frank, et al.
```

d. Journal with continuous pagination throughout the annual volume

```
Paolucci, Anne.  "Comedy and Paradox in Pirandello's

     Plays." Modern Drama 20 (1977): 321-39.
```

e. Journal with separate pagination for each issue

When each issue of a journal is paged separately, include the issue number (or month or season); page numbers alone will not locate the article since every issue begins with page 1.

```
Cappe, Walter H.  "Humanities at Large." The Center

     Magazine 11.2 (1978): 2-6.
```

Mangrum, Claude T. "Toward More Effective Justice."

Crime Prevention Review 5 (Jan. 1978): 1-9.

Brown, Robert. "Physical Illness and Mental Health."

Philosophy and Public Affairs 7 (Fall 1977): 18-19.

f. Monthly magazine

Miller, Mark Crispin. "The New Wave in Rock." Horizon

Mar. 1978: 76-77.

Davis, Flora, and Julia Orange. "The Strange Case of

the Children Who Invented Their Own Language."

Redbook Mar. 1978: 113, 165-67.

g. Weekly magazine

Eban, Suzy. "Our Far-Flung Correspondents." The New

Yorker 6 Mar. 1978: 70-81.

"Philadelphia's Way of Stopping the Shoplifter." Busi-

ness Week 6 Mar. 1972: 57-59.

h. Newspaper

Tanner, James. "Disenchantment Grows in OPEC Group with

Use of U.S. Dollar for Oil Pricing." Wall Street

Journal 9 Mar. 1978: 3.

List the edition and section of the newspaper if specified, as in the examples below:

Southerland, Daniel. "Carter Plans Firm Stand with

Begin." Christian Science Monitor 9 Mar. 1978,

western ed.: 1, 9.

Malino, Emily. "A Matter of Placement." <u>Washington</u>

      <u>Post</u> 5 Mar. 1978: L 1.

i. Editorial

If the section or part is labeled with a numeral rather than a letter, then the abbreviation "sec." or "pt." must appear before the section number. For example, see the unsigned editorial below.

Signed:

Futrell, William. "The Inner City Frontier." Editorial.

      <u>Sierra</u> 63.2 (1978): 5.

Unsigned:

"Criminals in Uniform." Editorial. <u>Los Angeles Times</u>

      7 Apr. 1978, pt. 2: 6.

j. Letter to the editor

Korczyk, Donna. Letter. <u>Time</u> 20 Mar. 1978: 4.

k. Critical review

Andrews, Peter. Rev. of <u>The Strange Ride of Rudyard</u>

      <u>Kipling: His Life and Works</u>, by Angus Wilson.

      <u>Saturday Review</u> 4 Mar. 1978: 24-25.

Daniels, Robert V. Rev. of <u>Stalinism: Essays in Histor-</u>

      <u>ical Interpretations</u>, ed. Robert C. Tucker. <u>The</u>

      <u>Russian Review</u> 37 (1978): 102-03.

"Soyer Sees Soyer." Rev. of <u>Diary of an Artist</u>, by

      Ralph Soyer. <u>American Artist</u> Mar. 1978: 18-19.

Rev. of <u>Charmed Life</u>, by Diane Wynne Jones. <u>Booklist</u> 74

(Feb. 1978): 1009.

l. Published interview

Leonel J. Castillo, Commissioner, Immigration and Natu-

ralization Service. Interview. "Why the Tide of

Illegal Aliens Keeps Rising." <u>U.S. News and World</u>

<u>Report</u> 20 Feb. 1978: 33-35.

m. Published address or lecture

Trudeau, Pierre E. "Reflections on Peace and Security."

Address to Conference on Strategies for Peace and

Security in the Nuclear Age, Guelph, Ont., Can.,

27 Oct. 1983. Rpt. in <u>Vital Speeches of the Day</u>

1 Dec. 1983: 98-102.

9b–5 Sample bibliographic references to nonprint materials

Since nonprint materials come in many forms and with varied information, the rule to follow when dealing with them is to provide as much information as is necessary for retrieval.

a. Address or lecture

O'Banion, Terry. "The Continuing Quest for Quality."

Address to California Assn. of Community Colleges.

Sacramento. 30 Aug. 1983.

Schwilck, Gene L. "The Core and the Community." Lec-

ture to Danforth Foundation. St. Louis, 16 Mar.

1978.

For how to handle the reprint of an address or lecture appearing in a periodical, see Section 9b–4m.

b. Artwork

> Angelico, Beato. <u>Madonna dei Linaioli</u>. Museo de San
>
>   Marco, Firenze.

For how to handle an illustration in a book of art, see Section 9b–6a.

c. Computer source

A computer citation will refer to either: (1) a computer program, that is, information received directly from a data bank, or (2) a written publication retrieved by a computer base.

(I) COMPUTER PROGRAM

First, list the primary creator of the database as the author. Second, give the title of the program underlined, followed by a period. Third, write "Computer software," followed by a period. Fourth, supply the name of the publisher of the program, followed by a comma and the date the program was issued. Finally, give any additional information necessary for identification and retrieval. This additional information should include, for example, the kind of computer for which the software was created, the number of kilobytes (units of memory), the operating system, and the program's form (cartridge, disk, or cassette):

> Moshell, J. M., and C. E. Hughes. <u>Imagination: Picture</u>
>
>   <u>Programming</u>. Computer software. Wiley, 1983.
>
>   Apple II/IIe, 64KB, disk.

(II) SOURCE RETRIEVED FROM A DATABASE

Entire articles and books are now being stored in huge data banks, with companies like ERIC, CompuServe, The Source, Mead Data Control (Nexis, Lexis), and many others providing the access service. These sources should be listed as if they appeared in print, except that you will also list the agency providing the access service. If possible, list any code or file associated with the source:

```
Cohen, Wilbur J.  "Lifelong Learning and Public Policy."

     Community Services Catalyst 9 (Fall 1979): 4-5.

     ERIC.  1982.  Dialog file 1: item EJ218031.
```

d. Film

Film citations should include the director's name, the title of the film (underlined), the name of the leading actor(s), the distributor, and the date of showing. Information on the producer, writer, and size or length of the film also may be supplied, if necessary to your study:

```
Ross, Herbert, dir.  The Turning Point.  With Anne Ban-

     croft, Shirley MacLaine, Mikhail Baryshnikov, and

     Leslie Brown.  Twentieth Century-Fox, 1978.
```

e. Interview

Citations of interviews should specify the kind of interview, the name (and, if pertinent, the title) of the interviewed person, and the date of the interview:

```
Witt, Dr. Charles.  Personal interview.  18 Feb. 1984.


Carpenter, Edward, librarian at the Huntington Library,

     Pasadena.  Telephone interview.  2 Mar. 1978.
```

f. Musical composition

Whenever possible, cite the title of the composition in your text, for instance:

```
Bach's Well-Tempered Clavier is a principal

     keyboard . . .
```

However, when opus numbers would clutter the text, cite the composition more fully in "Works Cited":

```
Grieg, Edvard.  Minuet in E Minor, op. 7, no. 3.
```

g. Radio or television program

Citations should include the title of the program (underlined), the network or local station, and the city and date of broadcast. If appropriate, the title of the episode is listed in quotation marks before the title of the program, while the title of the series, neither underlined nor in quotation marks, comes after the title of the program. The name of the writer, director, narrator, or producer may also be supplied, if significant to your paper:

<u>Diving for Roman Plunder</u>. Narr. and dir. Jacques

    Cousteau. KCET, Los Angeles. 14 Mar. 1978.

"Chapter 2." Writ. Wolf Mankowitz. <u>Dickens of London</u>.

    Dir. and prod. Marc Miller. Masterpiece Theatre.

    Introd. Alistair Cooke. PBS. 28 Aug. 1977.

<u>Dead Wrong</u>. CBS Special. 24 Jan. 1984.

h. Recording (disc or tape)

For commercially available recordings, cite the following: composer, conductor, or performer; title of recording or of work(s) on the recording; artist(s); manufacturer; catalog number; and year of issue (if not known, state "n.d."):

Beatles, The. "I Should Have Known Better." <u>The</u>

    <u>Beatles Again</u>. Apple Records, SO-385, n.d.

Bach, Johann Sebastian. Toccata and Fugue in D Minor,

    Toccata, Adagio, and Fugue in C Major, Passacaglia

    and Fugue in C Minor; Johann Christian Bach. Sin-

    fonia for Double Orchestra, op. 18, no. 1. Cond.

    Eugene Ormandy. Philadelphia Orchestra. Columbia,

    MS 6180, n.d.

Eagle, Swift. <u>The Pueblo Indians</u>. Caedmon, TC 1327,

n.d.

<u>Shakespeare's Othello</u>. With Paul Robeson, José Ferrer,

Uta Hagen, and Edith King. Columbia, SL-153, n.d.

Dwyer, Michael. Readings from Mark Twain. Rec. 15 Apr.

1968. Humorist Society. San Bernardino.

Wilgus, D. K. Irish Folksongs. Rec. 9 Mar. 1969. U of

California, Los Angeles, Archives of Folklore. T7-

69-22. 7¹/₂ ips.

Burr, Charles. Jacket notes. <u>Grofe: Grand Canyon</u>

<u>Suite</u>. Columbia, MS 6003, n.d.

i. Theatrical performance

Theatrical performances are cited in the form used for films, with added information on the theater, city, and date of performance. For opera, concert, or dance productions you may also wish to cite the conductor (cond.) or choreographer (chor.). If the author, composer, director, or choreographer should be emphasized, supply that information first:

<u>Getting Out</u>. Dir. Gordon Davidson. By Marsha Norman.

With Susan Clark. Mark Taper Forum, Los Angeles.

2 Apr. 1978.

This citation emphasizes the author:

Durang, Christopher. <u>Beyond Therapy</u>. Dir. John Madden.

With John Lithgow and Dianne Wiest. Brooks Atkin-

son Theater, New York. 26 May 1982.

This citation emphasizes the conductor:

```
Conlon, James, cond.  La Bohème.  With Renata Scotto.

    Metropolitan Opera.  Metropolitan Opera House, New

    York.  30 Oct. 1977.
```

This citation emphasizes the conductor and the guest performer:

```
Commissiona, Sergiu, cond.  Baltimore Symphony Orchestra.

    With Albert Markov, violin.  Brooklyn College, New

    York.  8 Nov. 1978.
```

This citation emphasizes the choreographer:

```
Baryshnikov, Mikhail, chor.  Swan Lake.  American Ballet

    Theatre, New York.  24 May 1982.
```

9b–6 Sample bibliographic references to special items

No standard form exists for every special item you might use in your paper. Again, as a general rule arrange the information in your bibliographic entry in the following order: author, title, place of publication, publisher, date, and any other information helpful for retrieval. Some examples of common citations follow:

a. Artwork, published

```
Healy, G. P. A.  The Meeting on the River Queen.  White

    House, Washington, DC.  Illus. in Lincoln: A Pic-

    ture Story of His Life.  By Stefan Lorent.  Rev.

    and enl. ed. New York: Harper, 1957.
```

For how to handle an artwork you actually have experienced, see Section 9b–5*b*.

b. The Bible

When referring to the Bible, cite the book and chapter within your text (the verse, too, may be cited when necessary):

```
The city of Babylon (Rev. 18.2) is used to

    symbolize . . .
```

or

```
In Rev. 18:2 the city of Babylon is used as a symbol

    of . . .
```

In "Works Cited" the following citation will suffice if you are using the King James version:

```
The Bible
```

If you are using another version, specify which:

```
The Bible, Revised Standard Version
```

c. Classical works in general

When referring to classical works that are subdivided into books, parts, cantos, verses, and lines, specify the appropriate subdivisions within your text:

```
Ovid makes claims to immortality in the last lines of

The Metamorphoses (3. Epilogue).
```

```
Francesca's speech (5.118-35) is poignant because . . .
```

In "Works Cited" these references will appear as follows:

```
Ovid.  The Metamorphoses.  Trans. and introd. Horace

    Gregory.  New York: NAL, 1958.
```

```
Alighieri, Dante.  The Inferno.  Trans. John Ciardi.  New

    York: NAL, 1954.
```

d. Dissertation

Unpublished: The title is placed within quotation marks and the work identified by "Diss.":

```
Cotton, Joyce Raymonde.   "Evan Harrington: An Analysis

     of George Meredith's Revisions."  Diss.  U of

     Southern California, 1968.
```

Published: The dissertation is treated as a book, except that the entry includes the label "Diss." and states where and when the dissertation originally was written:

```
Cortey, Teresa.  Le Rêve dans les contes de Charles

     Nodier.  Diss.  U of California, Berkeley, 1975.

     Washington, DC: UP of America, 1977.
```

e. Footnote or endnote citation

A bibliographical reference to a footnote or endnote in a source takes the following form:

```
Faber, M. D.  The Design Within: Psychoanalytic Ap-

     proaches to Shakespeare.  New York: Science House,

     1970.
```

In other words, no mention is made of the note. However, mention of the note should be made within the text itself:

```
In Schlegel's translation, the meaning is changed (Faber

     205, n. 9).
```

The reference is to page 205, note number 9, of Faber's book.

f. Manuscript or typescript

A bibliographical reference to a manuscript or typescript from a library collection should provide the following information: the author, the title or a description of the material, the material's form (ms. for manuscript, ts. for typescript), and any identifying number. If possible, give the name and location of the library or institution where the material is kept.

```
Chaucer, Geoffrey.  Ellesmere ms., E126C9.  Huntington

     Library, Pasadena.
```

The Wanderer. Ms. Exeter Cathedral, Exeter.

Cotton Vitellius. Ms., A. SV. British Museum, London.

g. Pamphlet or brochure

Citations of pamphlets or brochures should conform as nearly as possible to the format used for citations of books. Give as much information about the pamphlet as is necessary to help a reader find it. Underline the title:

Calplans Agricultural Fund. An Investment in California

  Agricultural Real Estate. Oakland: Calplans Secu-

  rities, n.d.

h. Personal letter

Published:

Wilde, Oscar. "To Mrs. Alfred Hunt." 25 Aug. 1880.

  The Letters of Oscar Wilde. Ed. Rupert Hart-Davis.

  New York: Harcourt, 1962. 67-68.

Unpublished:

Thomas, Dylan. Letter to Trevor Hughes. 12 Jan. 1934.

  Dylan Thomas Papers. Lockwood Memorial Library.

  Buffalo.

Personally received:

Highet, Gilbert. Letter to the author. 15 Mar. 1972.

i. Plays

(I) CLASSICAL PLAY

In your text, provide parenthetical references to act, scene, and line(s) of the play:

Cleopatra's jealousy pierces through her words:

> What says the married woman? You may go;
>
> Would she had never given you leave to come:
>
> Let her not say 'tis I that keep you here;
>
> I have no power upon you; hers you are.
>
> (1.3.20-23)

The reference is to Act 1, Scene 3, lines 20–23. In "Works Cited" the play will be cited as follows:

Shakespeare, William. <u>Antony and Cleopatra</u>. <u>The Complete Works of Shakespeare</u>. Ed. Hardin Craig and
David Bevington. Rev. ed. Glenview: Scott, 1973.
1073-1108.

NOTE: When the play is part of a collection, list the pages that cover the entire play.

(II) MODERN PLAY

Many modern plays are published as individual books:

Miller, Arthur. <u>The Crucible</u>. New York: Bantam, 1952.

However, if published as part of a collection, the play is cited as follows:

Chekhov, Anton. <u>The Cherry Orchard</u>. 1903. <u>The Art of
Drama</u>. Ed. R. F. Dietrich, William E. Carpenter,
and Kevin Kerrane. 2nd ed. New York: Holt, 1976.
134-56.

NOTE: The page reference is to the entire play.

j. Poems

(I) CLASSICAL POEM

> Lucretius [Titus Lucretius Carus]. <u>Of the Nature of</u>
>
>   <u>Things</u>. Trans. William Ellery Leonard. <u>Back-</u>
>
>   <u>grounds of the Modern World</u>. Vol. 1 of <u>The World</u>
>
>   <u>in Literature</u>. Ed. Robert Warnock and George K.
>
>   Anderson. New York: Scott, 1950. 343-53.

Or, if published in one book:

> Dante [Dante Alighieri]. <u>The Inferno</u>. Trans. John
>
>   Ciardi. New York: NAL, 1954.

(II) MODERN POEM

Modern poems are usually part of a larger collection:

> Moore, Marianne. "Poetry." <u>Fine Frenzy</u>. Ed. Robert
>
>   Baylor and Brenda Stokes. New York: McGraw, 1972.
>
>   372-73.

NOTE: Cite pages covered by the poem.

Or, if the poem is long enough to be published as a book, use the following format:

> Byron, George Gordon, Lord. <u>Don Juan</u>. Ed. Leslie A.
>
>   Marchand. Boston: Houghton, 1958.

k. Public documents

As a general rule, follow this order: Government; Body; Subsidiary bodies; Title of document (underlined); Identifying code; Place, publisher, and date of publication. Most publications by the federal government are printed by the Government Printing Office, which is abbreviated as "GPO":

(I) THE CONGRESSIONAL RECORD

A citation to the *Congressional Record* requires only title, date, and page(s):

Cong. Rec. 15 Dec. 1977, 19740.

(II) CONGRESSIONAL PUBLICATIONS

United States. Cong. Senate. Permanent Subcommittee on Investigations of the Committee on Government Operations. Organized Crime--Stolen Securities. 93rd. Cong., 1st sess. Washington: GPO, 1973.

United States. Cong. House. Committee on Foreign Relations. Hearings on S. 2793, Supplemental Foreign Assistance Fiscal Year 1966--Vietnam. 89th Cong., 2nd sess. Washington: GPO, 1966.

United States. Cong. Joint Economic Committee on Medical Policies and Costs. Hearings. 93rd Cong., 1st sess. Washington: GPO, 1973.

(III) EXECUTIVE BRANCH PUBLICATIONS

United States. Office of the President. Environmental Trends. Washington: GPO, 1981.

United States. Dept. of Defense. Annual Report to the Congress by the Secretary of Defense. Washington: GPO, 1984.

United States. Dept. of Education. National Commission

    on Excellence in Education. <u>A Nation at Risk: The</u>

    <u>Imperative for Educational Reform</u>. Washington:

    GPO, 1983.

United States. Dept. of Commerce. Bureau of the Cen-

    sus. <u>Statistical Abstracts of the United States</u>.

    Washington: GPO, 1963.

(IV) LEGAL DOCUMENTS

When citing a well-known statute or law, a simple format will suffice:

US Const. Art. 1, sec. 2.

15 US Code. Sec. 78j(b). 1964.

US CC Art. 9, pt. 2, par. 9-28.

Federal Trade Commission Act. 1914.

When citing a little-known statute, law, or other legal agreement, provide all the information needed for retrieval:

"Agreement Between the Government of the United States

    of America and the Khmer Republic for Sales of

    Agricultural Commodities." <u>Treaties and Other In-</u>

    <u>ternational Agreements</u>. Vol. 26, pt. 1. TIAS No.

    8008. Washington: GPO, 1976.

Names of court cases are abbreviated and the first important word of each party is spelled out: "Brown v. Board of Ed." stands for "Oliver Brown versus the Board of Education of Topeka, Kansas." Cases, unlike laws, are italicized in the text but not in "Works Cited." Text: *Miranda v. Arizona.* "Works Cited": Miranda v. Arizona. The following information must be supplied in the order listed: (1) name of the first plaintiff and the first defendant; (2) volume, name, and page (in that order) of the law report cited; (3) the place and name of the court that decided the case; and (4) the year in which the case was decided:

```
Richardson v. J. C. Flood Co.  190 A. 2d 259.  D.C. App.

    1963.
```

Interpreted, the above means that the Richardson v. J. C. Flood Co. case can be found on page 259 of volume 190 of the Second Series of the *Atlantic Reporter*. The case was settled in the District of Columbia Court of Appeals during the year 1963.

For further information on the proper form for legal citations, consult *A Uniform System of Citation*, 12th ed. (Cambridge: Harvard Law Rev. Assn., 1976).

l. Quotation in a book or article used as a source

(I) QUOTATION IN A BOOK

```
MacDonald, Dwight.  As quoted in John R. Trimble.  Writ-

    ing With Style: Conversations on the Art of

    Writing.  Englewood Cliffs: Prentice, 1975.
```

(II) QUOTATION IN AN ARTICLE

```
Grabar, Oleg.  As quoted in Katharine Slater Gittes.

    "The Canterbury Tales and the Arabic Frame Tradi-

    tion."  PMLA 98 (1983): 237-51.
```

m. Report

Titles of reports in the form of pamphlets or books require underlining. When a report is included within the pages of a larger work, the title is set off in quotation marks. The work must be identified as a report:

```
The Churches Survey Their Task.  Report of the Confer-

    ence on Church, Community, and State.  London:

    Allen & Unwin, 1937.
```

```
Luxenberg, Stan.  "New Life for New York Law."  Report

    on New York Law School.  Change 10 (Nov. 1978):

    16-18.
```

n. *Table, graph, chart, or other illustration*

If the table, graph, or chart has no title, identify it as a table, graph, or chart:

> National Geographic Cartographic Division. Graph on im-
>
> ports drive into U.S. market. <u>National Geographic</u>
>
> 164 (July 1983): 13.

NOTE: The descriptive label is not underlined or set off in quotation marks.

> Benson, Charles S. "Number of Full-Time Equivalent Em-
>
> ployees, by Industry, 1929-1959." Table. <u>The Eco-</u>
>
> <u>nomics of Public Education</u>. Boston: Houghton,
>
> 1961. 208.

This time the table has a title, so it is set off in quotation marks.

NOTE: The in-text citation should refer to "Table A.1."

o. *Thesis*

See Section 9b–6d, "Dissertation."

9c Reference List (APA style)

Your reference list will contain the following elements listed in this order: author, year of publication, title, place of publication, and publisher.

The job of preparing your reference list will be easy if you took care to copy your sources accurately onto your bibliography cards. The following rules must be observed:

- Start your reference list on a new page, regardless of how much blank space is left on the last page of your paper.
- Center the title "Reference List" on the page, two inches from the top. Leave four spaces between the title and the first entry (see Section 9a–2).
- List all entries in alphabetical order (see Section 9a–1). Anonymous works are listed alphabetically according to the first word of the title, omitting *a*, *an*, or *the* if one of these words begins the title.

- List the names of all initial authors in inverted order.
- Second and subsequent entries by the same author(s) are listed with three hyphens followed by a period: ---.
- Indent the second line of each entry three spaces.
- Double-space throughout the reference list.
- Place a period followed by one space between all units.

Study the reference list at the end of the sample student paper.

9c–1 General order for bibliographic references to books in "Reference List"

Your reference list for books will contain the following elements, listed in the order indicated below:

- Name(s) of author(s) in inverted order, with only the initials of first and middle names.
- Year of publication in parentheses, followed by a period.
- Title of the book, underlined, with only the initial letter of the first word capitalized, followed by a period. (In two-part titles separated by a colon, the initial letter of the first word in the second title also is capitalized.)
- Place of publication, followed by a colon.
- Name of publisher, followed by a period. (The name of the publisher is listed in as brief a form as is intelligible. Terms like *Publisher, Co.,* and *Inc.* are omitted. However, names of university presses and associations are spelled out.)

9c–2 Sample bibliographic references to books

a. Book by a single author

Jones, E. (1931). <u>On the nightmare</u>. London: Hogarth.

A period is placed after the author's name (the period following an initial serves this purpose), after the final parenthesis of the publication date, after the title, and at the end of the entry. A colon separates the city from the publisher.

b. Book by two or more authors

Terman, L. M. & Merrill, M. A. (1937). <u>Measuring</u>
<u>intelligence</u>. Cambridge, Mass.: The Riverside Press.

With two names, use an ampersand (&) before the second name and do not use a comma to separate the names. With three or more names, use an ampersand before the last name and use commas to separate the names (Bowen, B. M., Poole, K. J., & Gorky, A.). Give the surnames and initials of all authors, no matter how many there are. Separate the names with commas and use an ampersand between the last two names.

c. Edited book

```
Friedman, R. J. & Katz, M. M. (Eds.).  (1974).  The

     psychology of depression: Contemporary theory and

     research.  New York: Wiley.
```

Give the surname and initials of all editors, regardless of how many there are. Show "Ed." or "Eds." in parentheses after the name(s), followed by a period. When referring to an article or chapter in an edited book, use the following form:

```
Waxer, P.  (1979).  Therapist training in nonverbal be-

     havior.  In A. Wolfgang (Ed.), Nonverbal behavior:

     Applications and cultural implications (pp. 221-240).

     New York: Academic Press.
```

Precede the name of the editor(s) with the word "In." When an editor's name is not in the author position, *do not* invert his name. Place "Ed." or "Eds." in parentheses after the name(s), followed by a comma. The title of the article or chapter is *not* placed within quotation marks and only the initial letter in the title is capitalized. Give inclusive page numbers for the article or chapter in parentheses after the title of the book. Precede the page number(s) by "p." or "pp."

d. Translated book

The translator of a book (name *not* inverted) is placed within parentheses after the book title and is followed by "Trans." with a period after the end parenthesis:

```
Rank, O.  (1932).  Psychology and the soul (William

     Turner, Trans.).  Philadelphia: Univ. of Pennsylvania

     Press.
```

e. Book in a foreign language

```
Saint-Exupéry, A. de. (1939). Terre des hommes. Paris:

    Gallimard.
```

NOTE: Titles of foreign books are in lower case except for the initial letter.

f. Revised edition of a book

Give the edition ("rev. ed.," "4th ed.," and so on) in parentheses following the title. Place a period after the final parenthesis:

```
Boulding, K. (1955). Economic analysis (3rd ed.). New

    York: Harper.
```

g. Book by a corporate author

When a book is authorized by an organization rather than a person, the name of the organization appears in the author's place:

```
Committee of Public Finance. (1959). Public finance.

    New York: Pitman.
```

When the corporate author is also the publisher, place the word "Author" in place of the publisher:

```
Commission on Intergovernmental Relations. (1955).

    Report to the President. Washington, DC: Author.
```

h. Multivolume book

When citing a multivolume source, place the number(s) of the volume(s) actually used in parentheses immediately following the title. Use Arabic numerals for the volume number(s).

```
Reusch, J. (1980). Communication and psychiatry. In

    H. I. Kaplan, A. M. Freedman, & B. J. Sadock (Eds.),

    Comprehensive textbook of psychiatry (Vol. 1).

    Baltimore: Williams & Wilkins.
```

If a multivolume book was published over a number of years, list the years in parentheses following the author's name:

```
Brady, V. S.   (1978-82).
```

i. Unpublished manuscript

Treat an unpublished manuscript the way you would a book except that instead of the place of publication and publishers, you will write "Unpublished manuscript":

```
Hardison, R.   (1983).   On the shoulders of giants.

   Unpublished manuscript.
```

NOTE: For a publication of limited circulation, supply in parentheses, immediately after the title, an address where the publication can be obtained.

9c–3 General order for bibliographic references to periodicals in "Reference List"

Entries for periodicals in your reference list will contain the following elements, in the order indicated:

- Name(s) of author(s) in inverted order with only the initials of first and middle names.
- Year of publication in parentheses, followed by a period. (For magazines issued on a specific day or month, give the year followed by the month or by the month and day.)
- Title of article not enclosed in quotation marks and with only the initial letter of the first word capitalized, followed by a period.
- Name of the journal or magazine, underlined, with the first word and all other words except articles and prepositions capitalized, followed by a comma.
- Volume number, underlined, followed by a comma. (Do not give volume numbers of periodicals issued on a specific date.)
- Page references, followed by a period.

9c–4 Sample bibliographic references to periodicals

a. Journal article, one author

```
Harvey, O. L.   (1980).   The measurement of handwriting

   considered as a form of expressive movement. Quar-

   terly Review of Biology, 55, 231-249.
```

b. Journal article, up to six authors

```
Rodney, J., Hollender, B., & Campbell (1983).  Hypnotiz-

    ability and phobic behavior.  Journal of Abnormal

    Psychology, 92, 386-389.
```

Use an ampersand preceded by a comma in front of the last author. Name each author. If the article has more than six authors, use this shortened form for in-text parenthetical references:

```
(Frey et al. 1981).
```

c. Journal article, paginated anew in each issue

```
Rosenthal, G. A.  (1983).  A seed-eating beetle's adap-

    tations to poisonous seed.  Scientific American,

    249(6), 56-67.
```

If the journal begins each issue with page 1, supply the volume number, underlined, followed immediately by the issue number in parentheses, a comma, and then the page number(s) and a period.

d. Journal with continuous pagination throughout the annual volume

```
Anthony, R. G. & Smith, N. S.  (1977).  Ecological rela-

    tionships between mule deer and white-tailed deer in

    southeastern Arizona.  Ecological Monographs, 47,

    255-77.
```

Most scholarly journals are paginated continuously throughout the year, so volume and page numbers are all the reader requires for retrieval.

e. Magazine article, issued monthly

```
Canby, T. Y.  (1983, September).  Satellites that serve

    us.  National Geographic, pp. 281-300.
```

In parentheses after the author, place the year followed by a comma and the month. Place a period after the closing parenthesis. Use "p." or "pp." in front of page number(s).

f. Magazine article, issued on a specific day

Andersen, K. (1983, September 5). Private violence.

Time, pp. 18-19.

In parentheses after the author, place the year followed by a comma and the month and date. Place a period after the closing parenthesis. Use "p." or "pp." in front of page number(s).

g. Newspaper article

Goodman, E. (1983, December 23). Bouvia case crosses

the "rights" line. Los Angeles Times, Part 2, p. 5.

Place the exact date in parentheses following the author and indicate the section and page(s) following the newspaper title. Use Arabic numerals throughout the entry. Use "p." or "pp." for page(s). If the newspaper article has no author, begin with the title or headline of the article. Alphabetize works with no author by the first significant word in the title:

"Sad plight of anorexics." (Full title is "The sad

plight of anorexics.")

h. Editorial

Guion, R. M. (1983). Comments from the new editor

[Editorial]. Journal of Applied Psychology, 68, 547.

When citing an editorial, place the word "Editorial," followed by a period, after the title of the editorial. If the editorial has no title, "Editorial" immediately follows the date. Otherwise, treat the entry like any other magazine or journal article.

i. Letter to the editor

Jones, L. (1983, November). Bite the bullet [Letter to

the editor]. Psychology Today, p. 5.

NOTE: When the month of the magazine is given in parentheses after the author, use "p." or "pp." for page(s). Place "Letter to the editor" in brackets immediately following the title.

j. Review

```
Boorstein, J. K.   (1983, November/December).   On welfare

    [Review of Dilemmas of welfare policy: Why work

    strategies haven't worked].   Society, pp. 120-122.
```

Place "Review of," followed by the title of the work being reviewed, in brackets immediately following the title of the review.

9c–5 Sample bibliographic references to nonprint materials

Since nonprint materials come in many forms and with varied information, the rule to follow when dealing with them is to provide as much necessary information as is available.

a. Computer sources

List the primary creator of the database as the author, followed by the date (in parentheses) when the program was produced. Then give the title of the program and, immediately following the title, identify the source [in brackets] as a computer program. Supply the location and name of the publisher of the program. Finally, enclose in parentheses any additional information necessary for identification and retrieval. This additional information should include the kind of computer for which the software was created. Computer citations will refer to material of two kinds: (1) Computer programs—that is, information received directly from data banks—and (2) written publications retrieved by a computer base. Examples of both kinds of citations follow:

(I) COMPUTER PROGRAM

```
Poole, L. & Barchers, M.   (1977).   Future value of an

    investment [Computer program].   Berkeley, CA: Adam

    Osborne & Associates.   (Basic for a Wang 2200).
```

Fernandes, F. D. (1972). <u>Theoretical prediction of</u>

   <u>interference loading on aircraft stores</u>. [Computer

   program]. Pomona, CA: General Dynamics, Electro Dy-

   namics Division. (1650 card images, Fortran IV, for

   CDC-6000. Available through the University of Geor-

   gia, Athens, Georgia).

NOTE: To cite a manual for a computer program, give the same information as you would for a computer program, but in brackets after the title identify the source as a computer manual:

<u>Move-it: Inter-computer communication system</u>. (1982).

   [Computer manual]. Canoga Park, CA: Wolfe Software

   Systems.

(II) SOURCE RETRIEVED FROM A DATA BANK

Ulmer, C. (1981). Competence based instruction. <u>Commu-</u>

   <u>nity College Review</u>, <u>8</u>(4), 51-56; rpt. Los Angeles:

   ERIC, File 1, EJ27541.

Sources retrieved from a data bank are cited the way you would the original source. Follow the original source citation with a semicolon and "rpt.", followed by the city and company providing the computer source service. Add a code, file, or record number when applicable.

b. Film

Cotton, D. H. (Producer) & Correll, J. B. (Director).

   (1980). <u>The management of hypertension in pregnan-</u>

   <u>cies</u> [Film]. Houston: University of Texas.

When citing a film, name the producer (title in parentheses), followed by the director (title in parentheses), and then the date of production (in parentheses). Always specify the medium in brackets so that the material cannot be confused with a book or some other source.

c. Recording (cassette, record, tape)

```
Bronowski, J. (Speaker). (1983). The mind (Cassette

    Recording BB 4418.01). Los Angeles: Pacifica Tape

    Library, 5316 Venice Blvd., Los Angeles, CA 90019.
```

When citing a recording, name the primary contributor (Speaker, Narrator, Panel Chair, Forum Director, and so on), followed by the date of production. If the recording has a number, list it in parentheses after specifying the kind of recording. Finally, list the place of publication and the publisher, supplying an exact address if one is available.

9c–6 Sample bibliographic references to special items

Sources come in such varied forms that a sample cannot be supplied for every possibility. When listing a source for which there is no exact model, provide enough information to make it possible for your reader to trace the source. In general, follow this order: (1) person or organization responsible for the work; (2) year the work was published, produced, or released; (3) title of the work; (4) identifying code, if applicable; (5) place of origin; and (6) publisher. Study the following samples:

a. Government documents

(1) CONGRESS

```
U.S. Cong. House. (1977). U.S. assistance programs in

    Vietnam. 92d Cong., 2d sess. Washington, DC: U.S.

    Government Printing Office.


U.S. Cong. Senate. (1970). Separation of powers and

    the independent agencies: Cases and selected

    readings. 91st Cong., 1st sess. Washington, DC:

    U.S. Government Printing Office.


U.S. Cong. Joint Committee on Printing. (1983). Con-

    gressional directory. 98th Cong., 1st sess. Wash-

    ington, DC: U.S. Government Printing Office.
```

(II) EXECUTIVE BRANCH

Johnson, L. B. (1968). <u>Economic report of the President</u>. Washington, DC: U.S. Government Printing Office.

Executive Office of the President. (1981). <u>Environmental trends</u>. Washington, DC: U.S. Government Printing Office.

NOTE: U.S. Government Printing Office may be abbreviated as U.S.G.P.O.

b. Legal references

The only kinds of legal references a student paper is likely to cite are references to court cases or statutes. Since legal references can be complex, consult *A Uniform System of Citation,* 12th Edition (Cambridge: Harvard Law Review Association, 1976), if your paper relies heavily on legal references. For common kinds of citations, follow these sample entries:

(I) COURT CASE

In general, use the following order when citing court decisions: (1) plaintiff v. defendant; (2) volume, name, and page of law report cited; and (3) in parentheses, the name of the court that decided the case.

Clark v. Sumner. 559 S.W.2d. 914 (Tex. civ. app. 1977).

Explanation: The case can be found in the second series, volume 559, beginning on page 914, of the *Southwestern Reporter.* The case was decided by the Texas Civil Court of Appeals in 1977.

(II) STATUTE

When citing commonly known statutes or laws, a simple format will suffice:

U.S. Const. Art. III, sec. 2.

15 U.S. Code, sec. 78j. (1964).

Sherman Antitrust Act. (1890).

For lesser-known statutes, supply additional information:

```
90 U.S. Statutes at Large. 505 (1976).

Nuclear Waste Policy Act, Part I, sec. 112 (a).

Energy Conservation and Production Act, Title I, Part A,
    sec. 101, 42 U.S.C. 6901, 1976.
```

(III) TREATY

```
"Technical Cooperation Agreement Between the Government
    of Royal Kingdom of Saudi Arabia and the Government
    of the United States of America." Treaties and Other
    International Agreements. Vol. 26, Part 1, TAIS No.
    8072. Washington, D.C.: U.S.G.P.O., 1976.
```

9c–7 Sample bibliographic references to a report

```
Organization for Economic Cooperation and Development.
    (1983). Assessing the impacts of technology on soci-
    ety. (Report). Washington, D.C.: U.S.G.P.O.
```

Place "Report" in parentheses after the title. If a code has been assigned to the report, add it also:

```
(Report No. CSOS-R-292).
```

If the publisher is the same as the author, place the word "Author" where you would normally give the name of the publisher:

```
California Postsecondary Education Commission. (1982).
    Promises to keep: Remedial education in California's
    public colleges and universities. (Report). Sacra-
    mento, CA: Author.
```

9d   Works Cited (numbers system)

Your "Works Cited" list should be arranged in alphabetical order and numbered consecutively. Of course, the numbers will not appear in consecutive order in your text. (Some authorities prefer that you forgo an alphabetical arrangement in favor of consecutive numbering according to the order in which the sources appear in the text for the first time.) Study the sample below excerpted from an alphabetical/consecutive number listing. In listing works, follow the APA "Reference List" format as explained in Section 9c.

Works Cited

1. Albert, N. & Beck, A. T. (1975). Incidence of depression in early adolescence: A preliminary study. Journal of Youth and Adolescence, 4, 301-306.

2. American Heart Association. (1978). Guidelines for a weight control component in a smoking cessation program [Pamphlet]. Dallas: Author.

3. Hankin, J. R. & Locke, B. Z. (1982). The persistence of depressive symptomatology among prepaid group practice enrollees: An exploratory study. American Journal of Public Health, 72, 1000-1007.

4. Kovacs, M. & Beck, A. T. (1977). An empirical-clinical approach toward a definition of childhood depression. In J. G. Schulterbrandt & A. Ranskin (Eds.), Depression in childhood. New York: Raven, 1-25.

5. Nunnaly, J. C. (1967). Psychometric theory. New York: McGraw-Hill.

6.   Wahrheit, G. J., Holzer, C. E., & Schwab, J. J.

(1973). An analysis of social class and racial

differences in depressive symptomatology: A com-

munity study. <u>Journal of Health and Social</u>

<u>Behavior,</u> <u>14</u>, 291-299.

NOTE: Each of the sources cited by number in the text will correspond to one of the numbered sources listed above.

10

MECHANICS

10a   Using numbers in the paper

10a–1 Numerals

The rule of thumb on the use of numerals is this: use a numeral only if the number cannot be spelled out in two words or less. The MLA prefers that writers spell out numbers from one to nine; use numerals for all numbers 10 and above. For the Roman numeral "one," use a capital "I"; for the Arabic numeral "one," use either the number "1" on your typewriter keyboard, or the lower-case letter "l." Dates and page numbers are usually *not* spelled out: "November 19" or "19 November," and "page 36," are preferred to "the nineteenth of November" and "the thirty-sixth page." Also, do not begin a sentence with a numeral.

> *Wrong*   25,500 voters hailed the passage of the bill.

> *Right*   The bill was hailed by 25,500 voters.

10a–2 Percentages and amounts of money

Figures of percentages or amounts of money are governed by the rule for numerals. Figures or amounts that can be written out in two words or less may be spelled out; otherwise, they must be expressed as numerals.

May be spelled out:	thirteen percent	thirteen Deutsche Marks
	eighty-three percent	fifty British pounds
	ten francs	thirty-six dollars

Should be expressed as numerals:	133%	185 DM
	83.5%	£ 550
	103 fr	$366

10a–3 Dates

Consistency is the prime rule governing the treatment of dates in the paper. Write either "19 November 1929" or "November 19, 1929," but not a mixture of both. Write either "June 1931" or "June, 1931," but not both. (Note: if a comma is placed between the month and the year, a comma must also follow the year, unless some other kind of punctuation mark is necessary.) The MLA prefers that writers not use a comma between the month and year. Centuries are expressed in lower-case letters:

```
in the thirteenth century
```

A hyphen must be added when the century is used as an adjective:

```
twelfth-century literature

seventeenth- and eighteenth-century philosophy
```

Decades can either be written out:

```
during the thirties
```

or expressed in numerals:

```
during the 1930s

during the '30s
```

The term "B.C." (meaning before Christ's birth) follows the year; "A.D." (meaning after Christ's birth) precedes the year. The MLA recommends omitting the periods in these abbreviations:

```
in 55 BC

in AD 1066
```

When using both a Western and a non-Western date, place one or the other in parentheses:

```
1912 (Year One of the Republic)
```

Both "in 1929–30" and "from 1929 to 1930" are correct, as is "from 1929–30 to 1939–40." However, do not write "from 1951–72"; confusion may result from the absence of the preposition "to" after 1951. Rather, write "1951 to 1972."

10a–4 Numbers connected consecutively

When connecting two numbers, give the second number in full for all numbers from one through ninety-nine. For numbers from one hundred on, give only the last two figures of the second number, if it is within the same hundred or thousand:

```
        4-5

       15-18

      106-07

      486-523

      896-1025

     1860-1930

     1860-75

     1608-774

   13,456-67

   13,456-14,007
```

The above examples follow the style of the *MLA Handbook*. However, APA and other styles tend to show all digits of the second number, in all cases.

10a–5 Roman numerals

The following require capital Roman numerals: major divisions of an outline (see Section 4b–1); people in a series, such as monarchs, who share a common name:

```
Henry VIII, King of England
```

The following do not require capital Roman numerals: volumes, books, and parts of major works; acts of plays.

Use lower-case Roman numerals for pages from prefaces, forewords, or introductions to books.

The following do not require lower-case Roman numerals: chapters of books, scenes of plays, cantos of poems, or chapters of books from the Bible.

10b Titles

The rules that follow apply to titles used in your text. For how to handle titles in notes or bibliography, consult the section on the style you are using in Chapters 8 and 9. The APA, for example, has a special way of handling titles.

10b–1 Italicized titles

Certain titles must be italicized and therefore underlined in typewritten work. Underlined titles include the following:

Published books
A Farewell to Arms

Plays
The Devil's Disciple

Long poems
Enoch Arden

Pamphlets
The Biology of Cancer: A Guide to Twelve College
        Lectures

Newspapers
Los Angeles Times, *but* Stoneham Gazette

(Underline only those words that appear on the masthead of the paper.)

Magazines and journals
U.S. News and World Report; Shakespeare Quarterly

Classical works
Plutarch's Parallel Lives

Films
Gone with the Wind

Television and radio programs
60 Minutes (CBS); The Music of Your Life (KNXT)

Ballets
The Sleeping Beauty

Operas
Carmen

Instrumental music listed by name
Brahms's Rinaldo

NOTE: Instrumental music listed by form, number, and key is not underlined:

Brahms's Piano Concerto no. 1, opus 15 in D minor

Paintings
Regnault's Three Graces

Sculptures
```
Michelangelo's Madonna and Child
```

Ships
```
U.S.S. Charr
```

Aircraft
```
the presidental aircraft Air Force One
```

NOTE: An initial *a, an,* or *the* is italicized and capitalized when it is part of the title:

```
The Grapes of Wrath
```

After the use of the possessive case, delete *The, A,* or *An,* in a title:

```
Henry James's Portrait of a Lady
```

(The full title is *The Portrait of a Lady.*)

10b–2 Titles within quotation marks

The following items should be placed within quotation marks:

Short stories
```
"The Black Cat"
```

Short poems
```
"The Road Not Taken"
```

Songs
```
"A Mighty Fortress Is Our God"
```

Newspaper articles
```
"It's Drag Racing without Parachutes"
```

Magazine or journal articles
```
"How to Cope with Too Little Time and Too Many Meetings"
```

Encyclopedia articles
```
"Ballet"
```

Subdivisions in books
```
"The Solitude of Nathaniel Hawthorne"
```

Unpublished dissertations
```
"The Local Communications Media and Their Coverage of
    Local Government in California"
```

Lectures
"The Epic of King Tutankhamun: Archeological Superstar"

Television episodes
"Turnabout," from the program <u>The World of Women</u>

NOTE: Sacred writings, series, editions, societies, conventional titles, and parts of books neither use underlining nor are enclosed in quotation marks.

Sacred writings
the Bible, the Douay Version, the New Testament, Matthew, the Gospels, the Talmud, the Koran, the Upanishads

Series
Masterpiece Theatre, the Pacific Union College Lyceum Series

Editions
the Variorum Edition of Spenser

Societies
L'Alliance française, the Academy of Abdominal Surgeons

Conventional titles
Kennedy's first State of the Union Address

Parts of books
Preface
Introduction
Table of Contents
Appendix
Index

10b–3 Titles within titles

If a title enclosed by quotation marks appears within an underlined title, the quotation marks are retained. If an underlined title appears within a title enclosed by quotation marks, the underlining is retained:

Book <u>"The Sting" and Other Classical Short Stories</u>

Article "Textual Variants in Sinclair Lewis's

<u>Babbitt</u>"

Single quotation marks are used with a title requiring quotation marks appearing within another title also requiring quotation marks:

Article   "Jonathan Swift's 'Journal to Stella'"

A title that normally would be underlined, but that appears as part of another title, is neither underlined nor placed in quotation marks. For example, the title of the book *The Great Gatsby* would normally be underlined. But when this title forms part of the title of another book, such as *A Study of* The Great Gatsby, only "A Study of" is underlined:

<u>A Study of</u> The Great Gatsby

10b–4 Frequent reference to a title

If the research paper refers frequently to the same title, subsequent reference to the title may be abbreviated, once the full title initially has been used. In abbreviating, always use a key word:

<u>Return</u> *for* <u>Return of the Native</u>

<u>Tempest</u> *for* <u>Tempest in a Teapot</u>

"The Bishop" *for* "The Bishop Orders His Tomb at Saint

   Praxis"

UNESCO *for* United Nations Educational, Scientific, and

   Cultural Organization

For citation of titles in subsequent references in notes, see Section 8g–8.

10c   Italics

In typewritten work, italics are indicated by underlining. Words making up a phrase or title may be continuously, rather than separately, underlined.

■   Underline phrases, words, letters, or numerals cited as linguistic examples:

One cannot assume that the Victorian word <u>trump</u> is an

amalgamation of <u>tramp</u> and <u>chump</u>.

■ Underline foreign words in English texts:

```
It seems clearly a case of noblesse oblige.

He used the post hoc ergo propter hoc fallacy.
```

NOTE: Exceptions to the rule include quotations entirely in another language, titles of articles in another language, and words anglicized through frequent use, such as: détente, laissez faire, gestalt, and et al. In papers dealing with the arts, foreign expressions commonly used in the field need not be underlined: hubris, mimesis, leitmotif, pas de deux.

See Section 10b–1 for italics in titles.

10d Names of persons

■ In general, omit formal titles (Mr., Mrs., Miss, Ms., Dr., Professor) when referring to persons, living or dead, by their last names. However, convention dictates that certain persons be referred to by title:

```
Mme de Staël, Mrs. Humphry Ward
```

■ It is acceptable to use simplified names for famous people:

```
Dante for Dante Alighieri

Vergil for Publius Vergilius Maro

Michelangelo for Michelangelo Buonarroti
```

It is also acceptable to use an author's pseudonym rather than the author's real name:

```
George Sand for Amandine-Aurore-Lucie Dupin

Mark Twain for Samuel Clemens

Molière for Jean-Baptiste Poquelin
```

The *von, van, van der,* and *de* of foreign names usually are not included in references to people:

```
Goethe (Hans Wolfgang von Goethe)

Frontenac (Louis de Frontenac)

Ruysdael (Salman van Ruysdael)
```

However, certain names traditionally are not used with the last name alone:

```
Van Dyck  not  Dyck

De Gaulle  not  Gaulle

von Braun  not  Braun

O. Henry  not  Henry
```

10e   Hyphenating words

■   Is possible, avoid dividing a word at the end of a typewritten line. But if a word must be divided for the sake of a balanced margin, make the division at the end of a syllable:

```
de-ter-mined    haz-ard-ous

i-vo-ry         grad-u-al

con-clud-ing    dress-er
```

Correct syllabification of words is listed in a dictionary. College dictionaries indicate the syllables of words with dots: bru·tal·i·ty; far·ci·cal.

■   Never hyphenate a one-syllable word, such as "twelfth," "screamed," or "brought."

■   Do not end or begin a line with a single letter:

```
a-mend, bur-y
```

■   Make no division that might cause confusion in either the meaning or pronunciation of a word:

```
sour-ces, re-creation
```

■   Divide hyphenated words only at the hyphen:

```
editor-in-chief, semi-retired
```

- Do not divide proper names, such as "Lincoln" or "Italy."
- Do not end several consecutive lines with a hyphen.

10f   Handling foreign-language words

Words or phrases from a foreign language must be reproduced with all their accent marks. If you are doing a lengthy paper on a foreign language or on comparative literature, consider renting a typewriter with an international keyboard. Otherwise, the accent marks of foreign words must be written in by hand. Pay special attention to the following:

- It is not necessary to accent the capital letters of French and Spanish words:

  énormément, *but* Enormément *or* ENORMEMENT

- For German words with the umlaut, use two dots rather than an "e," even for initial capitals:

  Überhaupt *not* Ueberhaupt

  fröhlich *not* froehlich

- Proper names retain their conventional spelling:

  Boehm *not* Böhm

  Dürrenmatt *not* Duerrenmatt

- Digraphs (two letters that represent only one sound) can be typed without connection (ae, oe), can be written in by hand (æ, œ), or can be connected at the top (a͞e, o͞e). In American English, the digraph "ae" is being abandoned:

  archeology *not* archaeology

  medieval *not* mediaeval

  esthetic *not* aesthetic

10g   Abbreviations

Following is a list of abbreviations commonly encountered in research. The MLA favors dropping periods whenever possible.

10g–1 Abbreviations and reference words commonly used

AD, A.D.	*anno Domini* 'in the year of the Lord.' No space between; precedes numerals (AD 12).
anon.	anonymous
app.	appendix
art., arts.	article(s)
assn.	association
assoc.	associate, associated
b.	born
BC, B.C.	before Christ. No space between; follows numerals (23 BC).
bibliog.	bibliography, bibliographer, bibliographical
biog.	biography, biographer, biographical
bk., bks.	book(s)
©	copyright (© 1975)
c., ca.	*circa* 'about.' Used with approximate dates (c. 1851).
cf.	*confer* 'compare.' Do not use "cf." if "see" is intended.
ch., chs.	chapter(s)
chor., chors.	choreographed by, choreographer(s)
col., cols.	column(s)
comp., comps.	compiled by, compiler(s)
cond.	conducted by, conductor
Cong.	Congress
Cong. Rec.	*Congressional Record*
d.	died
dir., dirs.	directed by, director(s)
diss.	dissertation
E, Eng.	English
ed., eds.	edited by, editor(s), editions(s)
e.g.	*exempli gratia* 'for example.' Preceded and followed by a comma.
enl.	enlarged (as in "rev. and enl. ed.")
esp.	especially (as in "124–29, esp. 125")
et al.	*et alii* 'and others'
etc.	*et cetera* 'and so forth.' Do not use in text.
ex., exs.	example(s)
f., ff.	and the following (with no space after a numeral) page(s) or line(s). Exact references are preferable: 89–90 instead of 89f.; 72–79 instead of 72ff.
facsim. (or facs.)	facsimile
fig., figs.	figure(s)
fol., fols.	folio(s)
Fr.	French
front.	frontispiece
Ger.	German
Gk.	Greek
GPO	Government Printing Office, Washington, D.C.

hist.	history, historian, historical
ibid.	*ibidem* 'in the same place,' i.e., in the cited title. Avoid using. Cite instead the author's last name and the page number.
i.e.	*id est* 'that is.' Preceded and followed by a comma. Do not use in text.
illus.	illustrated (by), illustrator, illustration(s)
intro. (or introd.)	introduced by, introduction
ips	inches per second (used on labels of recording tapes)
It.	Italian
jour.	journal
L., Lat.	Latin
l., ll.	line(s). MLA style now uses "line" or "lines" instead of "l" or "ll."
lang., langs.	language(s)
LC, L. C.	Library of Congress. Typed with a space between when periods are used.
loc. cit. (not l.c.)	*loco citato* 'in the place (passage) cited.' Avoid using. Repeat the citation in shortened form.
MA, M.A.	Master of Arts. No space between.
mag.	magazine
ME	Middle English
ms, mss (or ms., mss.)	manuscript(s). Capitalized and followed by a period when referring to a specific manuscript.
MS, M.S.	Master of Science. No space between.
n., nn.	note(s)
narr., narrs.	narrated by, narrator(s)
NB, N.B.	*nota bene* 'take notice, mark well.' Not spaced.
n.d.	no date (in a book's imprint). No space between.
no., nos.	number(s)
n.p.	no place (of publication); no publisher. Not spaced.
n. pag.	no pagination. Space between.
OE	Old English
op.	opus (work)
op. cit.	*opere citato* 'in the work cited.' Avoid using. Repeat citation in shortened form.
p., pp.	page(s).
par., pars.	paragraph(s)
passim	'throughout the work, here and there' (as "84, 97, and passim")
PhD., Ph.D.	Doctor of Philosophy. No space between.
philos.	philosophical
pl., pls.	plate(s)
pref.	preface
prod., prods.	produced by, producer(s)
pseud.	pseudonym
pt., pts.	part(s)
pub., pubs.	published by, publication(s)
rept., repts.	reported by, report(s)

rev.	revised (by), revision; review, reviewed (by). Spell out "review," if there is any possibility of ambiguity.
rpm	revolutions per minute (used on recordings)
rpt.	reprinted (by), reprint
sc.	scene
sec., secs.	section(s)
ser.	series
sic	'thus, so.' Put between square brackets when used to signal an editorial interpolation.
soc.	society
Sp.	Spanish
st., sts.	stanza(s)
St., Sts.	Saint(s)
supp., supps.	supplement(s)
Tech rep.	Technical report
TLS	typed letter signed
trans. (or tr.)	translated by, translator, translation
ts.	typescript. Cf. "ms."
v., vs.	versus 'against.' Cf. "v., vv."
v., vv. (or vs., vss.)	verse(s)
vol., vols.	volume(s)

10g–2 The Bible and Shakespeare

Use the following abbreviations in notes and parenthetical references; do not use them in the text (except parenthetically).

a. The Bible

OLD TESTAMENT (OT)

Gen.	Genesis	Eccl.	Ecclesiastes
Exod.	Exodus	Song. Sol.	Song of Solomon
Lev.	Leviticus	(also Cant.)	(also Canticles)
Num.	Numbers	Isa.	Isaiah
Deut.	Deuteronomy	Jer.	Jeremiah
Josh.	Joshua	Lam.	Lamentations
Judg.	Judges	Ezek.	Ezekiel
Ruth	Ruth	Dan.	Daniel
1 Sam.	1 Samuel	Hos.	Hosea
2 Sam	2 Samuel	Joel	Joel
1 Kings	1 Kings	Amos	Amos
2 Kings	2 Kings	Obad.	Obadiah
1 Chron.	1 Chronicles	Jon.	Jonah
2 Chron.	2 Chronicles	Mic.	Micah
Ezra	Ezra	Nah.	Nahum
Neh.	Nehemiah	Hab.	Habakkuk

Esth.	Esther	Zeph.	Zephaniah
Job	Job	Hag.	Haggai
Ps.	Psalms	Zech.	Zechariah
Prov.	Proverbs	Mal.	Malachi

SELECTED APOCRYPHAL AND DUETEROCANONICAL WORKS

1 Esd.	1 Esdras	Bar.	Baruch
2 Esd.	2 Esdras	Song 3	Song of the
Tob.	Tobit	Childr.	Three
Jth.	Judith		Children
Esth.	Esther	Sus.	Susanna
(also Apocr.)	Apocrypha	Bel and Dr.	Bel and the
Wisd. Sol.	Wisdom of		Dragon
(also Wisd.)	Solomon	Pray. Man.	Prayer of
	(also Wisdom)		Manasseh
Ecclus.	Ecclesiasticus	1 Macc.	1 Maccabees
(also Sir.)	(also Sirach)	2 Macc.	2 Maccabees

NEW TESTAMENT (NT)

Matt.	Matthew	1 Tim.	1 Timothy
Mark	Mark	2 Tim.	2 Timothy
Luke	Luke	Tit.	Titus
John	John	Philem.	Philemon
Acts	Acts	Heb.	Hebrews
Rom.	Romans	Jas.	James
1 Cor.	1 Corinthians	1 Pet.	1 Peter
2 Cor.	2 Corinthians	2 Pet.	2 Peter
Gal.	Galatians	1 John	1 John
Eph.	Ephesians	2 John	2 John
Phil.	Philippians	3 John	3 John
Col.	Colossians	Jude	Jude
1 Thess.	1 Thessalonians	Rev. (also	Revelation (also
2 Thess.	2 Thessalonians	Apoc.)	Apocalypse)

SELECTED APOCRYPHAL WORKS

G. Thom.	Gospel of	G. Pet.	Gospel of Peter
	Thomas		
G. Heb.	Gospel of the		
	Hebrews		

b. Shakespeare

Ado	*Much Ado about Nothing*	*MND*	*A Midsummer Night's*
Ant	*Antony and Cleopatra*		*Dream*
AWW	*All's Well That Ends Well*	*MV*	*The Merchant of Venice*
AYL	*As You Like It*	*Oth.*	*Othello*

Cor.	*Coriolanus*
Cym.	*Cymbeline*
Err.	*The Comedy of Errors*
F1	First Folio ed. (1623)
F2	Second Folio ed. (1632)
Ham.	*Hamlet*
1H4	*Henry IV, Part I*
2H4	*Henry IV, Part II*
H5	*Henry V*
1H6	*Henry VI, Part I*
2H6	*Henry VI, Part II*
3H6	*Henry VI, Part III*
H8	*Henry VIII*
JC	*Julius Caesar*
Jn.	*King John*
LC	*A Lover's Complaint*
LLL	*Love's Labour's Lost*
Lr.	*King Lear*
Luc.	*The Rape of Lucrece*
Mac.	*Macbeth*
MM	*Measure for Measure*
Per.	*Pericles*
PhT	*The Phoenix and the Turtle*
PP	*The Passionate Pilgrim*
Q	Quarto ed.
R2	*Richard II*
R3	*Richard III*
Rom.	*Romeo and Juliet*
Shr.	*The Taming of the Shrew*
Son.	*Sonnets*
TGV	*The Two Gentlemen of Verona*
Tim.	*Timon of Athens*
Tit.	*Titus Andronicus*
Tmp.	*The Tempest*
TN	*Twelfth Night*
TNK	*The Two Noble Kinsmen*
Tro.	*Troilus and Cressida*
Ven.	*Venus and Adonis*
Wiv.	*The Merry Wives of Windsor*
WT	*The Winter's Tale*

11

FINISHED FORM
OF THE PAPER

11a   Finished form of the paper

11b   Outline

11c   Title page

11d   Abstract

11e   Text

11f   Tables, charts, graphs, and other
illustrative materials

11g   Content notes and endnotes

11h   Bibliography

11a Finished form of the paper

In its finished form the paper consists of the following parts:

> Outline (if required)
> Title page
> Abstract (if required)
> Text of the paper
> Content notes (if required)
> Endnotes or footnotes (if required)
> Works Cited (or Reference List)

The paper should be neatly typed on one side only of each page with a fresh black ribbon. Papers typed in script characters are frequently more difficult to read and therefore unacceptable. Use heavy (20-pound) $8^1/_2'' \times 11''$ white bond paper. Erasable bond smudges too easily for a teacher to pencil in corrections; therefore it should not be used. If you must use erasable bond, have the paper photocopied on plain (uncoated) paper and submit the photocopy. Do not staple the pages or submit the paper inside a folder. Simply clip the pages together with a paper clip and submit the paper as a loose-leaf manuscript. Give the paper a thorough proofreading before submitting it to the teacher for evaluation.

11b Outline

The outline that precedes the text of the paper should look uncluttered and balanced. Use small Roman numerals to paginate all pages of the outline. These are not included in the total count of the paper. Place your name, the instructor's name, the name of the course for which the paper was written, and the date in the upper left-hand corner of the paper, just as you are required to do on the title page (see Fig. 11–1).

11c Title page

A separate title page is not required for papers following the MLA style. Instead, the first page should contain the full title of the paper, your name, the instructor's name, the course for which the paper was written, the date, and the opening text of your paper. The following facsimile of a typical opening page includes marginal measurements and line spacing. (See also the first page of the sample paper on page 238.)

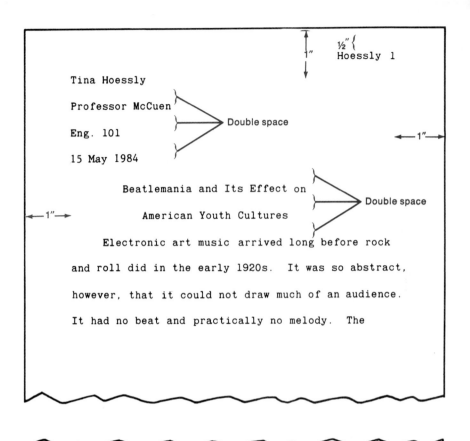

Figure 11–1   Sample student title page (MLA style)

This first page, and all subsequent pages, must contain one-inch margins on all sides. All pages, including the first, are numbered. From page 2 on, type your last name before the page number in case a page is misplaced. Except for titles of published works appearing within it, the title of the paper is neither underlined nor entirely placed in capitals. If the title takes up two or more lines, position the extra lines so as to form a double-spaced inverted pyramid, with each line centered on the page:

```
       Early English Novels: The Development of a

            New and Influential Stereotype

               of the Feminine Role
```

Do not use a period at the end of the title.

Papers written in the APA style do require a title page. See the sample student paper on page 267 for specific directions on handling the title page.

11d Abstract

Papers written for the social sciences require an abstract, that is, a summary of the paper's major findings. The abstract must be written in coherent paragraph form and should not exceed one page. See the sample student paper on pages 267–91.

11e Text

- Use normal paragraphing throughout the paper. If your paper contains subdivisions, use subtitles either centered on the page or aligned with the left margin. Underline but do not capitalize subtitles. Separate subtitles from the last line of the previous section by quadruple spacing.
- Double-space the text, including quotations. Footnotes are double-spaced between notes but single-spaced within (see p. 143).
- Number pages, including the first, consecutively in the upper right-hand corner of the paper. Numbers are not followed by hyphens, parentheses, periods, or other characters. "Notes" and "Works Cited" begin on new pages but are numbered as part of the general sequence (see sample student paper, pp. 263–64).
- Note that numerals are placed one half space above the line within the text of the paper. Each superscript numeral should be placed as near as possible to the end of the cited material to which it refers (see Section 8g–4).
- Unless otherwise indicated by your teacher, place each footnote on the bottom of the same page on which its numeral occurs. The first line of each footnote is indented five spaces; second and subsequent lines are aligned with the left margin. For both footnotes and endnotes use elevated numerals (a half space above the line) and follow the numerals with one space. (See p. 143.)

- For parenthetical citations, see Sections 8d and 8e.
- If possible use pica type, which is easier to read than elite. Script type and other artistic typefaces are often difficult to read and therefore unacceptable. If in doubt, consult your teacher.
- Avoid multiple corrections. If a correction is unavoidable, type it, or write it in legibly with black ink, *above* the line involved. Do not use the margins. If corrections are extensive, retype the page.
- We encourage all students to learn word processing on a computer. The advantage in terms of correcting, editing, revising, and producing a clean final copy are manifold.

11f Tables, charts, graphs, and other illustrative materials

Papers in many fields frequently require tables, graphs, charts, maps, drawings, and other illustrations. For example, a paper on the decline of basic skills among high school students may include a graph that plots this decline over the past five years. An economics paper may require charts that explain certain economic changes. An anthropology paper may include drawings of primitive artifacts. A history paper may illustrate some historic battle with a map. A biology paper may include drawings of enlarged cells. The possibilities are nearly endless. The general rule, however, is for all illustrative materials to appear as close as possible to the part of the text that they illustrate.

11f–1 Tables

Tables are usually labeled, numbered with Arabic numerals, and captioned. Both labels and captions are capitalized as you would a title (do not use all capital letters). The source of the table and accompanying notes should be placed flush left at the bottom of the table. If no source is listed, a reader will assume that the table is your original work. Indicate notes to tables with lower-case letters, or with asterisks and crosses if you need additional indicators, to avoid confusion with endnotes, footnotes, or other textual notes. (See Fig. 11–2, p. 232.)

11f–2 Other illustrative materials

Other illustrative materials should be labeled "Fig." or "Figure" and numbered with Arabic numerals: Fig. 3. Each figure should be captioned and capitalized with a title:

Fig. 12. Chart Tracing the Development of the Alphabet

Again, the source of the illustration and any notes should be placed flush left immediately below the illustration. If no source is cited, a reader will assume that the illustration is your original work. Indicate notes to illustrations with lower-case letters, asterisks, and crosses, so as to avoid confusion with other footnote or endnote numbers in the text. A few sample illustrations follow:

11g   Content notes and endnotes

If you are using the parenthetical style of documentation, content notes, numbered consecutively, would appear at the end of the paper under the heading "Notes." If you are using endnotes, they appear on a separate page at the end of the paper, preceded by the heading "Notes." Any content notes appear either at the bottom of the appropriate page or on a separate page along with the endnotes. (See Section 8h, pp. 157–60.)

Table 2

Significance of Differences Between Mean Grade Point Averages of Male Achievers and Underachievers from Grade One Through Eleven

Grade	Mean grade point average		F	P	t	P
	Achievers	Under-achievers				
1	2.81	2.56	1.97	n.s.†	1.44	n.s.
2	2.94	2.64	1.94	n.s.	1.77	n.s.
3	3.03	2.58	1.49	n.s.	2.83	.01*
4	3.19	2.72	1.03	n.s.	2.96	.01*
5	3.28	2.75	1.02	n.s.	3.71	.01*
6	3.33	2.67	1.33	n.s.	4.46	.01*
7	3.25	2.56	1.02	n.s.	5.80	.01*
8	3.36	2.50	1.59	n.s.	6.23	.01*
9	3.25	2.14	1.32	n.s.	10.57	.01*
10	3.13	1.87	1.30	n.s.	10.24	.01*
11	2.81	1.85	4.05	.02**	5.46	.01*

* Yields significance beyond the .01 level.

** Yields significance beyond the .02 level but below the .01 level.

† No significance.

Figure 11–2   Sample table

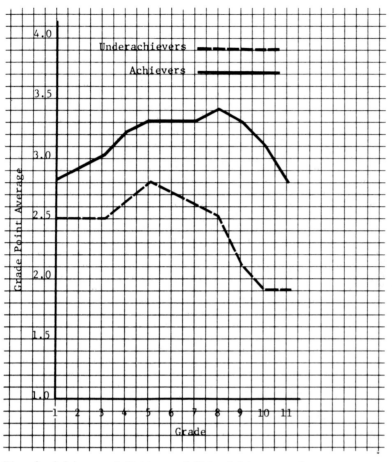

Fig. 1. Achievement Pattern of Male Achievers and
Underachievers from Grades One Through Eleven

Figure 11–3   Sample line graph

Fig. 2. African Doll (Akua'ba)
Source: American Museum of
  Natural History

Figure 11–4   Sample illustration

Figure 11–5   Sample map

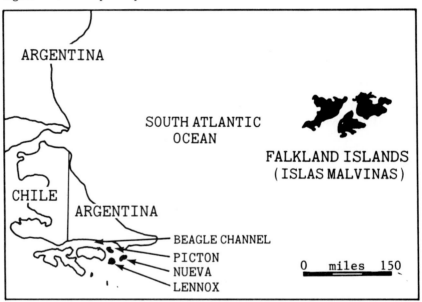

Fig. 3. Islands Involved in the Beagle Channel Dispute
Source: U.S. Government Printing Office, 1984

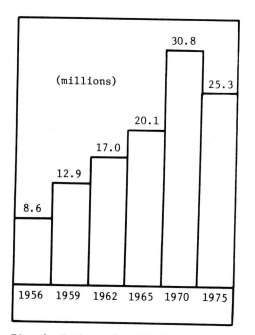

Fig. 4. Number of individuals owning shares in public corporations

Source: New York Stock Exchange

Figure 11–6   Sample bar graph

11h Bibliography

The bibliography appears on a separate page at the end of your paper, marked by the centered heading "Works Cited" or "Reference List." (For sample "Works Cited" pages, see Fig. 9–1, p. 166, and student paper, p. 264; for sample "Reference List," see student paper, p. 289.)

SAMPLE
STUDENT
PAPERS

The following samples were researched and written by college freshmen. Except for a few minor corrections, they are reproduced as they were submitted. The accompanying marginal annotations clarify the format of the paper, explain specific problems, or draw attention to important aspects of research.

12a Entire paper using the author-work style of documentation (MLA)

}*1 inch margin*

i

Double-space throughout the body of the outline.

Butch Mulcahey

Professor McCuen } *double space*

English 101 } *space*

13 January 1984

} *double space*

The title, centered on the page, appears in the outline.

The Certainties of Hawthorne's Moral } *double space*

Ambiguity in <u>The Scarlet Letter</u>

} *quadruple space*

Place the thesis at the beginning of the outline, although it may not be the first sentence of the paper. The thesis in the outline may be worded more succinctly than in the paper. The outline leaves out the details of the paper, mentioning only major points.

Thesis: Hawthorne's moral ambiguity suggests

certainties that transcend in impor-

tance the ambiguity, which several

critics claim to be the novel's

fault.

I. There are matters of interpretation

of Hawthorne's concerns upon which

most critics agree.

A. Most critics agree that

Hawthorne concerns himself with

the consequences of sin rather

than with the sin itself.

*Use small
Roman
numerals for
paginating the
outline.*

ii

*Use standard
outline symbols.
For a full
discussion of
how to write the
outline, see
Section 4b.*

    B.   Hypocrisy is generally believed to be what Hawthorne considered the most grave consequence of sin.

    C.   A common interpretation is that Hawthorne's moral seems to follow logically from his concern with the gravity of hypocrisy.

II. Beyond this level of generally accepted interpretation, however, some critics suggest that the value of the moral diminishes in the presence of ambiguity in the novel.

    A.   Some argue that Hawthorne's definition of sin itself is ambiguous and has at best only a cloudy, tentative meaning.

    B.   Some, especially Jeffrey Duncan, suggest that Hawthorne's plea that men "be true" is paradoxical.

    C.   Hyatt H. Waggoner questions

iii

whether salvation is possible
from Hawthorne's proposed morality, observing the dark and uncertain conclusion that Hester
and Dimmesdale seem to share.

III. Undoubtedly these ambiguities exist;
however, they do not destroy the
"blossom" of wisdom that Hawthorne
wishes to convey, but rather they
enrich its meaning by implying important certainties in life.

A. Hawthorne defines sin ambiguously because he wants to show
the absolute relativity of it in
this world.

B. Hawthorne also asserts his belief that the existence of sin
is certain.

C. Finally, he implies in his ambiguity the most important certainty that he wishes to
present, the certainty of
tragedy in life.

Neither the
introduction
nor the
conclusion
carries a special
label.

Mulcahey 1

The name of the student, professor, and class, as well as the date, are repeated on the title page of the paper.

Butch Mulcahey

Professor McCuen

English 101

13 January 1984

} *double space*

The Certainties of Hawthorne's Moral

Ambiguity in <u>The Scarlet Letter</u>

} *quadruple space*

The title is centered (and double-spaced if more than one line).

A quotation from a primary source creates an effective opening.

"Be true! Be true! Be true! Show
freely to the world, if not your worst, yet
some trait whereby the worst may be in-
ferred!" Nathaniel Hawthorne (242) impresses
upon his readers this singular statement in
order to "relieve the darkening close of a
tale of human frailty and sorrow" (56). The
tale, of course, is <u>The Scarlet Letter</u>, and
the statement represents the "sweet moral
blossom" which at the end of the first chapter Hawthorne promises to present to his
readers. He hopes that this "moral blossom"
will project a brightening ray of wisdom into
the darkness of the fateful triangle of sin
in which his three main characters seem tragically entrapped. Yet, despite Hawthorne's

Mulcahey 2

stated intention, several critics suggest
that his "blossom" lacks the sweetness he
wishes it to have, that his conclusion lacks
moral value because of the ambiguity and
paradox found in the development of
Hawthorne's view of morality.[1] And, of
course, the critics observing these ambiguities and paradoxes make valid points, for
such moral uncertainty undeniably exists in
The Scarlet Letter. However, Hawthorne's
moral ambiguity is not the book's fault
but its strength. It will be seen that
Hawthorne's moral ambiguity actually enhances
the wisdom, the "blossom," which the reader
is to receive. It does not confuse the meaning of Hawthorne's conclusion, but rather it
redefines and enriches it by implying certainties concerning sin which transcend in
importance the ambiguities.

Despite the controversy concerning
Hawthorne's view of morality, there are nevertheless interpretations of his moral concerns upon which most critics agree.

An elevated numeral indicates a content note. Such super-scripts are not used for in-text documentation.

The thesis is placed in a classical position, at the end of the first paragraph.

A transitional paragraph alerts the reader to what is coming—matters upon which critics agree.

Mulcahey 3

One observation accepted almost without debate is that Hawthorne concerns himself with the consequences of sin rather than the action of sin. Several critics assert that, regardless of its background, the book obviously does not deal with the sin of adultery. Arlin Turner, for instance, draws attention to the fact that Hawthorne begins the novel in medias res, long after Hester Prynne and Arthur Dimmesdale have committed the initial sin of passion (Turner 56). Apparently, then, Hawthorne wishes to deal with the consequences of sin and to study them exclusively. As W. C. Brownell notes, the word adultery does not even appear in the text of the novel (245). Brownell further suggests that the entire book ultimately fails to support a study of original sin. He comments, "As a story of illicit love its omissions are too great, its significance is not definite enough, its detail has not enough richness; the successive scenes of which it is composed have not an effective enough cohesion" (246).

A Latin expression is underlined to indicate italics.

Note the in-text citations to "Works Cited."

A word referred to as a word is underlined to indicate italics.

Since the author (Brownell) is named, only the page is cited within parentheses.

A direct quotation is smoothly introduced by "He comments."

Mulcahey 4

Certain critics of form indicate that the structure of the novel does support very well Hawthorne's study in consequences. Gordon Roper considers the entire progress of <u>The Scarlet Letter</u> to be divided into four separate parts, in each of which a single activating force affects three other forces in the novel (49-52). The initial sin is seen simply as the force which triggers the mechanism of the whole development of the book. What results is a study in the reactions of the three main characters to this sin. Another pattern observed by critic Roy Male is the symmetrical approach of the characters to their ends, as Hester Prynne becomes a repentant sinner, Dimmesdale a partially repentant sinner, and Chillingworth an unrepentant sinner (91). Both of these patterns uphold the presumption that Hawthorne places his major emphasis on the effects of sin on the characters.

Critics also commonly agree on what Hawthorne considers the most grave conse-

Coherence is maintained by reminding the reader of the continuing topic at hand— common agreement.

Mulcahey 5

quence of sin. Although interpretations of
this consequence vary, Hawthorne is generally
thought to concentrate much of his concern on
the dangers of hypocrisy. Brownell interprets the novel as an attempt to study pre-
dominantly the problems resulting from
concealment of sin, whereby concealment itself is considered a serious sin (247). And,
of course, this form of hypocrisy pervades
the novel, as all three of Hawthorne's main
characters are continuously guilty of it.

Coherence is achieved by repeating the phrase "is guilty because."

Hester is guilty because she refuses to reveal her partner in adultery; Dimmesdale is
guilty because he conceals both his guilt in
the adultery and his sin of concealment; and
Chillingworth is guilty because he conceals
both his identity and his vengeful purpose.
More accurately, however, Hawthorne's study
of hypocrisy stands as a study of human per-
fidy and especially self-delusion. Undoubtedly, Arthur Dimmesdale serves as the
ultimate example of this type of hypocrisy.
Religious and philosophical explanations

Mulcahey 6

A popular phrase is placed in quotation marks.

would summarize Dimmesdale's dilemma as the "skeptical predicament." Dimmesdale assumes that flesh and spirit are separate and different, that the sins of one are not necessarily the sins of the other. He lives a double life, damning his flesh while pridefully glorifying his spirit and maintaining his elevated ministerial image in the Puritan society. Consequently, he absolutely distorts his sense of which life is real, and his life becomes totally false (Davidson 86). He loses his sense of his true humanity. Here one can see, then, why Hawthorne considered hypocrisy such a dangerous sin.

The clarity of Hawthorne's extensive study of hypocrisy emerges not only in Dimmesdale, whose hypocrisy is obvious, but also in Roger Chillingworth. Chillingworth practices the most intense forms of hypocrisy. He attempts to punish sin despite the fact that he himself is not free from it. He assumes the role of Dimmesdale's presumably helpful physician while, ironically, he

Mulcahey 7

knowingly inflicts the minister's harm
(Turner 102). He thus becomes the most false
of Hawthorne's characters, and he concludes
the story as a demon, a dehumanized mortal.
In this respect, Hawthorne's concern with the
dangers of hypocrisy is once again reflected.
As many critics have indicated, this concern
seems ever-present.

Paraphrase and personal comment are integrated nicely.

From these interpretations of Hawthorne's concern with hypocrisy, his moral
seems to follow logically. "Be true" is obviously the morality he prescribes for avoiding the terrible suffering of Dimmesdale as
well as that of the other characters guilty
of hypocritical sins. "Being true," as Roy
Male indicates, involves each character's direct confrontation of his own guilt (96).
Each character who fulfills this requirement
of Hawthorne's moral is believed to achieve
salvation. Hester, of course, must embrace

Bracketed words help the reader understand the quotation in proper context.

her guilt from the beginning of the novel.
Her resulting ignominy is what makes her a
heroine. It causes her to "[stand] erect,

Mulcahey 8

and [think]," questioning her punishment and
the society which inflicts it (Carl Van Doren
69-70). Her salvation is seen in her humbler
spirit and her greater sympathy for human
fault as well as her increased generosity.
Dimmesdale appears to achieve his salvation
in the final scaffold scene, where he con-
fronts and resists Roger Chillingworth, the
strong advocate of hypocrisy. In fact, his
conclusion has been interpreted to be almost
Christlike (Waggoner, <u>The Presence</u> 66).
Pearl, who is Hawthorne's symbol of truth,
reaches a proportionately happy conclusion,
becoming "the richest heiress of her day, in
the New World" (243). From these observa-
tions, Hawthorne's view of morality seems
very beneficial, and indeed proves to be,
without further interpretation, the "sweet
moral blossom" the reader anticipates.

Beyond this level of interpretation,
however, several critics suggest that the
value of Hawthorne's proposed morality diminishes because of his ambiguity. They contend

Van Doren's first name is cited so he will not be confused with Mark Van Doren, who is cited later.

Since two of Waggoner's works appear in "Works Cited," a key word from the title appears here.

Here the student writer moves to negative criticism of the novel's ambiguity.

Mulcahey 9

that his moral solution cannot possibly be useful in the definite sense he wishes it to be, because its meaning lacks certainty as a result of the novel's atmosphere of ambiguity and paradox.

Some argue that Hawthorne's concept of sin itself is indefinite, that <u>sin</u> has at most only a cloudy, tentative meaning in the novel. Jeffrey Duncan asserts that Hawthorne entertains at least two possibilities about "the essential nature" of the reality of sin and evil. In one, sin is only "committed in the flesh"; in the other, sin exists only in the human mind--in thoughts--and "sins of the flesh" only exist in the mind's interpretation of actions (61). Duncan concludes of Hawthorne's presentation of sin that "reality [hangs] in the balance, a moot point, indeterminable" (61). Thus it is argued that Hawthorne's sin cannot be definitely perceived, that what may be considered sin in one sense may not be considered sin in another sense. Arlin Turner observes this am-

Here sin *is referred to as a word.*

Direct quotation and paraphrase smoothly alternate, adding to the smooth flow of the paper.

Mulcahey 10

biguity to be especially true in the presen-

tation of the sin of adultery: "The trans-

gression of Hester and Dimmesdale stands

condemned by the laws of society but in an

absolute sense is condemned only mildly if at

all by the author and the reader . . ."

*Parenthetical
documentation
is placed inside
the fourth
period because
the page
citation is part
of the context of
the sentence.*

(Turner 59). The adultery of Hester and

Arthur seems acceptable in the context of <u>The

Scarlet Letter</u>, yet it is not condoned in a

general sense. According to this interpreta-

tion, the gravity of this sin is uncertain

and almost arbitrary. The obvious implica-

tion of these arguments is that sin cannot be

conquered if its true nature is unknown.

In a similar argument, Hawthorne's plea

that man "be true" is proven to be inherently

and irreconcilably paradoxical. Duncan indi-

cates first of all that Hawthorne does not

explain to what one should be true (Duncan

52). The perfect example of this ambiguity

occurs in chapter 18 of the novel, when

Hester dicards her scarlet "A" and proposes

that she and Dimmesdale flee from the Puritan

community. As revealed in Pearl's disap-

proval of this act, Hawthorne censures the

idea, showing Hester as trying to ignore the

fact of her own sinfulness. Yet, as John

Gerber notes, she is true to the natural pas-

sion that she has demonstrated throughout the

book; therefore she does not in essence com-

mit what Hawthorne considers a sin (107).

Thus Hester can be considered a sinner or she

can be absolutely justified, regardless of

her actions. Likewise, Roger Chillingworth,

the undisputed antagonist of the novel, can

be considered totally justified in his ac-

tions, for he is true to his own antagonism

throughout the novel.

Furthermore, Duncan contends that

Dimmesdale's final moment of truth, his ap-

parent salvation through confession, is "per-

fectly ambiguous" because of an endless

paradox in his "being true." Duncan proposes

that the minister's confession may be inter-

preted in several different ways: (1) he may

be false in his confession in the sense that

Mulcahey 12

he confesses in such a way as to appear to the Puritan community as the Christlike saint which he is not; (2) his confession may be as sincere and true as common interpretation contends; (3) he may be perfectly false in confession, in which case he is perfectly true to himself (69-70). An endless cycle of paradox results, which Duncan interprets to mean that Dimmesdale's truth may be false and his falsity may in fact be truth. Whether Dimmesdale gains his salvation from his "being true" is therefore indefinite and ultimately irreconcilable. Once more the usefulness of Hawthorne's morality is questioned.

In one essay, Hyatt H. Waggoner questions whether salvation ever comes about by Hawthorne's proposed morality, observing the dark and uncertain conclusion which both Hester and Dimmesdale appear to share. He asserts that neither Hester nor Dimmesdale achieves a glorious salvation: ". . . For Hester there is no escape, only sublimation

Three ellipsis dots are used to indicate a word or words omitted at the start of the quotation.

Mulcahey 13

and self-control. For Dimmesdale there is

only public confession of guilt and submis-

sion to a will he conceives as higher than

his own" (The Presence 69). Waggoner further

declares that the final images of the novel

are gloomy and pessimistic. He suggests that

the imagery of the final tombstone inscrip-

tion "ON A FIELD, SABLE, THE LETTER A, GULES"

(Hawthorne 245) implies all of the negative-

ness of Hawthorne's dual symbols and none

of the positiveness. The scene, he believes,

is absolutely void of the relieving gleam of

hope which Hawthorne had promised, and death

or guilt seems to be all that is left to

Hester and Arthur in the end (The Presence

70). "Being true" apparently has not brought

them to a happier state than they had experi-

enced without "being true." Thus, Waggoner

concludes that Hawthorne does not succeed in

lightening the dark close of his story. He

notes that both Hawthorne and his wife wept

miserably when Hawthorne had read the conclu-

sion aloud (The Presence 72). This reaction

Since the author (Waggoner) is mentioned twice earlier in the paragraph, only an abbreviated title is necessary.

Mulcahey 14

suggests to Waggoner that even Hawthorne himself tended to feel that ambiguity of his
moral, that he also had doubts concerning the
ultimate value of his "moral blossom."

These arguments have unanswerable validity. Such ambiguity undeniably exists in <u>The
Scarlet Letter</u>, as Hawthorne's tears apparently attest. In fact, Hawthorne's ambiguity
even serves as the cement which bonds the
entire novel together, allowing illusions to
assume a sense of reality and binding abstract ideas to materialistic symbols such as
the scarlet "A." Contrary to what the critics cited suggest, however, the ambiguity
does not destroy the true purpose of the
story, nor does it confuse the "blossom" of
wisdom which Hawthorne wishes to imply to the
reader. Instead, it solidifies the certainties which Hawthorne had felt to be true
throughout his life.

In Waggoner's opinion, Hawthorne defines
sin ambiguously not because he doubted his
own concept of sin but because he wished to

*The student
author now
leads the reader
back to his
original thesis.*

Mulcahey 15

show the relativity it assumes in this world.
He used ambiguity as an expression of his own
"existentially oriented" religious beliefs,
and he based his view of life on his own
experience ("Art and Belief" 67). Just as
Hawthorne's convictions depended on his own
perception of life, the reality of the nature
of sin in <u>The Scarlet Letter</u> varies relative
to the perception of the characters of the
novel. As John Gerber states, "Sin [in
Hawthorne's novel] . . . is a violation of
only that which the sinner thinks he vio-
lates." The inevitable conclusion of this
statement is that a uniform definition of sin
cannot exist and indeed is not supposed to
exist in <u>The Scarlet Letter</u>. Hawthorne is
certain that sin is relative and dependent on
man himself. For instance, Hester Prynne
realizes that she has sinned against the
Puritan society, but she hardly views her
adultery in the sense that the Puritan community views it. She does not consider it a
breach of God's law, but a breach of the law

Key words from Waggoner's other work are cited to avoid confusion.

Words are added in brackets to clarify the context.

Mulcahey 16

of order and Puritan orthodoxy (Gerber 108).

Although the society's and Hester's views

are very different, both nevertheless have a

sense of reality with respect to those who

conceive them.[2] Hawthorne is certain, then,

that man's concept of sin is definite only

with respect to himself.

Thus Hawthorne's purpose is not to de-

fine sin but to juxtapose his characters'

relative concepts of sin and let the reader

observe the results. R. W. B. Lewis main-

tains that the novel is merely a showcase in

which the characters and the Puritan society

are measured against each other (74). It was

therefore Hawthorne's intention to have the

entire effect of the novel on the reader

depend on the reader's determination of this

measurement. For instance, a reader with a

strong religious background might consider

adultery a serious sin, while on the other

hand a romantic might believe the act of pas-

sion to be totally justified.

Hawthorne does not intend to imply, how-

Mulcahey 17

ever, that sin does not really exist because it is merely a formulation of each man's mind. Strongly implicit in <u>The Scarlet Letter</u> is that sin is inevitable despite its relativity. As an American writer who partially refuted the ideas of Transcendentalism, Hawthorne was certain that sin and evil were real enough so that they could not be relinquished, as Ralph Waldo Emerson had thought, by "self-reliance" or by simply imagining that they did not exist (Mark Van Doren 137). He saw the certainty of the existence of sin not as a result of dogma, but as a direct implication of the relativity of sin. Men perceive sin with respect to their own convictions, and therefore their perceptions are necessarily various. And since men interact with each other in a society, they must perceive sin in each other and attempt to impress their concepts of sin upon others. Such is the case with the Puritan society of Hawthorne's novel, of which the adulterers are influenced members. "In the

Van Doren's full name is given to avoid confusing him with Carl Van Doren, cited earlier.

Mulcahey 18

minds of [Hawthorne's] characters, their sins
are absolute, for they have broken God's
laws; and they see themselves and their relations with people and institutions about them
in the light of that assumption" (Turner 57).
The main characters are convinced that they
are sinners, despite their ability to believe
otherwise. That their sins depend on their
own relative perceptions does not make these
sins any less real to them. Therefore,
Hawthorne's grand implication of sin's definite existence is finally revealed. Because
he shows the nature of sin's reality to vary
from man to man, sin must always exist; for
if a man does not see sin in himself, he must
surely see it in others, and vice versa. In
either case, the existence of sin will be
definite.

   And if the certainty of sin does not lie
in man's perception of it, Hawthorne implies
that evil must exist in the punishment of sin
and the resulting suffering of his characters. If it is certain that one can justify

Mulcahey 19

Hester's adultery in her naturally passionate and wild nature, then surely the Puritan society has sinned against her by punishing her action. In this case, the sin committed is that of human injustice, which occurs "because men fumbled in their understanding of justice" (Mark Van Doren 138). In either sense, some form of sin has occurred, and Hawthorne shows evil and suffering to be tragically inevitable.

These ideas concerning human beings and their perceptions of sin imply the most important certainty which Hawthorne wishes finally to give to his readers. This is the certainty of tragedy in life. In his study of the consequences of sin, Hawthorne asserts a belief that "retribution for sin is certain," and apparent in the entire progress of the novel is an assumed inevitability, a fatefulness surrounding the destinies of the characters (Turner 58). Chillingworth serves as the constant symbol, or indeed the mechanism, of this fatefulness. It is he who

Mulcahey 20

makes Hester and Arthur tragic victims of

destiny. This fact is clear in his statement

to Hester in chapter 14:

} *double space*

*A colon precedes
long quotations.
The quotation
is double-spaced
and indented
ten spaces. The
final period is
placed before the
documentation
parentheses.
Double-space
above and
below the
quotation.*

It is not granted me to pardon. I

have no such power as thou tellest

me of. By thy first step awry thou

didst plant the germ of evil; but

since that moment, it has all been

dark necessity. . . . It is our

fate. Let the black flower blossom

as it may. (167)

} *double space*

double space

It is also made definite by the entrapment of

Hester, Dimmesdale, and Chillingworth. For

instance, the plans of Hester and Dimmesdale

to escape by boat are spoiled by Chilling-

worth himself, who plans to board the same

ship. All three characters are deterministi-

cally tied to their destinies, and the occur-

rence of tragedy in their conclusions is

certain.

However, the certainty of tragedy in

life that Hawthorne wishes to demonstrate is

ironically most apparent in the ambiguity of

Mulcahey 21

the moral itself. The inevitable tragedy im-

plied by the ambiguity of the moral exists in

what Roy Male calls its "eternal paradox."

Man's knowledge, represented by the wisdom of

Hawthorne's final moral, may be "insanity to

God," while celestial truth may likewise seem

insane in the social world (Male 94). In

this respect, tragedy exists in the fact that

man cannot be absolutely sure of the nature

of ultimate truth, that his worldly percep-

tions do not reflect necessarily the truths

of the spirit. The ambiguity of Hawthorne's

moral thus converts itself into an absolute

certainty, the certainty that any of man's

attempts to solve the eternal problem of sin,

including that of Hawthorne, is unavoidably

vested with tragic uncertainty. The weeping

of Hawthorne which Waggoner notes is not for

his ambiguous moral but for the impending

tragedy which it implies.

The student author moves toward his conclusion.

The "blossom" which Hawthorne presents

to the reader therefore reveals its highest

meaning. It is not represented by definite

Mulcahey 22

moral advice but by tragic wisdom. It is the
sad knowledge that the reader finally shares
with Hester Prynne, the knowledge that sin is
"a problem for which there is no solution in
life," the knowledge which makes "the life
of Hester [increase], not [diminish] . . ."
(Mark Van Doren 132). The "blossom" of wisdom serves for the reader the same purpose
that Pearl serves for Hester, reminding her
of her guilt and sin and causing her to "look
with warm sympathy into the hearts of sin-

Once again the thesis is emphasized.

ners" (Turner 61). Hawthorne's "moral blossom" therefore does not lose its value or its
sweetness. It gives to readers a renewed
hope that although they cannot conquer the
problem of sin altogether, they can still

The paper has come full circle, beginning with a reference to the "moral blossom" and ending with this same reference. The final sentence is a strong conclusion.

benefit from its tragedy. At this point, the
"blossom" is in full bloom.

Notes

Content notes are on a separate page entitled "Notes."

1 It is useful to compare Hawthorne's moral ambiguity and paradox with that of Milton in <u>Paradise Lost</u>.

A reference to another work for comparison

2 Only in the forest (symbolizing a moral wilderness away from society) can Hester and Dimmesdale escape the strict Puritan code and acknowledge their bond.

A note of further explication

Mulcahey 24

Works Cited

Brownell, W. C. "This New England Faust."

The Scarlet Letter: <u>An Authoritative</u>

<u>Text, Backgrounds and Sources,</u>

<u>Criticism</u>. Ed. Sculley Bradley and oth-

ers. 2nd ed. New York: Norton, 1978.

291-293.

Davidson, Edward H. "Dimmesdale's Fall."

<u>Twentieth Century Interpretations of</u>

The Scarlet Letter. Ed. John C. Gerber.

Englewood Cliffs: Prentice, 1968.

82-105.

Duncan, Jeffrey L. "The Design of

Hawthorne's Fabrications." <u>The Yale Re-</u>

<u>view</u> 71 (Oct. 1981): 51-71.

Gerber, John C. "Form and Content in <u>The</u>

<u>Scarlet Letter</u>." <u>The New England Quar-</u>

<u>terly</u> 17 (1944): 25-55.

Hawthorne, Nathaniel. <u>The Scarlet Letter</u>.

New York: NAL, 1959.

Lewis, R. W. B. "The Return into Time:

Hawthorne." <u>Hawthorne: A Collection of</u>

<u>Critical Essays</u>. Ed. A. N. Kaul Engle-

"Works Cited" must begin on a new page. The title of the novel is not underlined since it is part of a title that must be underlined (see Section 10b–3, p. 217–18).

Citation of a work within an edited collection (see Section 9b–2h, p. 174).

Citation of a journal article (see Section 9b–4d, p. 180).

Mulcahey 25

wood Cliffs: Prentice, 1966. 72-95.

Male, Roy R. <u>Hawthorne's Tragic Vision</u>. New
    York: Norton, 1957.

Roper, Gordon. "The Four Part Structure."
    <u>Twentieth Century Interpretations of</u>
    The Scarlet Letter. Ed. John C. Gerber.
    Englewood Cliffs: Prentice, 1968.
    49-52.

Turner, Arlin. <u>Nathaniel Hawthorne: An In-</u>
    <u>troduction and Interpretation</u>. New
    York: Barnes, 1961.

Van Doren, Carl. <u>The American Novel,</u>
    <u>1789-1939</u>. 2nd ed. New York:
    Macmillan, 1940.

Van Doren, Mark. "<u>The Scarlet Letter</u>."
    <u>Hawthorne: A Collection of Critical</u>
    <u>Essays</u>. Ed. A. N. Kaul. Englewood
    Cliffs: Prentice, 1966. 129-140.

Waggoner, Hyatt H. <u>The Presence of</u>
    <u>Hawthorne</u>. Baton Rouge: Louisiana State
    UP, 1979.

---. "Art and Belief." <u>Twentieth Century</u>
    <u>Interpretations of</u> The Scarlet Letter.

Citation of a book by a single author (see Section 9b–2a, p. 172).

Citation of a book in its second edition (see Section 9b–2m, p. 176).

The line indicates a repetition of Hyatt H. Waggoner as author.

Mulcahey 26

Ed. John C. Gerber.   Englewood Cliffs:

Prentice, 1968.   67-72.

12b   Entire paper using the author-date style
of documentation (APA)

The first page of the paper is the title page. It includes the full title of the paper, the name of the student, the name of the class, the name of the institution, and the date. All lines are centered on the page.

A running head (an abbreviated version of the title) is placed at the top right-hand side of each page. Do not use more than fifty characters (including spaces) for the running head.

The page number is placed one double-spaced line below the running head, beginning with the title page and going on through the entire paper, including the reference pages.

1

Passive Victims of Substance Abuse

Tracy Weed

English 101

Glendale Community College

June 2, 1989

Following the title page is the abstract, a brief summary of the paper's major ideas. The heading "Abstract" is centered at the top of the page. For a paper of ten pages or less, the abstract should be no longer than one page.

The abstract itself is written in coherent paragraph form but leaves out the minor points and details of the research.

Passive Victims

2

Abstract

For the past twenty years the United States has witnessed the proliferation of substance abuse, counteracted by treatment programs aimed at resolving addictions. Research indicates that addictive behavior affects all the people around the addict, most especially the spouses and the children. Every member of the addict's family is caught in the web of co-dependency, a behavioral syndrome characterized by an obsession with other people and other people's problems, and a denial of one's self and one's needs. Co-dependency is considered an illness that parallels the progressive deterioration in addiction. The most lamentable among the co-dependent victims are the children of addicts or alcoholics, termed CoAs. They develop coping and surviving skills that serve them well in childhood but can cripple their adult lives. There is no dispute about the fact that alcoholism and co-dependency are generational

Passive Victims

3

afflictions and that in order to stop the havoc they create, these innocent young victims must be identified. Only as society becomes aware of the patterns exhibited by these passive victims as a result of their dysfunctional home-lives can they be set free from the inevitable repetition of injurious patterns.

The body of the paper begins on page 4. The full title of the paper is centered at the top of the page. The text begins one double-spaced line below the title.

The intro-ductory paragraph contains no documentation, as it is the student's own conclusion. The final sentence is the thesis of the paper.

Passive Victims

4

Passive Victims of Substance Abuse

Since the mid-nineteen sixties, the United States has witnessed an ever-increasing portion of its population involved with illegal street drugs, so-called recre-ational drugs, and the use and abuse of le-gal, mind-altering substances, such as alcohol and prescription drugs. The nineteen eighties have seen the creation of treatment programs, offered to assist substance abusers of every kind in overcoming their addictions. Missing in this rush to treat and resolve ad-diction problems is an awareness of the pas-sive victims of substance abuse: the family members and significant others affected by their relationships to the abusers. The dev-astating impact of substance abuse on these passive victims is gradually coming to light, and the damage done to them urgently needs to be addressed. If we are to break this chain of substance abuse and addiction, all those touched must first be recognized and then

Passive Victims

5

helped to understand that they do not have to create an endless cycle of pernicious patterns.

Any addictive behavior, whether it involves the abuse of substances, such as alcohol and cocaine, or the excessive intake of high-calorie food resulting in extreme obesity "is one of the most pervasive and intransigent mental health problems facing society today" (Coleman, Butcher, & Carson, 1984, p. 367). It must be understood from the onset of this paper that all addictions evolve as ways to handle anxiety, conflict, and stress. All addictions provide a false sense of relief--"a quick fix"--and cause the build-up of tolerance so that when the substance is removed, withdrawal ensues (Peterson, 1987). The particular substance is not the critical factor. Disorders that have all the features of an addictive condition but do not involve addictive substances can be just as damaging and life threatening as those

The reference is to a quotation from a book by three authors. Always cite the specific page number of a quotation. Place the final period following the end parenthesis.

The reference is to an idea from one author. Only the author and date need to be cited.

Passive Victims

6

resulting from alcohol or other drugs. A
person can develop an overpowering need or
addiction to just about any substance or behavior. Witness the recovering alcoholic who
becomes a workaholic (Capell-Sowder, 1984).

In 1938, Menninger described addiction
as chronic suicide. Much later, Stanton
Peele (in Capell-Sowder, 1984) stated that
addictive disorders are not a sign of weak
moral character; rather, they represent disorders of self-control, a way of coping with
the world and the self, a way of interpreting
experience. Toby Rice Drews (1983) maintained that long-standing repression of feelings could lead to overeating, compulsive
sexual behavior, compulsive spending, alcohol
and drug use, obsessive or controlling ges-
tures, and other compulsive behaviors. Moreover, addicts often move from one addiction
to another in a compulsive repetitiveness
that aggravates and expresses denial
(V., 1984). They are trapped in the illusion

*Here the author
and date are
named in the
body of the text;
therefore, no
parenthetical
citation is
necessary. Since
the statement by
Stanton Peele
was found in a
book by Capell-
Sowder, the
word "in"
precedes the
parenthetical
citation.*

*Citing an
author in the
body of the text
and following
the name with
the year in
parentheses is
the most
common way of
handling a
citation in the
APA style.*

*The reason the
author's name*

Passive Victims

7

is a mere initial
("V.") is that he
or she is a
member of
Alcoholics
Anonymous, an
organization
that insists on
the anonymity
of its members.

that they hold the power to control the fast
high while in reality their lives are completely out of control.

The focus of this paper is on the families of alcoholics, particularly the children. Families of alcoholics are caught in
a web of addiction that causes their members
to become increasingly angry with the people
they love the most. There is a generational
link in alcoholism that was recognized as
long ago as Aristotle and the philosopher
Plutarch (Squires, 1987). According to a

In the text the
student writer
names the year
and title of the
magazine used.

January, 1988, <u>Newsweek</u> article, at least 28
million Americans are either living with or
have seen at least one of their parents in
the throes of addictive behavior (Leerhsen &
Nanuth, p. 62).

At the end of
the idea, she
provides the
names of the
two authors
and the page
reference within
parentheses.

The hallmark of the alcoholic family is
isolation from feelings, from other family
members who do not talk about the problem,
and from the world at large (Woititz, 1983).
Not really wanting to confront reality is the

biggest issue in the alcoholic home. The
family is not conscious that isolation and
non-confrontation provide the perfect environment for the alcoholic to continue in his
or her entrapment. By trying to conceal
their embarrassment, shame, and humiliation,
the family clears the way for the progression
of the disease. By protecting the alcoholic
from the world, the family unwittingly sets
in motion a cycle of addiction that can last
for generations. Families of serious substance abusers have many commonalities. They
are dysfunctional, chaotic, unpredictable,
and inconsistent. They are also abusive,
rigid, and neglectful. As the addictive disorder progresses, these families are trapped
in a divisive atmosphere about the problem
and become consumed with unspoken anger and
feelings of guilt, shame, anxiety, confusion,
and remorse (Squires, 1987). As the saying
goes in alcohol treatment circles, "The
alcoholic is addicted to alcohol, the non-

Passive Victims

9

drinking parent is addicted to the alcoholic,
and the children are left to fend for themselves" (Squires, 1987, p. 15).

    These dysfunctional families are highly
connected by their simultaneous denial of and
loyalty to the family secret. They suffer
undercurrents of tension and anxiety in the
face of constant unpredictability and chaos.
Their peculiar bonding, better described as
being fused or enmeshed, is an unhealthy system of corroding the mental, emotional, and
spiritual growth of each member. These
shame-based families have rigid rules: don't
ask questions; don't express your feelings;
don't betray the family; focus on the trou-
bled person's behavior to the exclusion of
all else. This is known as the family syndrome. In these families there is a blurring
of generational boundaries, a lack of consistent limits set by the parents, and a complete lack of structure. Perhaps the
situation is best summarized by the venerable

Neither author nor date is mentioned in the text. They are both placed within parentheses, followed by the page since a specific quotation is involved. As you can see, considerable flexibility exists for handling documentary citations. The main rule is to keep the body of the paper running smoothly.

Passive Victims

10

psychoanalyst Carl Jung (1983): "When an
inner situation is not made conscious, it
appears on the outside as fate" (p. 203).

All the family members of the alcoholic
are termed co-dependents, including the
spouse or significant other adult and the
children (Beattie, 1987). Co-dependency follows a remarkably parallel degenerative progression to the disease of the addict. What
begins as a little concern may trigger isolation, depression, emotional or physical illness, and suicidal fantasies (Beattie, 1987).
Adult co-dependents inevitably find their way
into relationships with needy people because
most co-dependents have been the victims of
physical, sexual, or emotional abuse and have
been neglected or abandoned in their families
of origin. They adopt this caretaking role
and develop a compulsion to ignore their own
needs in order to anticipate and serve others. They feel responsible for other adults
and compelled to solve others' problems.

*The author is
mentioned in
the text; the
quoted page is
placed within
parentheses
following the
quotation.*

*The next four
references are to
Beattie. Each
time both the
author and date
are cited.*

They may become so obsessed with others, that
they abandon their own routines and gradually
lose touch with the world outside their compulsion. These are the perfectionists who
are never satisfied with themselves; yet,
they build increasing tolerance to the unacceptable behavior of those around them.
Their self-image deteriorates as they live
through the addict's deteriorating behavior.
They compromise their value system for the
sake of clearly destructive relationships,
becoming hopelessly entangled in others'
lives and problems as if they had no choice.
They let their lives become chaotic by always
focusing outside themselves and living
through and with people who are out of control (Beattie, 1987).

    Co-dependents live in a profound state
of denial as an instinctive reaction to pain,
loss, and change. They use denial to shut
themselves away from facts and events that
are too disturbing to acknowledge (Beattie,

1987). They are reactionaries who forfeit
their power to think, to feel, or to behave
in their own best interest. They take other
people's loathsome behavior to be a reflec-
tion of their own lives. Desperate to find
love, they usually seek it from people inca-
pable of giving or loving (Beattie, 1987).
Ironically, they equate love with pain, and
often tolerate abuse just to keep others
close to them. This emotional insecurity is
fueled by a form of self-torture, a nameless
sense of being unfit for reality (Beattie,
1987), an antagonistic relationship to the
self, and the shame of feeling their entire
lives to be a dreadful mistake (Whitfield,
1987).

   Alcoholic or co-dependent parents who
are locked into their own narcissistic needs
cannot provide a mirror for their child and
therefore the child cannot develop an individual identity (V., 1987). Children from
alcoholic homes are robbed of their individ-

Passive Victims

13

ual identity and become subject to situa-

tional reinforcement or "people pleasing."

Similar to co-dependents, they feel their

very worth tied to their "performance," to

the reactions and judgments of others, and to

the outcome of situations. They are the for-

gotten victims of addiction, known in re-

search circles as Children of Alcoholics, or

CoAs. While adult co-dependents feel trapped

in their relationship with the alcoholic,

they could, in reality, leave. Unlike them,

the CoA has neither the choice nor the mobil-

ity to enter or exit the relationship to ei-

ther parent, and truly is trapped (Greenleaf,

1984). These children are not born with so-

cial skills, moral values or standards for

evaluating behavior, but they implicitly

learn from what they see in the environment

into which they are born. In other words,

they learn behavior from both the alcoholic

and the co-dependent parent. Consequently,

it is not sufficient to say that children are

Passive Victims

14

hurt by distorted parental behavior; what
they learn becomes the model not only for
their own behavior but their choice of future
relationships (Greenleaf, 1984). "It is an
unfounded platitude that children are re-
silient. The ability to bounce back into
health from repeated, long-term psychological
trauma requires a healthy, well-developed ego
not present until adulthood. When childhood
development is continually thwarted, there is
nothing to bounce back to" (Greenleaf, 1984,
p. 14).

CoAs span the social strata all the way
from the White House to the welfare rolls.
Often they appear as super achievers, honor
roll students, or varsity players. But in
reality they are masquerading behind the expertise of their long-practiced denial of
what goes on (Squires, 1987). They have
strong tendencies as children to look normal
because they do not want to draw attention to
themselves (Woititz, 1983).

Passive Victims

15

Krisberg (1986) describes three levels of stress among CoAs that create responses that greatly resemble Post Traumatic Stress Disorder. "For a child moderate stress is caused by continual parental fighting; severe stress is caused by the parents' divorce and persistent, harsh parental discipline; and extreme stress is caused by repeated physical and sexual abuse" (Whitfield, 1987, p. 57). The traumas hardest to treat are of human origin and have existed for a period of six months or more. They appear in the child as the absence of feeling and as a decreased interest in important life activities.

Former Secretary of Health, Education, and Welfare, Margaret Heckler (1986, January), stressed that one of the issues most urgently needing to be addressed is the under-reported crimes of family violence. "These crimes," says Heckler, "are usually committed in an atmosphere where alcohol and drug abuse are present; they are, in fact, a

*Here the
student deftly
mixes text and
documentation.
She names the
magazine and
author in the
text, placing the
year and month
of the issue in
parentheses
following the
title of the
magazine. At
the end of the
quotation she
cites the page
number within
parentheses.*

*The student
writer smoothly
integrates the
author, title of
work, and the
date—all in her
text. Do not
attempt to
crowd in so
much infor-
mation unless
doing so will
not mar the
coherence of
your text. The
next three
paragraphs are
based on
information
from the source
cited.*

by-product of such abuse" (p. 55).

Janet Geringer Woititz, President of
the Institute for Counseling and Training, in
Verona, New Jersey, commented on CoAs in
Newsweek (1987, January): "Violence, incest,
and sexual abuse are three times more common
in alcoholic households than in the general
population" (p. 65).

In her 1981 expose of the problems of
CoAs, It Will Never Happen to Me, author
Claudia Black describes the most common roles
these children adopt early in life as a means
of coping and surviving. One such role is
that of the "responsible" child who seldom
misbehaves, takes over household chores as
the home deteriorates, and creates structure
and organization. This child acts as an
adult because the adults are not available to
fill the child's needs. This child is never
exposed to models of either setting or
achieving long-term goals, and from the
effort of keeping the home functioning from

Passive Victims

17

crisis to crisis, has only practiced immedi-
ate, short-term goals for survival. Such a
child will grow into an adult who is completely unable to be spontaneous, who always
needs to be in control, and who is not able
to relate to others as equals. He or she
will eventually become isolated from all
intimate relationships.

Another common role is that of the
"adjuster." This role is characterized as
detachment from the deteriorating household.
The child does not attempt to prevent or
alleviate the chaotic situation and is not
highly visible in the home. He or she copes
by acting without thinking or feeling. This
is the role most permeated with denial. As
"adjusters" grow up, they continue to avoid
central positions and often feel victimized
and powerless. Their continued need for
movement creates a total lack of continuity
in their lives. They only know how to deal
with chaos, not with their own feelings.

Passive Victims

18

They feel lonely, inadequate, and depressed.

A third common role is that of the "placater." The "placater" is adept at focusing
attention away from himself or herself by
showing extreme sensitivity to others' feelings. The "placater" grows into a compulsive
rescuer and caregiver, the most obviously co-
dependent role, and as an adult will often
take up a caregiving profession. These care-
givers never consider what they want and
need; instead they seek out situations with
"takers" so that they can play out childhood
roles.

Finally, there is the role of "acting
out." The "acting out" child draws attention
by negative, disruptive behavior. Because
this child cannot be ignored, he or she is
the most likely one to have his or her problem addressed early and to receive professional attention. Children who "act out" are
often institutionalized, either in jail or
in a mental hospital, by their late teens.

As adults, they are unable to interact with others or to express their needs in acceptable ways. Often their early behavior causes life-long complications.

CoAs may exhibit some or each of these adaptive roles, which are progressive and may change in adulthood. All children reared in alcoholic homes have problems in adulthood with control, trust, identity, dependency, and expression of feelings (Black, 1981).

CoAs will experience great gaps in their development, especially in the area of self-esteem. They suffer from a lack of identity and from severe discrepancies in their self-image. Because of their compulsion for control, they tend toward an all-or-nothing thinking and reacting style. They have no role models and no exposure to healthy problem solving, having grown up, literally, from crisis to crisis (Whitfield, 1987). They lock themselves into a course of action without giving serious consideration to alterna-

Passive Victims

20

tives. They live with a sense of urgency, silent desperation, always thinking that "this is my last chance, it's now or never" (Woititz, 1983). They are terrified of losing control, which is tied to their early dependence on unpredictable, inconsistent adults. They have an unusually high tolerance for inappropriate behavior in the people around them.

Since self-esteem is based on respectful acceptance and concerned treatment from significant others, the lack of these in an alcoholic home makes it impossible for CoAs to feel good about themselves (Woititz, 1983). CoAs have extreme problems with their self-images because they internalize the early parental messages that they are unimportant and not cared about. They translate these messages into the belief that somehow their very existence is wrong and shameful, that they do not merit the right to be alive. Because they confuse loyalty with love, they

Passive Victims

21

remain in destructive friendships, love affairs, and marriages long after they would
be better dissolved. CoAs would rather en-
dure known pain than face the uncertainty of
starting fresh. Paradoxically, the only
frame of reference CoAs have in terms of intimate relationships is the push/pull of "I
want you, go away" (Woititz, 1983). Thus,
their fear of abandonment, sparked to life in
early childhood, overwhelms reason and leads
them to deny their loveableness. Emotional
insecurity urges them to maintain almost in-
tolerable relationships (Beattie, 1987).

The conclusion of the paper is a strong appeal for action on the part of the psychological community and parents. It is a restatement of the original thesis.

Changing CoAs' habitual behavior is
extremely difficult because it is the only
behavior they know and because it is inter-
locked with the unconscious of one or both
parents (V., 1987). The seven million CoAs
who are under the age of eighteen right now
are the hardest to reach because their parents' denial keeps them from treatment. For
these children, who never know what to expect

Passive Victims

22

when they come home from school each day,
life is a state of constant anxiety (Woititz,
p. 68). It should be a primary goal of the
psychological community and society in general to identify these passive victims and to
help them understand that they are not responsible for their parents' illness (Greenleaf, 1984). Only then can these children be
saved from the bondage of a life sentence to
a half-life of blindly repeating their parents' pain and misery.

Passive Victims

23

Reference List

Beattie, M. (1987). <u>Co-dependent no more</u>.

Center City, MN.: Hazelden.

Black, C. (1987). <u>It will never happen to</u>

<u>me</u>. Denver: M.A.C.

Blum, R. (1984). An argument for family re-

search. In B. G. Ellis (Ed.), <u>Drug</u>

<u>abuse from the family perspective</u>. (pp.

104-116). Washington, D.C.: U.S.G.P.O.

Capell-Sowder, K. (1984). On being addicted

to the addict: Co-dependent relation-

ships. In <u>Co-dependency: An emerging</u>

<u>issue</u>. (pp. 19-23). Deerfield Beach,

FL: Health Communications.

Coleman, J. C., Butcher, J. N., & Carson,

R. C. (1984). <u>Abnormal psychology and</u>

<u>modern life</u>. Glenville, IL.: Scott,

Foresman.

Ellis, B. G. (1980). <u>Drug abuse from the</u>

<u>family perspective</u>. Washington, D.C.:

U.S.G.P.O.

Greenleaf, J. (1984). Co-alcoholic/para-

alcoholic: Who's who and what's the

"Reference List" is centered at the top of a new page.

All of the references follow the APA rules for listing sources.

This anthology has no editor.

Passive Victims

24

difference? In <u>Co-dependency: An emerg-</u>
<u>ing issue</u>. (pp. 1-17). Deerfield
Beach, FL.: Health Communications.

Jung, C. J. (1983). The development of personality. In Storr, A. (Ed.), <u>The es-</u>
<u>sential Jung</u>. (pp. 191-228).
Princeton, N.J.: Princeton University.

Leerhsen, C., & Namuth, T. (1988, January
18). Alcohol and the family. <u>Newsweek</u>.
pp. 62-68.

Menninger, K. A. (1938). <u>Man against himself</u>.
New York: Harcourt, Brace & World.

Peterson, N. (1986, November). What about
the children? <u>McCalls</u>, 114(2)
pp. 103-104; rpt. Pasadena, CA.: Microcomputer Index, Dialog File 47,
04459707.

Squires, S. (1987, December 15). For families, a long road to happiness. <u>Wash-</u>
<u>ington Post</u>, Health, pp. 15-16.

V., R. (1987). <u>Family secrets</u>. San Francisco: Harper & Row.

Passive Victims

25

Weingarten, N. (1980). Treating adolescent
drug abuse as a sympton of dysfunction
in the family. In B. G. Ellis (Ed.),
<u>Drug abuse from the family perspective</u>
(pp. 57-61). Washington, D.C.:
U.S.G.P.O.

Whitfield, C. L. (1987). <u>Healing the child
within</u>. Deerfield Beach, FL.: Health
Communications.

Woititz, J. G. (1983). <u>Adult children of al-
coholics</u>. Pompano Beach, FL.: Health
Communications.

12c Excerpt from a paper using footnote documentation (traditional)

1

Elaine Spray

Professor McCuen } ⟍
                 } ── *double*
English 101   } ⟍ *space*
                 }
21 June 1984   }

} *double space*

Rasputin's Other Side

} *quadruple space*

The name "Rasputin" commonly evokes an image of unbridled, mystical evil. Few figures have fared as badly in the popular memory. In the 1930s, Lionel Barrymore transfixed thousands of movie goers by portraying him as a devilish, licentious, mysteriously hypnotic fiend. Hundreds of books published since his murder in 1916 unanimously agree on his subhumanity. Reporting a libel trial involving one of his murderers, United Press International in 1965 casually labeled Rasputin as mad, filthy, licentious, semiliterate, fiendish, and lecherous.[1] After

} *quadruple space*

[1] Dave Smith, "Casting a Light on } *single*
Rasputin's Shadow," <u>Los Angeles Times</u> } *space*
9 June 1977, pt. 4: 1.

The title is centered on the page.

An elevated numeral refers to footnote at bottom of page. For proper footnote format, see Fig 8–2, p. 143.

Spray 2

six decades of being judged a demoniacal libertine, Rasputin now deserves to be viewed
from another point of view--as a man who was
intensely religious, who passionately desired
peace, and who was deeply devoted to his family and friends.

Who was this so-called horror incarnate,
this man named Rasputin? It is said that on
the night of January 23, 1871, a great meteor
seared a flaming path across the skies of
Western Siberia, hurtled in an arc over the
little village of Pokrovskoye and, at the
very moment that the meteor burned out, a
seven-pound boy was born to Anna Egorovina,
the wife of Efim Akovlevich, a Russian
farmer. The couple named the boy, their second son, Grigori Efimovich Rasputin.

What was this second son, this Rasputin,
really like? "Supporters called him a spiritual leader and claimed he had healing pow-
ers; detractors called him a satyr and said
his depraved faithful were merely in awe of

Spray 3

his sexual endowments."[2] By the time he was

lured to his death in the basement of a

St. Petersburg palace in 1916, he had aroused

such intensities of hatred and loyalty that

the facts of his early life had already

become blurred and sensationalized. Was it

true that at sixteen he was already known in

his part of Siberia as an insatiable lecher

whom peasant girls found irresistible? Did

he really have gifts of second sight and

prophecy that cast a glow of religious mysti-

cism around him? Did he disappear from his

home for long intervals, wandering about Rus-

sia and even to the Holy Land as a starets,

a pilgrim of God, who was simultaneously a

drunkard and an insatiable womanizer? Was he

really a member of the secret group known as

the Khlysts, outlawed fanatics who held fren-

zied rites in torch-lit forest glades that

ended with wild, naked dancing and savage

sexual orgies?[3] In these suppositions--all

[2] Smith 10.

[3] E. M. Halliday, "Rasputin Reconsidered," _Horizon_ 8.4 (1967):83.

Spray 4

part of the legend before Rasputin died--
there is probably a kernel of truth.
Nevertheless, this remarkable man also
had another side, which has been entirely
overlooked.

To begin with, Rasputin was a man of
intense religious feelings. His love for
Christianity bordered on an exuberant devo-
tion. Maria Rasputin writes of her father's
simple peasant faith:

> Entering his fourteenth year, my
> father passed into a new phase, his
> interest, which soon blossomed into
> a preoccupation, with religion.
> Although he had not learned to read
> or write, skills he did not acquire
> until his later years in St.
> Petersburg, he possessed a remark-
> able memory and could quote whole
> passages of the Bible from having
> heard them read but once.[4]

[4] Maria Rasputin and Patte Barham,
Rasputin: The Man Behind the Myth (Englewood
Cliffs: Prentice, 1977) 15.

Long quotations are introduced by a colon, double-spaced, and indented ten spaces. Double-space before and after the long quotation.

Spray 5

Rasputin, moreover, taught a lofty, sub-lime sort of Christianity at a time when nu-merous Russian politicians were becoming suspicious of the Christian religion. Yet his teaching, made all the more simple by his innate ability to explain abstruse theologi-cal concepts in plain, comprehensible terms, was understood by even the most common plow-man. Consequently, as Christian Orthodoxy waned among those in power, Rasputin was sought out more and more by the ordinary man in the street.[5]

When Rasputin moved to St. Petersburg, he could often be found breakfasting with women followers and talking about God and the "Mysterious resurrection." Suddenly, he would begin to hum softly to himself. Soon the voices around him would join in, swelling to a loud chorus. Then he would leap from his seat and dance around the room.[6] This reli-

[5] M. Rasputin 130.

[6] René Fülöp-Miller, <u>Rasputin: The Holy Devil</u> (New York: Garden City Pub., 1927) 268.

Spray 6

gious demonstration was accepted as sincere
by the Russian peasants, with whom dance had
remained a rite of primitive religious activ-
ity, assuming the character of prayer.[7]

But a vital religion was not the only
positive force in the life of Rasputin. He
also expressed a passionate desire for peace
and political harmony in Russia. For instance, he was deeply concerned about the
Russian underdog. He had vague notions of
turning over the landowners' land to the
peasants, and the landowners' mansions to the
educational system. He was genuinely concerned about the treatment of Jews and other
minorities. His concern about the poor people caused many to liken him. . . .

[7] Fülöp-Miller 267.

Spray 7

"Works Cited" appears on a separate page.

Works Cited

Fülöp-Miller, René. <u>Rasputin: The Holy Devil</u>. New York: Garden City Pub., 1927.

Halliday, E. M. "Rasputin Reconsidered." <u>Horizon</u> 8.4 (1967): 81-87.

Massie, Robert K. <u>Nicholas and Alexandra</u>. New York: Atheneum, 1972.

Pares, Bernard. <u>The Fall of the Russian Monarchy</u>. New York: Knopf, 1939.

Rasputin, Maria, and Patte Barham. <u>Rasputin: The Man Behind the Myth</u>. Englewood Cliffs: Prentice, 1977.

Smith, Dave. "Casting a Light on Rasputin's Shadow." <u>Los Angeles Times</u> 9 June 1977, pt. 4: 1, 10, 11

Checklist for Preparing the Final Draft of the Research Paper

Subject

1. My subject meets the criteria of the assignment.
2. I have found enough sources to prove my thesis.
3. My title reveals my subject.

Sources

4. I have evaluated each source adequately.
5. I have summarized, para-phrased, or quoted properly to avoid plagiarism.
6. All assertions not my own are documented.

Organization

7. My thesis predicts and con-trols my paper.
8. My paper shows an orga-nized progression of thought (it follows the outline/abstract).

Writing

9. My opening paragraph is effective.
10. My writing is coherent.
11. I have avoided the passive voice whenever possible.
12. I have used concrete language.
13. I have been concise.
14. Spelling, punctuation, and other mechanical problems have been eliminated.
15. I have deleted all slang, con-tractions, and clichés.
16. I have checked my diction to assure that my words re-flect precisely what I want to say.

Form

17. The visual form of the pa-per adheres to the style sheet (MLA/APA) recom-mended for my subject.
18. All documentation is accu-rate and consistent with the appropriate style sheet.
19. All quotations have been in-tegrated into the text cor-rectly and smoothly.
20. I have given my paper a final proofreading.

GENERAL AND SPECIALIZED REFERENCES

A   A list of general references

B   A list of specialized references

*This appendix was prepared by Marshall E. Nunn, Reference Librarian Emeritus, Glendale Community College Library, Glendale, CA, with the assistance of Mrs. Barbara Peck (manuscript preparation) of the Glendale Community College Library and of Mr. John de La Fontaine (bibliographic searching) of the Occidental College Library, Los Angeles, CA.

A   A list of general references

There has been a veritable revolution in publishing since the last edition of this book. This increased growth has been, and continues to be, in the field of electronic publishing. Increasingly, more material is becoming available in four non-printed versions: on-line, CD-ROM, magnetic tape, and diskette. And more information is updated more frequently, sometimes daily, and made available on-line in a full-text format, especially with newspapers and journals. This bibliography recognizes these changes by noting which printed sources are available electronically, and, when appropriate, creating new sections for material on databases. There are also new listings for videos in the specialized references section.

This section will systematically list the common general references and give a brief description of the information they provide: general references index information available on a variety of subjects and specialized references index information on specific subjects.

A–1   Books and databases that list other books

The best efforts of ambitious bibliographers cannot produce an exhaustive list of all books in print. Nevertheless, many important references catalog the publication of books. The following are the prime sources for information about existing books.

a.   Books currently in print

<u>Books</u>
Books in Print. 8 vols. New York: Bowker, 1948–present. Published annually in September and updated by annual supplements in March. See also *Books in Print Online* in Database section.
Books in Print on Microfiche. New York: Bowker. Quarterly. Contains completely updated *Books in Print* and *Forthcoming Books* information totaling 885,000 titles.
Books in Print Supplement. 3 vols. New York: Bowker, 1975–present. Published annually in March. Citations are included in *Books in Print Online.*
Paperbound Books in Print. 3 vols. New York: Bowker, 1955–present. Semiannual.
Publishers' Trade List Annual. 4 vols. New York: Bowker, 1873–present. A compilation of yearly catalogs from almost all important publishers, arranged alphabetically by publisher's name. Contains data on books, software, microforms, maps, and calendars.
<u>Databases</u>
Books in Print Online. New York: Bowker. Complete records for titles that are in print, forthcoming, or out-of-print. Available from DIALOG Information Services, Inc.
Books in Print With Book Reviews Plus. New York: Bowker. Includes information on almost one million in-print books plus over 100,000 current, full-text book reviews. Available on CD-ROM from Bowker.
Subject Guide to Books in Print. 5 vols. New York: Bowker, 1957–present. Published

annually and simultaneously with *Books in Print.* A companion volume to *Books in Print, Paperbound Books in Print,* and *Publishers' Trade List Annual.* Available on CD-ROM, microfiche, on-line, and data tape.

b. Bibliographies

Bibliographic Index. Bronx, NY: H. W. Wilson, 1937–present. A subject list of bibliographies. Published in April and August, with an annual cumulation. Also available on-line from WILSONLINE and on magnetic tape from WILSONTAPE.

Cumulative Book Index. Bronx, NY: H. W. Wilson. "A world list of books in the English language." Monthly, with quarterly and semiannual/annual cumulations. Also available on-line from WILSONLINE, on CD-ROM from WILSONDISC, and on magnetic tape from WILSONTAPE.

The catalogs of national libraries come closer to achieving bibliographical universality than do any other listings. The most pertinent sources for the purposes of most students are the following:

National Union Catalog, Pre-1956 Imprints. A Cumulative Author List Representing Library of Congress Printed Cards and Titles Reported by Other American Libraries. 754 vols. London: Mansell, 1968–81. Note: Vols. 686–754 comprise a supplement.

National Union Catalog. New York: Rowan and Littlefield, 1963–83. Note: first quinquennial cumulation covers 1958–62; the entries for 1956–57 were combined with the 1953–55 annual volumes of the *Library of Congress Catalog.—Books: Authors* in a cumulation published in 1958 by J. W. Edwards, Ann Arbor, MI; 1958–62 cumulation published by Rowan and Littlefield, New York; 1963–1967 and 1968–1972 cumulations, J. W. Edwards, Ann Arbor; 1973–77 cumulation, Rowan and Littlefield, Totowa, NJ.

National Union Catalog, 1952–1955 Imprints: An Author List. 30 vols. Ann Arbor, MI: J. W. Edwards, 1961. Supplements the published *National Union Catalog* for 1956 and later imprint.

National Union Catalog. Books. Jan. 1983–present. Washington, DC: Library of Congress, 1983–present. Monthly. Published in microfiche format.

For information on the existence of incunabula—books published before 1500— see the following:

Goff, Frederick R. *Incunabula: A Third Census of Fifteenth Century Books Recorded in North American Collections.* Millwood, NY: Kraus International, 1973.

Stillwell, Margaret B. *The Beginning of the World of Books, 1450 to 1470.* New York: Bibliographic Society of America, 1972.

c. Book industry journals

(†Indicates title is available on-line from DIALOG in a full-text format.)

†*Publisher's Weekly.* New York: Bowker, 1872–present. Weekly record of all books published in the United States. Semiannual issues announce books scheduled for publication.

d. Books about book reviews

Book Review Digest. Bronx, NY: H. W. Wilson, 1905–present. Lists reviews and prints digests of reviews from ninety-five English language periodicals. Also available on-line from WILSONLINE, on CD-ROM from WILSONDISC, and on magnetic tape from WILSONTAPE.

A–2 Books and databases about periodicals and newspapers

Since its beginning in the eighteenth century, periodical literature—whether published weekly, monthly, seasonally, in serial form, or simply on a random basis—has become increasingly important for scholarly research, especially in any field where up-to-date knowledge is important. Millions of articles are published annually in periodicals, making a complete indexing of them nearly impossible. However, the following books and databases about periodicals are especially useful.

a. Periodical and newspaper directories

<u>Books</u>

Ayer Directory of Publications. Philadelphia: Ayer, 1880–1982. An annual list of newspapers and periodicals published in the United States. The directory is organized by states and cities and contains indexes.

IMS/Ayer Directory of Publications. 3 vols. Fort Washington, PA: IMS Press, 1983–85. Annual. Superseded *Ayer Directory of Publications.*

Editor & Publisher International Year Book. New York: Editor & Publisher, 1920/21–present. Provides information on newspapers, advertising agencies, syndicates, and other aspects of journalism in the U.S., Canada, and other countries.

Gale Directory of Publications and Broadcast Media. 3 vols. Detroit: Gale Research Co., 1990–present. Supersedes the three publications listed immediately above. Available on-line through DIALOG.

Standard Periodical Directory. New York: Oxbridge, 1964/65–present. Annual. Largest directory of periodicals in the U.S. and Canada, including more than 67,000 listings.

Ulrich's International Periodicals Directory. 3 vols. New York: Bowker, 1932–present. Annual. Supplemented by *Ulrich's Update.* Both titles are available on-line from DIALOG as part of *Bowker's International Serials Database*; this database is also available on magnetic tape from Bowker Electronic Publishing Co., NY. *Ulrich's on Microfiche* is updated quarterly.

<u>Databases</u>

Ulrich's Plus. New York: Bowker Electronic Publishing. Available on CD-ROM from Bowker.

b. Union lists of periodicals and newspapers

Union lists catalog and record the collection of periodical and newspaper titles available in various libraries. The following are among the most prominent union lists:

American Newspapers, 1821–1936: A Union List of Files Available in the United States and Canada. New York: Wilson, 1937. Catalogue files of newspapers in nearly 6,000 libraries and private locations.

Brigham, Clarence S. *History and Bibliography of American Newspapers, 1690–1820,* 2 vols. Worcester, MA: American Antiquarian Soc., 1947. The best list for anyone trying to find articles in old newspapers.

Brigham, Clarence S. *Additions and Corrections to History and Bibliography of American Newspapers, 1690–1820.* Worcester, MA: American Antiquarian Soc., 1961.

Magazines for Libraries. New York: Bowker, 1969–present. Kept up-to-date with supplements. A standard tool for librarians and library users, with good annotations.

Milner, Anita Cheek. *Newspaper Indexes: A Location and Subject Guide for Researchers.* Metuchen, NJ: Scarecrow, 1977–present. Three volumes of this guide have been published.

New Serial Titles: A Union List of Serials Commencing Publication After Dec. 31, 1949. Washington, DC: U.S. Library of Congress, 1953–present. Monthly and quarterly.

New Serial Titles, 1950–1970 Cumulative. 4 vols. New York: Bowker, 1973.

New Serial Titles, 1950–1970 Subject Guide. 2 vols. New York: Bowker, 1975.

Newspapers in Microform: United States, 1948–1983. 2 vols. Washington, DC: U.S. Library of Congress, 1984.

Union Lists of Serials in Libraries of the United States and Canada. 3d ed. 5 vols. Bronx, NY: H. W. Wilson, 1965.

c. Indexes of periodicals and newspapers

An index lists topics of magazine and newspaper articles alphabetically, giving each article's title and page number. William Poole, working with a group of dedicated librarians, compiled the first American index in 1802. His index is still in use, along with the following:

Index to U.S. Government Periodicals. Chicago: Infodata International, 1970–present. Quarterly, with an annual cumulation.

Index to the Times, 1906–72. London: The Times, 1907–73. Superseded by *The Times Index.*

Magazine Index. Foster City, CA: Information Access Co., 1978–present. Irregular. Also available on-line from DIALOG, on CD-ROM as *Magazine Index Plus,* and on magnetic tape from Information Access Co.

National Newspaper Index. Foster City, CA: Information Access Co., 1979–present. Indexes the *New York Times, Wall Street Journal, Christian Science Monitor, Washington Post,* and *Los Angeles Times.* Monthly. Microfilm. Also available on-line through DIALOG, on microfiche, and on CD-ROM and magnetic tape from Information Access Co.

Newsbank. New Canaan, CT: News Bank, Inc., 1970–present. An index to American newspapers. Articles on current topics of interest to students and other researchers are reproduced on microfiche, each month, accompanied by a monthly printed index. There is also a CD-ROM index: The *Newsbank Electronic Information System* available from News Bank, Inc.

The Times Index, 1973–present. Reading, Eng.: Newspaper Archive Developments, 1973–present. Monthly, with annual cumulations. Supersedes *Index to the Times.*

Poole's Index to Periodical Literature. Rev. ed. 6 vols. Boston: Houghton, 1882–1908. This pioneer work indexes close to 600,000 articles in American and English periodicals. Contains a subject index only.

Reader's Guide to Periodical Literature, 1900–present. Bronx, NY: H. W. Wilson, 1905–present. Published in seventeen separate paper issues per year plus quarterly and annual cumulations. This guide is by far the most popular periodical index. Contains an author, subject, and title index to 200 general magazines with a separate listing of book reviews. Available on-line through WILSON-LINE, WILSONDISC CD-ROM search system, WILSONTAPE database licensing service, and WILSONSEARCH software, from 1983.

Social Sciences and Humanities Index. Bronx, NY: Wilson, 1965–1974. Since 1974, published separately as *Social Sciences Index* and *Humanities Index;* these two titles are available on-line from WILSONLINE, on CD-ROM from WILSONDISC, and on magnetic tape from WILSONTAPE.

A–3 Books and databases about general knowledge: encyclopedias

The encyclopedia is the czar of general knowledge books and a good place to begin research on almost any topic. While they seldom treat a topic in minute detail, encyclopedias are usually factual and current. Among the best are the following:

Books

Academic American Encyclopedia. 21 vols. Danbury, CT: Grolier, 1991. Available on-line from Delphi (Grolier), on CD-ROM from Grolier Electronic Pub., and on CD-ROM as *The Software Toolworks™ Illustrated Encyclopedia* from Grolier Electronic Pub.

The Cambridge Encyclopedia. David Crystal, ed. Cambridge, Eng: Cambridge Univ. Press, 1990. A most excellent and comprehensive one-volume encyclopedia.

Collier's Encyclopedia. 24 vols. New York: Macmillan, 1991. Accompanied by a *Year Book.*

Concise Columbia Encyclopedia. 2d ed. New York: Columbia Univ. Press, 1989. A very good one-volume encyclopedia.

Encyclopaedia Britannica. 32 vols. Chicago: Encyclopaedia Britannica, 1991. Supplemented by the *Britannica Book of the Year.*

Encyclopedia Americana. 30 vols. Danbury, CT: Grolier, 1991. Accompanied by *Americana Annual* volumes.

Random House Encyclopedia. New rev. ed. New York: Random, 1990. The emphasis is on color illustrations in this one-volume encyclopedia.

Databases

Compton's Multimedia Encyclopedia. San Francisco: Britannica Software. Contains the complete text of the 26-volume *Compton's Encyclopedia.* On CD-ROM from Britannica Software.

Information Finder. Chicago: World Book. Contains the full text of *The World Book Encyclopedia* (1989 ed.), plus the full text of *The World Book Dictionary* (1989 ed.). Available on CD-ROM from World Book.

A–4 Books, databases, and journals about words: dictionaries

Dictionaries were originally invented to list equivalent words in two languages, as an aid in translating from one language to another. Sumerian clay tablets listed Sumerian words beside their Semitic-Assyrian equivalents. By the seventeenth century, *dictionary* had come to mean a book that explained the etymology, pronunciation, meaning, and correct usage of words. Nathan Bailey's Universal *Etymological English Dictionary*, published in 1721, was the first comprehensive dictionary in English.

Modern dictionaries provide information about the meaning, derivation, spelling, and syllabication of words, and about linguistic study, synonyms, antonyms, rhymes, slang, colloquialisms, dialect, and usage. Unabridged dictionaries contain complete information about words; abridged dictionaries condense their information so as to be more portable. Some titles are now available in databases.

a. General dictionaries

Books

The American Heritage Dictionary of the English Language. 3d ed. Boston: Houghton Mifflin, 1992.

Corbeil, Jean C. *The Facts on File Visual Dictionary*. New York: Facts on File, 1986.

The Oxford Dictionary of New Words: A Popular Guide to Words in the News. Comp. by Sara Tulloch. Oxford: Oxford Univ. Press, 1991.

The Oxford English Dictionary. 2d ed. Prepared by J. A. Simpson and E. S. Weiner. 20 vols. Oxford: Clarendon, 1989. A monumental work that presents the historical development of each word in the English language since 1150, illustrating correct usage with varied quotations. Also available on CD-ROM from Tri Star Pub., Horsham, PA.

Random House Webster's College Dictionary. New York: Random, 1991.

Third Barnhart Dictionary of New English. Robert K. Barnhart and Sol Steinmetz, eds., with Clarence L. Barnhart. Bronx, NY: H. W. Wilson, 1990.

Webster's New World College Dictionary. 3d ed. Englewood Cliffs, NJ: Prentice-Hall, 1989.

Webster's Ninth New Collegiate Dictionary. Springfield, MA: Merriam-Webster, 1991. Also available on CD-ROM; updated periodically; with audio pronunciation from Highlighted Data, Inc., Arlington, VA.

Webster's Third New International Dictionary of the English Language Unabridged. Springfield, MA: Merriam-Webster, 1986.

The World Book Dictionary. Clarence L. Barnhart, ed. 2 vols. Chicago: World Book, 1990.

Databases

The Amazing Moby. Eden Prairie, MN: ALDE Pub. An electronic dictionary. Available on CD-ROM from ALDE Pub.

The American Heritage Electronic Dictionary. Boston: Houghton Mifflin. Contains the complete text of *The American Heritage Dictionary and Roget's II, The New Thesaurus* on diskette, from Houghton Mifflin.

Journals

The Barnhart Dictionary Companion: A Quarterly to Update General Dictionaries. New York: Springer-Verlag, 1981–present. A periodical.

b. Specialized dictionaries

Barnhart Dictionary of Etymology. Robert K. Barnhart, ed. Bronx, NY: H. W. Wilson, 1988.

Clark, John O. *Word for Word: A Dictionary of Synonyms.* New York: Holt, 1990.

Craigie, William A., and James R. Hulbert. *Dictionary of American English on Historical Principles.* 4 vols. Chicago: Univ. of Chicago Press, 1936–44. A valuable work for anyone interested in how English developed during Colonial times. Indicates which words originated in America and which in other English-speaking countries. Excludes dialects and slang.

Dictionary of American Regional English. Frederic G. Cassidy, ed. Cambridge, MA: Belknap Press, 1985–present. The first two volumes of this landmark set have been published.

Partridge, Eric. *Dictionary of Slang and Unconventional English.* Paul Beale, ed. 8th ed. New York: Macmillan, 1984.

Thesaurus of American Slang. Robert L. Chapman, ed. New York: HarperCollins, 1989.

Thorne, Tony. *The Dictionary of Contemporary Slang.* New York: Pantheon, 1990.

Wentworth, Harold, and Stuart B. Flexner. *Dictionary of American Slang.* 2d supplemented ed. New York: Crowell, 1975. A comprehensive listing of American slang, including taboo words and expressions.

Young, Sue. *The New Comprehensive American Rhyming Dictionary.* 1st ed. New York: Morrow, 1991.

c. Dictionaries of synonyms and antonyms

Dictionaries of synonyms and antonyms list the equivalents and opposites of words. Among the best-known are the following:

American Heritage Dictionary Editors. *The Right Word, no. III.* Rev. ed. Boston: Houghton Mifflin, 1991.

Roget's International Thesaurus. 5th ed. Robert L. Chapman, ed. New York: HarperCollins, 1992.

Urdang, Laurence. *The Oxford Thesaurus.* New York: Oxford Univ. Press, 1992.

A–5 Books and databases about places

Reference books on places come in two forms: atlases and gazetteers.

a. Atlases

An atlas is a bound collection of maps, sometimes amplified by charts, tables, and plates, that provides information about the people, culture, and economy of the countries covered. Among the most comprehensive and useful atlases are the following:

Books

Britannica Atlas. Chicago: Encyclopaedia Britannica, 1990.

Goode, J. Paul. *Goode's World Atlas.* 18th ed. Chicago: Rand McNally, 1990.

Maps on File. New York: Facts on File, 1981–present. With loose-leaf annual updates.

National Geographic Society. *National Geographic Atlas of the World.* 6th ed. Washington, DC: National Geographic Society, 1990.

New York Times. *The Times Atlas of the World.* 8th ed. New York: Random, 1990.
Rand McNally and Company. *The New International Atlas.* Anniversary ed. Jon Leverenz, ed. Chicago: Rand McNally, 1990.
Rand McNally and Company. *Rand McNally . . . Commercial Atlas & Marketing Guide.* Chicago: Rand McNally, 1876–present. Annual.
Rand McNally Encyclopedic World Atlas. Rev. 1990 ed. Chicago: Rand McNally, 1990.
Databases
The Electronic Map Cabinet. Arlington, VA: Highlighted Data, Inc. Available on CD-ROM from the producer.
Rand McNally's America: Family United States Atlas. Los Angeles: Philips, Interactive Media of America. Available on CD-ROM from the provider.
The Software Toolworks™ World Atlas. Novato, CA: Software Toolworks, Inc. Available on CD-ROM and diskette from the provider.
The USA Fact Book. St. Paul, MN: Quanta Press, Inc. Available on CD-ROM from Quanta Press.

b. Gazetteers

A gazetteer is a geographical dictionary or index that gives basic information about the most important regions, cities, and natural features of the countries of the world. The best general gazetteers are the following:
Books
Cambridge World Gazetteer: A Geographical Dictionary. Daniel Munro, ed. Cambridge, Eng.: Cambridge Univ. Press, 1990.
Canby, Courtlandt. *The Encyclopedia of Historic Places.* 2 vols. New York: Facts on File, 1984.
Chambers World Gazetteer: An A-Z of Geographical Information. 5th ed. Edinburgh: Chambers, 1988.
Modern Geography: An Encyclopedic Survey. Gary S. Dunbar, ed. New York: Garland, 1991.
Worldmark Encyclopedia of the Nations. 7th ed. 5 vols. New York: Worldmark Press, 1988.
Databases
Place Name Index. Grand Rapids, MN: Wayzata Technology, Inc. Available on CD-ROM from the provider.

A–6 Books and databases about people

Biographical reference books are classified under four primary headings: (a) general biography of deceased persons; (b) general biography of living persons; (c) national biography of deceased persons; and (d) national biography of living persons.

a. General biography of deceased persons

Cambridge Biographical Dictionary. Magnus Magnusson, general ed. Cambridge, Eng.: Cambridge Univ. Press, 1990.

De Ford, Miriam A. *Who Was When?: A Dictionary of Contemporaries.* 3d ed. New York: H. W. Wilson, 1976.

Encyclopedia of World Biography: 20th Century Supplement. McGraw-Hill Encyclopedia of World Biography. 4 vols. Palatine, IL: Jack Heraty & Associates, 1987.

Great Lives From History: Ancient and Medieval Series. 5 vols. Pasadena, CA: Salem Press, 1988.

Great Lives From History. Renaissance to 1900 Series. 5 vols. Pasadena, CA: Salem Press, 1989.

The McGraw-Hill Encyclopedia of World Biography. 12 vols. New York: McGraw, 1973.

Phillips, Lawrence B. *The Dictionary of Biographical Reference.* New ed. Detroit: Gale, 1981. A reprint of an 1888 imprint.

Slocum, Robert B. *Biographical Dictionaries and Related Works: An International Bibliography of More Than 16,000 Collective Biographies.* 2d ed. 2 vols. Detroit: Gale, 1986. This work lists all major biographical works. An excellent place to begin finding biographies.

Thinkers of the Twentieth Century. 2d ed. Roland Turner, ed. Chicago: St. James, 1987.

b. General biography of living persons

Books

Biographical Books, 1876–1949. New York: Bowker, 1983.

Current Biography. Vol. 1–present. Bronx, NY: H. W. Wilson, 1940–present. Monthly, except December, with annual cumulative volume.

Current Biography Cumulated Index, 1940–1990. Bronx, NY: H. W. Wilson, 1991.

International Who's Who. London: Europa, 1935–present. Issued annually. Provides sketches of important people all over the world.

Who's Who in the World. Wilmette, IL: Marquis Who's Who, 1971/72–present.

Databases

Gale Biographies. Dayton, OH: Mead Data Central, Inc. (MDC), NEXIS. Available on-line from Mead Data Central, Inc.

The New York Times Biographical File. Dayton, OH: Mead Data Central, Inc. (MDC), NEXIS. Available on-line from the provider.

c. National biography of deceased persons (American and British)

Appleton's Cyclopaedia of American Biography. 7 vols. New York: Appleton, 1887–1900.

Concise Dictionary of American Biography. 4th ed. Complete to 1970. New York: Scribner's, 1990. A one-volume edition of the large set.

Dictionary of American Biography. 22 vols. New York: Scribner's 1928–58. (See preceding entry: *Concise Dictionary of American Biography.*)

Dictionary of American Biography. Comprehensive Index: Complete Through Supplement Eight. New York: Scribner's, 1990.

Dictionary of American Biography. Supplement. New York: Scribner's, 1973–present.

The Dictionary of National Biography, the Concise Dictionary. 2 vols. New York: Oxford Univ. Press, 1930–1982.

Dictionary of National Biography: From the Earliest Times to 1900. 22 vols. London: Oxford Univ. Press, 1921–1922. *Supplement.* London: Oxford Univ. Press, 1912/21–present. So far seven supplementary volumes have been published.

Notable American Women, 1607–1950: A Biographical Dictionary. 3 vols. Cambridge, MA: Belknap Press of Harvard Univ. Press, 1971.

Notable American Women: The Modern Period: A Biographical Dictionary. Cambridge, MA: Belknap Press of Harvard Univ. Press, 1980.

Van Doren, Charles L. *Webster's American Biographies.* Springfield, MA: G. & C. Merriam, 1974.

Who Was Who. 1897/1916–present. New York: St. Martin's, 1920–present. A companion volume to *Who's Who.*

Who Was Who: A Cumulated Index, 1897–1980. London: Adam and Charles Black, 1981.

Who Was Who in America. 1897/1942–present. Chicago: Marquis, 1943–present. A companion volume to *Who's Who in America.* Includes a historical volume for 1607/1896.

d. National biography of living persons (American and British)

<u>Books</u>

National Cyclopaedia of American Biography. 63 vols. New York: J. T. White, 1889–1984. A monumental work that presents a complete political, social, commercial, and industrial history in the form of sketches of individuals, deceased and living, who helped shape America.

Who's Who. London: Black, 1849–present. Annual. Contains excellent biographical sketches of prominent people living in Great Britain and its commonwealth.

Who's Who in America. Chicago: Marquis, 1899/1900–present. Editions come out biennally. Identifies people of special prominence in all lines of work. Supplemented by *Who's Who in the East, Who's Who in the West, Who's Who in the Midwest, Who's Who in the South and Southwest,* and *Who's Who in the West*—all issued by the Marquis Company.

Who's Who of American Women. Chicago: Marquis, 1958–present. Biennial. A dictionary identifying American women who have made a name for themselves in various fields.

Many countries and professions now publish "Who's Who" rosters. Examples include the following:

The Asian Who's Who
Who's Who in Africa South of the Sahara
Who's Who in Canada
Who's Who in Germany
Who's Who in the Middle East
Who's Who in the People's Republic of China
Who's Who in American Education
Who's Who in Art
Who's Who in Electronics
Who's Who in Entertainment
Who's Who in Finance & Industry
Who's Who in Nobel Prize Winners
Who's Who in Technology

Ask your librarian about other areas in which a "Who's Who" roster is published. There are too many to include here.

Databases
The Marquis Who's Who database is on-line through DIALOG Information Services, Inc. In addition, the following "Who's Who" are available on-line:
Almanac of American Politics
American Men and Women of Science Online
Bio Doc. Corresponds to _Who's Who in Europe_
International Who's Who in Science
Who's Who in Technology, plus many other sources in _Gale Biographies_
Consult the latest edition of _Directory of Online Databases_ for complete information. Also, the following biographical reference works are available on portable databases (CD-ROM, diskette, or magnetic tape):
Congress Stack
Dun's Million Dollar Disc
The Government Disc
International Who's Who in Science
Marquis Who's Who in Finance and Industry
Standard and Poor's Corporations
Who's Who in Electronics
Who's Who in Science and Technology
Consult the latest edition of _The Directory of Portable Databases_ for complete information.

e. Indexes to biographical material

Almanac of Famous People. 4th ed. Detroit: Gale, 1989–present. Biennial supplements issued between editions. Formerly titled _Biography Almanac._
Bio-base [microform]. Detroit: Gale, 1978–present. Microfiche.
Biography and Genealogy Master Index. 2d ed. Detroit: Gale, 1980–present. A consolidated index to biographical sketches in current and retrospective biographical dictionaries.
Biographical and Genealogy Master Index Supplement. Detroit: Gale, 1982–present. Annual.
Biography Index. Bronx, NY: H. W. Wilson Co., 1946–present. Quarterly, plus annual and two-year cumulations. Also available on-line through WILSONLINE, on machine-readable tape through WILSONTAPE, and on CD-ROM through WILSONDISC and WILSONSEARCH.
Biography Master Index. Detroit: Gale. Available on-line from DIALOG. Corresponds to _Biography and Genealogy Master Index._
New York Times Obituaries Index. 2 vols. New York: New York Times, 1970–80. Vol. 1, 1858–1968. Vol. 2, 1969–1978.
Falk, Byron A. _Personal Name Index to "The New York Times Index," 1851–1974._ 22 vols. Succasunna, NJ: Roxbury Data Interface, 1976–1983.
———. _Supplement._ Verdi, NV: Roxbury Data Interface, 1984–present.
Historical Biographical Dictionaries Master Index. 1st ed. Detroit: Gale, 1980.

A–7 Books and databases about government publications

The work of government bureaucracy is reflected in government publications. The most important references that list government publications are the following:

Books

Ames, John G. *Comprehensive Index to the Publications of the United States Government, 1881–1893.* 2 vols. Washington, DC: GPO, 1905. This work will help a researcher locate government information by subject or title. Covers a decade of post-Civil War times.

Bailey, William G. *Guide to popular U.S. Government Publications.* 2d ed. Littleton, CO: Libraries Unlimited, 1990.

Catalog of the Public Documents of Congress and of All Departments of the Government of the United States for the Period March 4, 1893–December 31, 1940. 25 vols. Washington, DC: GPO, 1896–1945.

Congressional Information Service. *CIS U.S. Serial Set Index.* Washington, DC: Congressional Information Service, 1975–present.

Government Reference Books. Littleton, CO: Libraries Unlimited, 1968/69–present. A biennial guide to U.S. government publications, with index.

Guide to U.S. Government Publications. McLean, VA: Documents Index, 1973–present. Quarterly updating supplements are issued between editions. Also available on microfiche.

Monthly Catalog of United States Government Publications. Washington, DC: GPO, 1895–present. Published under the title *Catalogue of United States Public Documents,* from 1895–1907. Monthly, with semiannual and annual indexes.

Morehead, Joe. *Introduction to United States Government Information Sources.* By Joe Morehead and Mary Fetzer. 4th ed. Littleton, CO: Libraries Unlimited, 1992.

Pokorny, Elizabeth J. *U.S. Government Documents: A Practical Guide.* By Elizabeth J. Pokorny and Suzanne M. Miller. Littleton, CO: Libraries Unlimited, 1989.

Poore, Benjamin P. *A Descriptive Catalogue of the Government Publications of the United States, September 5, 1774–March 4, 1881.* Washington, DC: GPO, 1885. A 1392-page compilation, invaluable to the student of early U.S. history.

U.S. Congress. *United States Government Publications* [microform]: serial set. Washington, DC: GPO, 1817–present. Microopaque. Readex Microprint Corp.

U.S. Government Books. Washington, DC: GPO, 1982–present. Quarterly.

U.S. Superintendent of Documents. *Checklist of United States Public Documents, 1789–1909.* 3d ed., rev. and enl. Washington, DC: GPO, 1911.

———. *Monthly Catalog.* Volumes for Jan. 1984–present also available on microfiche.

Zwirn, Arnold. *Access to U.S. Government Information: Guide to Executive and Legislative Authors and Authority.* New York: Greenwood Press, 1989.

Databases

CIS Index to Publications of the U.S. Congress. Washington, DC: Congressional Information Service. Citations, with abstracts, to publications published by U.S. Congressional committees and subcommittees. Available on-line from DIALOG; also available on CD-ROM under the title *Congressional Masterfile I and II* from Congressional Information Service.

Federal Index. Gaithersburg, MD: National Standards Assn., Inc. Contains citations to the *Congressional Record, Federal Register,* and the *Weekly Compilation of Presidential Documents, 1976–1980.* Available on-line from DIALOG.

GPO Monthly Catalog. Washington, DC: GPO. Corresponds to the *Monthly Catalog of United States Government Publications.* Available on-line from DIALOG. Also available on CD-ROM from OCLC Online Computer Library Center, Dublin, OH.

GPO Sales Publications Reference File. Washington, DC: U.S. Government Printing Office (GPO)—Superintendent of Documents. Corresponds to the microfiche *GPO Sales Publications Reference File.* Available on-line from DIALOG. Also available on CD-ROM as *The Publications Reference File on CD-ROM* from News-Bank/Readex.

Foreign countries have their own government printing offices, catalogs, indexes, and databases. Consult with your reference librarian for their availability and use.

A–8 Books and databases about nonbooks

In recent years nonbooks have become a necessary and distinctive part of library collections. Materials stored on microform, film, video, sound recordings, and databases are often valuable to researchers.

a. General guides

Audiovisual Materials. 4 vols. Washington, DC: Library of Congress, 1980–1983, 1979–1982.

Educators Guide. Series. Randolph, WI: Educators Progress Service. Includes guides to free audio and video materials, films, filmstrips and slides, microcomputers, and personalized reading instruction.

Media Resource Catalog from the National Audiovisual Center. Capitol Heights, MD: The Center, 19??–present. Kept up-to-date by supplements and by a *Quarterly Update.*

Media Review Digest. Ann Arbor, MI: Pierian Press, 1973/74–present. Annual with semiannual supplements. A guide to reviews and descriptions of nonbook materials.

The Video Source Book. Syosset, NY: National Video Clearinghouse, 1979–present. Also available on diskette from Gale Research Co., Detroit.

b. Indexes of microforms

Bibliographic Guide to Microform Publications. Boston: G. K. Hall, 1987–present. Annual. Includes catalog records for microform publications in the New York Public Library and the Library of Congress.

Dissertation Abstracts International. Ann Arbor, MI: University Microfilms International, 1969–present. Monthly. The publisher produces microform copies of dissertations on demand. Available also on-line from DIALOG; also available on CD-ROM through *Dissertation Abstracts Ondisc.*

Guide to Microforms in Print. Author, Title. Westport, CT: Microform Review, 1978–present. Annual.

Index to Microform Collections. 2 vols. Ann Niles, ed. Westport, CT: Meckler, 1984–88.

Microform Research Collections: A Guide. 2d ed. Suzanne C. Dodson, ed. Westport, CT: Meckler, 1984.

Newspapers in Microform. Ann Arbor, MI: University Microfilms International, 19–present.

Newspapers in Microform: United States, 1948–1983. 2 vols. Washington, DC: Library of Congress, 1984. A companion volume to *Newspapers in Microform: Foreign Countries, 1948–1983,* also published by the Library of Congress, 1984.

Serials in Microform. Ann Arbor, MI: University Microfilms International, 1972—present. Annual.

U.S. National Archives and Records Administration. *Microfilm Resources for Research: A Comprehensive Catalog.* Washington, DC: The Archives, 1990.

c. Guides to films

<u>Books</u>

American Film Institute. *The American Film Institute Catalog of Motion Pictures Produced in the United States.* New York: Bowker, 1971–1988. *Feature Films, 1911–1920.* 2 vols. *Feature Films, 1961–1970,* 2 vols.

American Folklore Films and Videotapes: A Catalog. Center for Southern Folklore. 2d ed. New York: Bowker, 1982–present.

Bowker's Complete Video Directory. New York: Bowker, 1990–present. Annual. Has occasional supplements.

Dimmitt, Richard B. *A Title Guide to the Talkies: A Comprehensive Listing of 16,000 Feature-Length Films From October, 1927 Until December, 1963.* 2 vols. New York: Scarecrow, 1965.

Educational Film & Video Locator of the Consortium of Colleges and University Media Centers and R. R. Bowker. 4th ed. New York: Bowker, 1990–present.

Feature Films: *A Directory of Feature Films on 16 mm and Videotape Available for Rental, Sale, and Lease.* 8th ed.–present. New York: Bowker, 1985–present. Editor: 8th ed.–present, James L. Limbacher. Irregular.

The Film File. Minneapolis, MN: Media Referral Service, 1981–present.

Guide to Government-loan Films. 1st ed., 1969/70–present. Alexandria, VA: Serina Press. Title varies slightly.

Halliwell, Leslie. *Halliwell's Film Guide.* 7th ed. New York: Harper & Row, 1989.

International Film Guide. 26 vols. New York: A. S. Barnes, 1964–1988. Annual, 1964–1989.

International Motion Picture Almanac. New York: Quigley Publications. Annual. Began in 1956.

Leonard Maltin's TV Movies and Video Guide. New York: New American Library, 1986–present. Annual.

Library of Congress Catalog. Motion Pictures and Filmstrips. 9 vols. Washington, DC: The Library, 1955–73. Also published by J. W. Edwards, Ann Arbor, MI.

Marill, Alvin H. *Movies Made For Television: The Telefeature and the Mini-Series, 1964–1986.* New York: New York Zeotrope, 1987.

Museum of Modern Art (New York, NY). *The Film Catalog: A List of Holdings in the Museum of Modern Art.* Jon Gartenberg and others, eds. Boston: G. K. Hall, 1985.

Nash, Jay Robert. *The Motion Picture Guide.* J. Robert Nash et al., eds. 12 vols. Chicago: Cinebooks, 1985–87. Kept up-to-date by annual supplements, beginning with 1986.

Nowlan, Robert A. *The Films of the Eighties: A Complete, Qualitative Filmography.* By Robert A. Nowlan [and] Gwendolyn Wright Nowlan. Jefferson, NC: McFarland, 1991.

Pitman, Randy. *Video Movies: A Core Collection for Libraries.* By Randy Pitman and Elliott Swanson. Santa Barbara, CA: ABC-CLIO, 1990.

U.S. Library of Congress. *Films and Other Materials for Projection.* 8 vols. Washington, DC: Library of Congress. Supersedes *Library of Congress Catalog. Motion Pictures and Filmstrips.*

Film catalogs are available from many colleges and universities, such as the following:

Brigham Young University

Indiana University

Iowa State University

Kent State University

UCLA

University of Colorado at Boulder

University of Illinois

University of Minnesota

University of Utah

Databases

Movie Database and Software Potpourri. Parsippany, NJ: Bureau of Electronic Publishing, Inc. Includes more than 500 references to movies, with title, release date, producer, and much other information. Available on CD-ROM.

d. Guides to sound recordings: music

Books

Bibliography of Discographies. Michael H. Gray et al., comps. 3 vols. New York: Bowker, 1977–83.

CD Review Digest. 3 vols. Voorheesville, NY: Peri Press, 1987–89. Quarterly. Ceased with vol. 3, no. 1, 1989. Split into: *CD Review Digest. Classical* and *CD Review Digest. Jazz, Popular, etc.*

CD Review Digest. Classical. Voorheesville, NY: Peri Press, 1989–present. Quarterly.

CD Review Digest. Jazz, Popular, etc. Voorheesville, NY: Peri Press, 1989–present. Quarterly.

Gray, Michael H. *Classical Music Discographies, 1976–1988: A Bibliography.* New York: Greenwood, 1989. Supplement to: *Bibliography of Discographies.* 1977.

Greenfield, Edward. *The Penguin Guide to Compact Discs, Cassettes, and LPs.* New York: Penguin, 1986.

Harris, Steve. *Film, Television, and Stage Music on Phonograph Records: A Discography.* Jefferson, NC: McFarland, 1988.

Library of Congress Catalog: Music and Phonorecords, 1953–1972. Washington, DC: Library of Congress, 1953–present.

Music, Books on Music, and Sound Recordings. Washington, DC: Library of Congress. Began with Jan/June, 1973; ceased with 1989. Also available on microfiche from Advanced Library Systems.

The Music Catalog. Washington, DC: Library of Congress, 1991–present. Quarterly, on microfiche, 1981–present.

Penguin Guide to Compact Discs & Cassettes Yearbook. New York: Penguin, 1991–present. Annual. Supplement to *Penguin Guide to Compact Discs.*

Rodgers and Hammerstein Archives of Recorded Sound. *Dictionary Catalog of the Rodgers and Hammerstein Archives of Recorded Sound.* 15 vols. Boston: Hall, 1981.

Rust, Brian A. L. *The American Record Label Book.* New York: Da Capo, 1984.

Schwann. 5 vols. Boston: ABC Consumer Magazines, Inc., 1986–89. "The world's most consulted record and tape guide." Continued by *Schwann Opus* and *Schwann Spectrum.*

Schwann Opus. Vol. 1, no. 1 (Spring 1990)–present. Chatsworth, CA: ABC Consumer Magazines, 1990–present. Quarterly.

Schwann Spectrum. Feb. 1990–present. Chatsworth, CA: Schwann. Quarterly. With *Schwann Opus*; continues *Schwann.*

Tudor, Dean. *Popular Music, an Annotated Guide to Recordings.* Littleton, CO: Libraries Unlimited, 1983.

Databases

CD Guide Optical Edition. Hancock, NH: WGE Publishing, Inc. Available on CD-ROM from WGE Publishing.

Music Library: Musical Sound Recordings. Dublin, OH: OCLC Online Computer Library Center, Inc. Available on CD-ROM from OCLC Online Computer Library Center.

e. Guides to sound recordings: speeches, readings, and oral history

Columbia University. Oral History Research Office. *The Oral History Collection of Columbia University.* Elizabeth Mason and Louis M. Starr, eds. New York, 1979.

Hoffman, Herbert H. *International Index to Recorded Poetry.* New York: H. W. Wilson, 1983.

On Cassette. 3 vols. New York: Bowker, 1989–91. Annual. Merged with *Words on Tape* to form *Words on Cassette.*

On Cassette: A Comprehensive Bibliography of Spoken Word Audio Cassettes. 2 vols. New York: Bowker, 1985–87. Annual. Covered years 1985–86/1987.

Perks, Robert. *Oral History: An Annotated Bibliography.* London: British Library National Sound Archive, 1990.

Smith, Allen. *Directory of Oral History Collections.* Phoenix: Oryx, 1988.

U.S. Library of Congress. Poetry Office. *Literary Recordings: A Checklist of the Archive of Recorded Poetry and Literature in the Library of Congress.* Rev., enl. ed. Washington, DC: GPO, 1981.

Words on Cassette. 7th ed. New Providence, NJ: Bowker, 1992–present. Annual. Formed by the union of: *Words on Tape* and *On Cassette.*

Words on Tape. Westport, CT: Meckler, 1984–91. Biennial. "An international guide to the audio cassette market." Merged with: *On Cassette* to form *Words on Cassette.*

f. Books about databases

Directory of Online Databases. Detroit: Gale, 1979–present. Published twice a year. Also available on-line, together with the *Directory of Portable Databases,* as the

Cuadra Directory of Databases from Data-Star, London, Eng.; available as well on diskette and magnetic tape from Gale with the title *Directory of Online and Portable Databases.*

Directory of Portable Databases. Detroit: Gale, 1990–present. Describes products on CD-ROM, diskette, and magnetic tape. Published twice a year. See notes under *Directory of Online Databases* for availability in electronic and other forms.

B   A list of specialized references

A specialized reference classifies and indexes information about a specific subject. Depending on the complexity of your topic, you may or may not have to consult a specialized reference. Numerous such references exist, covering virtually all subjects. A complete listing of all the specialized references on popular subjects such as history and literature, for instance, would easily fill an entire book.

Specialized references are listed here in alphabetical order by subject and are restricted to those most likely to be useful in student research.

B–1 Art

Books

American Art Directory. New York: Bowker, 1952–present. Updated annually.

Art & Architecture Thesaurus. Toni Petersen, director. New York: Oxford Univ. Press, 1990. Also available on-line through RLIN and on computer diskettes through the publisher.

Art Books, 1950–1979. New York: Bowker, 1979.

Art Index. New York: Wilson, 1929/1932–present. An index to articles in over 200 domestic and foreign art periodicals. Quarterly, with an annual cumulation. Also available on-line through WILSONLINE, on CD-ROM from WILSON-DISC, and on magnetic tape through WILSONTAPE.

Atkins, Robert. *Artspeak: A Guide to Contemporary Ideas, Movements, and Buzzwords.* New York: Abbeville, 1990.

Bibliography of the History of Art: BHA = Bibliographie d'Histoire de l'Art. Santa Monica, CA: J. Paul Getty Trust, Getty Art History Information Program. 1991–present. Quarterly, with an annual cumulation.

Chiarmonte, Paula L. *Women Artists in the United States: A Bibliography and Resource Guide on the Fine and Decorative Arts, 1750–1986.* Boston: G. K. Hall, 1990.

Contemporary Artists. 3d ed. Colin Naylor, ed. Chicago: St. James, 1989.

Contemporary Designers. Colin Naylor, ed. 2d ed. Chicago: St. James, 1990.

Denvir, Bernard. *The Thames and Hudson Encyclopaedia of Impressionism.* New York: Thames and Hudson, 1990.

Ehresmann, Donald L. *Fine Arts: A Bibliographic Guide to Basic Reference Works, Histories, and Handbooks.* 3d ed. Littleton, CO: Libraries Unlimited, 1990.

Encyclopedia of Architecture: Design, Engineering & Construction. Joseph A. Wilkes, editor-in-chief. 5 vols. New York: Wiley, 1988–89.

Encyclopedia of World Art. 17 vols. New York: McGraw-Hill, 1959–87.

Fleming, John. *The Penguin Dictionary of Decorative Arts.* John Fleming and Hugh Honour, eds. New ed. London: Viking, 1989.

Gardner, Helen. *Gardner's Art Through the Ages.* Horst de la Croix et al., eds. 9th ed. San Diego, CA: Harcourt Brace Jovanovich, 1991.

International Dictionary of Art and Artists, with a foreword by Cecil Gould; James Vinson, ed. 2 vols. Chicago: St. James, 1990.

Jones, Lois Swan. *Art Information: Research Methods and Resources.* 3d ed. Dubuque, IA: Kendall/Hunt, 1990.

Modern Arts Criticism. Vol. 1. Detroit: Gale, 1991–present.

Norman, Geraldine. *Nineteenth-Century Painters and Painting: A Dictionary.* Berkeley: Univ. of California Press, 1977.

The Oxford Companion to the Decorative Arts. New York: Oxford Univ. Press, 1985.

The Oxford Dictionary of Art. Ian Chilvers and Harold Osborne, eds. New York: Oxford Univ. Press, 1988.

Oxford Illustrated Encyclopedia of the Arts. New York: Oxford Univ. Press, 1990.

Parry, Pamela J. *Print Index: A Guide to Reproductions.* Westport, CT: Greenwood, 1983.

The Pelican History of Art. Nikolaus Pevsner, ed. Baltimore: Penguin, 1950–present. Some volumes issued in revised editions.

Petteys, Chris. *Dictionary of Women Artists: An International Dictionary of Women Artists Born Before 1900.* Boston: G. K. Hall, 1985.

Who's Who in American Art. New York: Bowker, 1936/37–present. Irregular.

World Artists 1980–1900: A Volume in the Wilson Biographical Series. Claude Marks, ed. New York: H. W. Wilson, 1991. Continues the editor's *World Artists 1950–1980.*

<u>Databases</u>

ART bibliographies MODERN. Santa Barbara, CA: ABC-CLIO. Contains citations from about 350 periodicals in the subjects of modern art and design. Available on-line through DIALOG.

Art: Impressionism. Los Angeles: Philips Interactive Media of America (PIMA). A companion to the same company's *Art: Italian Renaissance,* also available on CD-ROM from the producer.

Art Literature International. Williamstown, MA: J. Paul Getty Trust. Available on-line from DIALOG.

Arts & Humanities Search. Philadelphia: Institute for Scientific Information. Available on-line from DIALOG. Also available on magnetic tape from Institute for Scientific Information.

Avery Index to Architectural Periodicals. New York: Avery Architectural and Fine Arts Library, Columbia Univ. Available on-line from RLIN.

Treasures of the Smithsonian. Los Angeles: Philips Interactive Media of America (PIMA). Available on CD-ROM from the producer.

ART JOURNALS
Art & Antiques
Art in America
Art International
Artforum
ARTnews
Graphis

ART VIDEOS
Creativity With Bill Moyers (17-part series)
Frank Lloyd Wright: Prophet Without Honor

Smithsonian World Series
(All of these titles are available from PBS Video, Alexandria, VA.)

B–2 Business and economics

Books
Accountants' Handbook. D. R. Carmichael et al., eds. 7th ed. New York: Wiley, 1991.
Business Periodicals Index. New York: H. W. Wilson, 1959–present. Monthly (except August), with quarterly and annual cumulations. Also available on-line through WILSONLINE, on CD-ROM through WILSONDISC, and on machine-readable tape through WILSONTAPE.
A Concise Dictionary of Business. New York: Oxford Univ. Press, 1990.
Encyclopedia of American Business History and Biography. New York: Facts on File, 1988–present. Three volumes have been published.
Encyclopedia of Business Information Services. James Woy, ed. 8th ed. Detroit: Gale, 1990. Biennial, with periodic supplements.
Encyclopedia of Investments. Jack P. Friedman, editor-in-chief. 2d ed. Boston: Warren, Gorham & Lamont, 1990.
Freed, Melvyn N. *Business Information Desk Reference.* Melvyn N. Freed and Virgil P. Diodato, eds. New York: Macmillan, 1991.
Freeman, Michael J. *Atlas of the World Economy.* By Michael Freeman; Derek Aldcroft, consulting ed. New York: Simon & Schuster, 1991.
Handbook of Labor Statistics. U.S. Department of Labor, Bureau of Labor Statistics. Washington, DC: GPO, 1927–present. Irregular.
Ingham, John N. *Biographical Dictionary of American Business Leaders.* 4 vols. Westport, CT: Greenwood, 1983.
International Business Handbook. V. H. (Manek) Kirpalani, ed. New York: Haworth, 1990.
International Marketing Handbook. Detroit: Gale, 1981–present. Biennial, with supplements.
Investment Companies. New York: Arthur Weisenberger & Co., 1944–present. Annual. The "bible" for information on mutual funds and investment companies.
Johannsen, Hano. International Dictionary of Management. By Hano Johannsen and G. T. Page. 4th ed. New York: Nichols, 1990.
Mattera, Philip. *Inside U.S. Business: A Concise Encyclopedia of Leading Industries.* Homewood, IL: Business One Irwin, 1991.
Million Dollar Directory. Parsippany, NJ: Dun's Marketing Services, 1979–present. Annual. Also available on-line from DIALOG as *Dun's Million Dollar Directory* and on CD-ROM as *Dun's Million Dollar Disc* from Dun's Marketing Services.
Moody's Handbook of Common Stocks. New York: Moody's Investors Service, 1965–present. Quarterly.
Munn, Glenn G. *Encyclopedia of Banking & Finance.* By Glenn G. Munn et al. 9th ed., rev. and expanded. Chicago: St. James, 1991.
The New Palgrave: A Dictionary of Economics. John Eatwell et al., eds. 4 vols. Reprinted with corrections. New York: Stockton, 1991.
Pearce, David W. *The MIT Dictionary of Modern Economics.* David W. Pearce and Robert Shaw, eds. 4th ed. Cambridge, MA: MIT Press, 1992.
Rand McNally and Company. *Rand McNally Commercial Atlas & Marketing Guide.* Chicago: Rand McNally, 1983–present. Annual.

Rosenberg, Jerry M. *Dictionary of Business and Management.* 3d ed. New York: Wiley, 1992.

Shim, Jae K. *Encyclopedic Dictionary of Accounting and Finance.* By Jae K. Shim and Joel G. Siegel. Englewood Cliffs, NJ: Prentice-Hall, 1989.

Shook, R. J. *The Wall Street Dictionary.* New York: New York Institute of Finance, 1990.

Small Business Sourcebook. Detroit: Gale, 1983–present. Biennial. Updated between editions by supplements.

Thomas Register of American Manufacturers and Thomas Register Catalog File. New York: Thomas, 1905/06–present. Annual. Each edition is published in more than one volume. See also citation for this entry in databases section.

Who's Who in Economics: A Biographical Dictionary of Major Economists, 1700–1986. Mark Blaug, ed. 2d ed. Cambridge, MA: MIT Press, 1986.

Databases

ABI/INFORM. Louisville, KY: UMI/Data Courier. Available on-line from DIALOG and on CD-ROM as *ABI/INFORM Ondisc* from University Microfilms International, Ann Arbor, MI.

Business Dateline. Louisville, KY: UMI/Data Courier. Available on-line from DIALOG, and on CD-ROM as *Business Dateline Ondisc* from University Microfilms International, Ann Arbor, MI.

Dun's Electronic Business Directory. Parsippany, NJ: Dun's Marketing Services. Available on-line from DIALOG.

Dun's Market Identifiers (DMI). Parsippany, NJ: Dun's Marketing Services. Available on-line from DIALOG and on magnetic tape from Dun's Marketing Services.

ECONBASE: Time Series & Forecasts. Bala Cynwyd, PA. Available on-line from DIALOG.

Economic Literature Index. Pittsburgh: American Economic Assn. Available on-line from DIALOG and on CD-ROM as *EconLit* from Silver Platter, Norwood, MA.

F&S Index Plus Text. Cleveland: Predicasts. Available on CD-ROM from Silver Platter, Norwood, MA. See also: *PTS Marketing and Advertising Reference Service* in this section.

Investext. Boston: Thomson, Financial Networks, Inc. available on-line from DIALOG and on CD-ROM from Information Access Co., Foster City, CA.

PTS Marketing and Advertising Reference. Cleveland: Predicasts. Available on-line from DIALOG. See also: *F&S Index Plus Text* in this section.

Small Business Reports. Chappaqua, NY: Stevens Features. Available on-line from CompuServe Information Service, Columbus, OH.

Standard & Poor's Register—Biographical. New York: Standard & Poor's Corp. Available on-line and on CD-ROM from DIALOG.

Standard & Poor's Register—Corporate. New York: Standard & Poor's Corp. Available on-line and on CD-ROM from DIALOG.

Thomas Register Online. NewYork: Thomas. Available on-line from DIALOG; also available on CD-ROM as *Thomas Register of American Manufacturers* from DIALOG.

Wilson Business Abstracts. Bronx, NY: H. W. Wilson. Available on-line from WILSONLINE; on CD-ROM from WILSONDISC; and on machine-readable tape from WILSONTAPE.

BUSINESS AND ECONOMICS JOURNALS AND NEWSPAPERS

(†Indicates title is available on-line in a full-text format from Dow Jones Text Library.)

(††Title is available on-line in a full-text format from DIALOG.)
(†††Title is available on-line, full-text, from DIALOG under the title *Economic Literature Index.*)
American Economic Review
†*Barron's National Business and Financial Weekly*
†*Business Week*
††*Challenge*
†*Forbes*
†*Fortune*
††*Harvard Business Review*
†*Inc.*
†††*Journal of Economic Literature*
†*Los Angeles Business Journal*
†*Monthly Labor Review*
†*Wall Street Journal*

BUSINESS AND ECONOMICS VIDEOS
The Business File (28-part series)
The Entrepreneurs (6-part series)
Wall Street Investment Primer (2-part series)
(All of these titles are available from PBS Video, Alexandria, VA.)

B–3 Dance

American Dance Directory. New York: Assoc. of American Dance Companies, 1979/80–present.
Coe, Robert. *Dance in America*. New York: Dutton, 1985.
Cohen-Stratyner, Barbara Naomi. *Biographical Dictionary of Dance*. New York: Schirmer, 1982.
The Dance Anthology. Cobbett Steinberg, ed. New York: New American Library, 1980.
Kirstein, Lincoln. *Four Centuries of Ballet: Fifty Masterworks*. Mineola, NY: Dover, 1984.
Koegler, Horst. *The Concise Oxford Dictionary of Ballet*. 2d ed., updated. New York: Oxford, 1985.
Lawson, Joan. *A Ballet-Maker's Handbook: Sources, Vocabulary, Styles*. New York: Theatre Arts Books/Routledge, 1991.
New York Public Library. Dance Collection. *Bibliographic Guide to Dance*. Boston: G. K. Hall, 1975–present. Annual.
Robertson, Allen. *The Dance Handbook* by Allen Robertson and Donald Hutera. Boston: G. K. Hall, 1988.
Studwell, William E. *Ballet Plot Index: A Guide to Locating Plots and Descriptions of Ballets and Associated Materials* by William E. Studwell and David A. Hamilton. New York: Garland, 1987.

DANCE JOURNALS
Ballet Review
Dance Magazine

Dance Research Journal
New Dance Review

DANCE VIDEOS
(†Available from PBS Video, Alexandria, VA.)
(††Available from Kultur, West Long Branch, NJ.)
(†††Available from Music Video Distributors, Norristown, PA.)
†*Dance to the Music*
††*Giselle* (Nureyev)
†††*The Margot Fonteyn Story*

B–4 Ecology

This term encompasses energy, environmental, and conservation issues.
Books
California Environmental Directory: A Guide to Organizations and Resources. Edited by
   Thaddeus C. Trzyna. Claremont, CA: California Institute for Public Affairs,
   1977–present. Irregular.
Conservation Directory. Washington, DC: National Wildlife Federation, 1956–
   present. Annual.
Darnay, Arsen. *Statistical Record of the Environment.* Arsen J. Darnay, comp. and ed.
   Detroit: Gale, 1992.
Ecological Abstracts. Norwich, Eng.: Geo Abstracts, 1974–present. Monthly. Abstracts
   about 700 books, conference proceedings, reports, and dissertations.
Energy Statistics Yearbook. Department of International Economic and Social Affairs.
   Statistical Office. New York: United Nations, 1984–present. Annual.
Environment Abstracts Annual. New York: Bowker A&I Publishing, 1980–present.
Environmental Viewpoints. Detroit: Gale. Annual. Excerpts articles from over 100 pe-
   riodicals.
The Global Ecology Handbook: What You Can Do About the Environmental Crisis. The
   Global Tomorrow Coalition. Walter H. Carson, ed. Boston: Beacon Press, 1990.
*Hazardous Substance Resource Guide: Citizen's Guide to Home, Workplace, and Commu-
   nity Contaminants.* 1st ed. Richard Pohamish and Stanley A. Greene, eds. De-
   troit: Gale, 1992.
International Handbook of Pollution Control. New York: Greenwood, 1989.
Kreissman, Bernard. *California, an Environmental Atlas & Guide.* By Bern Kreiss-
   man; assisted by Barbara Lebisch. Davis, CA: Bear Klaw Press, 1991.
Mason, Robert J. *Atlas of United States Environmental Issues.* Robert J. Mason and
   Mark T. Mattson. New York: Macmillan, 1990.
Miller, E. Willard. *Environmental Hazards: Air Pollution: A Handbook for Reference.* By
   E. Willard Miller and Ruby M. Miller. Santa Barbara, CA: ABC-CLIO, 1989.
Pollution Abstracts. Bethesda, MD: Cambridge Scientific Abstracts, 1970–present.
   Bimonthly. Also available on-line from DIALOG and on magnetic tape from
   Cambridge Scientific Abstracts. (See also entry under *PoltoxI: NLM, CSA, FIS* in
   the Databases section.)
Sax, N. Irving. *Dangerous Properties of Industrial Materials.* 7th ed. 3 vols. New York:
   Van Nostrand Reinhold, 1989.
Solar Index. Denver: Solar Index, 1982–present. An annual periodical index.

Stevenson, L. Harold. *The Facts on File Dictionary of Environmental Science.* By L. Harold Stevenson and Bruce Wyman. New York: Facts on File, 1991.

Synerjy: A Directory of Energy Alternatives. New York: J. Twine, 1974–present. Updated semiannually; July issues are cumulative for one year.

Van der Leeden, Frits. *The Water Encyclopedia.* By Frits van der Leeden et al. 2d ed. Chelsea, MI: Lewis Publishers, 1990.

Weber, R. David. *Energy Update: A Guide to Current Reference Literature.* San Carlos, CA: Energy Information Press, 1991.

World Resources: A Report by the World Resources Institute for Environmental and Development. New York: Basic Books, 1986–present. Annual. Published since 1990 by Oxford Univ. Press.

<u>Databases</u>

Air/Water Pollution Report. Silver Spring, MD: Business Publishers, Inc. (BPI). Available on-line from DIALOG as part of the *PTS Newsletter Database.*

Energy Information Database. Eagan, MN: International Research and Evaluation (IRE). Available on-line from the producer.

Enviroline. New York: Bowker A&I Publishing. Available on-line from DIALOG; also available on CD-ROM as *Enviro/Energyline Abstracts Plus* and on magnetic tape from Bowker Electronic Publishing.

Environmental Bibliography. Santa Barbara, CA: International Academy at Santa Barbara Environmental Studies Institute. Available on-line from DIALOG; also available on CD-ROM from the provider under the title *Environmental Periodicals Bibliography.*

Global Environmental Change Report. Arlington, MA: Cutter Information Group. Available on-line from DIALOG as part of the *PTS Newsletter Database.*

PoltoxI: NLM, CSA, IFIS. Bethesda, MD: Cambridge Scientific Abstracts (CSA). Comprises seven databases. Available on CD-ROM from the producer. See also entry under *Pollution Abstracts* in the preceding section.

ECOLOGY JOURNALS
(†Indicates title is available on-line in a full-text format from DIALOG.)
Audubon
Conservationist
Ecology
†*Energy Journal*
Environment
Sierra: The Magazine of the Sierra Club
Solar Energy

ECOLOGY VIDEOS
Down the Shore
Icewalls (4-part series)
National Audubon Society Specials (continuing series)
(All of these titles are available from PBS Video, Alexandria, VA.)

B–5 Education

<u>Books</u>

Barrow, Robin. *A Critical Dictionary of Educational Concepts.* 2d ed. By Robin Barrow and Geoffrey Milburn. New York: Teachers College Press, Columbia Univ., 1990.

Berry, Dorothea M. *A Bibliographic Guide to Educational Research.* 3d ed. Metuchen, NJ: Scarecrow, 1990.

Bibliographical Guide to Education. Boston: G. K. Hall, 1978–present. Annual.

Buttlar, Lois. *Education: A Guide to Reference and Information Sources.* Englewood, CO: Libraries Unlimited, 1989.

Current Index to Journals in Education: CIJE. Phoenix: Oryx Press, 1969–present. See entry under ERIC in databases section.

Dejnozka, Edward L. *American Educators' Encyclopedia.* Rev. ed. Westport, CT: Greenwood, 1991.

Directory of American Scholars. Lancaster, PA: Science Press, 1942–present. Published since 1957 by R. R. Bowker, New York. Beginning with the 4th ed., each edition is published in several volumes, each devoted to a specific academic area.

Education Index. Bronx, NY: H. W. Wilson, 1929–present. Monthly, except July and August, plus annual cumulation. Also available on-line through WILSONLINE, on CD-ROM through WILSONDISC, and on machine-readable tape through WILSONTAPE.

The Educational Software Selector: T.E.S.S. New York: EPIE Institute and Teachers College Press, 1984–present. Annual.

Encyclopedia of Educational Research. 6th ed. Marvin C. Alkin, ed. New York: Macmillan, 1992.

The Encyclopedia of Higher Education. Burton R. Clark and Guy R. Neave, editors-in-chief. 4 vols. Oxford, Eng.: Pergamon, 1992.

Fact Book on Higher Education. New York: American Council on Education: Macmillan, 1984–present. Biennial.

Fraenkel, Jack R. *How to Design and Evaluate Research in Education.* New York: McGraw-Hill, 1990.

The International Encyclopedia of Education: Research and Studies. Torsten Husen and T. Neville Postlethwaite, eds. 10 vols. New York: Pergamon, 1985. Supplementary volume 1989–present. Also available on CD-ROM from the publisher.

The Mental Measurements Yearbook. O. K. Buros, ed. Lincoln, NE: Univ. of Nebraska, 1985–present. Also available on-line from BRS Information Technologies.

Shafritz, Jay M. *The Facts on File Dictionary of Education.* By Jay M. Shafritz et al. New York: Facts on File, 1988.

World Education Encyclopedia. George Thomas Kurian, ed. 3 vols. New York: Facts on File, 1988.

Databases

Educational Directory Online. Shelton, CT: Market Data Retrieval, Inc. Available on-line from DIALOG.

ERIC. Washington, DC: U.S. Department of Education, Educational Resources Information Center. Available on-line from DIALOG; also available on CD-ROM (*ERIC on Silver Platter*) from Silver Platter Information, Inc., Norwood, MA; and on magnetic tape from OCLC Online Computer Library Center, Inc., Dublin, OH.

Peterson's College Database. Princeton, NJ: Peterson's Guides. Available on-line from DIALOG; on CD-ROM from Silver Platter Information, Inc., Norwood, MA; on diskette from the provider under the title *Peterson's College Selection Service*; and on magnetic tape from the provider.

EDUCATION JOURNALS

American Educational Research Journal
American Journal of Education

Change
Chronicle of Higher Education
Harvard Education Review
Journal of Higher Education
Phi Delta Kappan
Resources in Education

EDUCATION VIDEOS
Learning in America (5-part series)
A Quest for Education
Who Will Teach for America?
(All of these titles are available from PBS Video, Alexandria, VA.)

B–6 Ethnic studies

a. General

<u>Books</u>
Cashmore, Ernest. *Dictionary of Race and Ethnic Relations.* 2d ed. London: Routledge, 1988.
Dictionary of American Immigration History. Francesco Cordasco, ed. Metuchen, NJ: Scarecrow, 1990.
Taylor, Charles A. *Guide to Multicultural Resources.* 1989–90 ed. Madison, WI: Praxis, 1989.
Weinberg, Meyer. *Racism in the United States: A Comprehensive Classified Bibliography.* New York: Greenwood, 1990.
Woll, Allen L. *Ethnic and Racial Images in American Film and Television: Historical Essays and Bibliography.* New York: Garland, 1987.
World Directory of Minorities. Minority Rights Group, ed. Chicago: St. James Press, 1990.
<u>Databases</u>
Ethnic News Watch. Stamford, CT: Soft Line Information. Available on CD-ROM from the provider.

ETHNIC STUDIES (GENERAL) JOURNALS
Ethnic and Racial Studies
Ethnic Forum
Journal of American Ethnic History
New Perspectives

ETHNIC STUDIES (GENERAL) VIDEOS
America Becoming
Journey to America
(Both titles are available from PBS Video, Alexandria, VA.)

b. American Indian studies

Brumble, H. David. *American Indian Autobiography.* Berkeley: Univ. of California Press, 1988.

Handbook of North American Indians. William C. Sturtevant, general ed. Washington, DC: Smithsonian Institution, 1978–present. In progress. A basic and valuable source.

Hoxie, Frederick E. *Native Americans: An Annotated Bibliography.* By Frederick E. Hoxie and Harvey Markowitz. Pasadena, CA: Salem Press, 1991.

Klein, Barry T. *Reference Encyclopedia of the American Indian.* 5th ed. West Nyack, NY: Todd Publications, 1990. Also available on diskette from Todd Publications, West Nyack, NY.

LePoer, Barbara A. *A Concise Dictionary of Indian Tribes of North America.* Algonac, MI: Reference Publications, 1979.

Martin, M. Marlene. *Ethnographic Bibliography of North America: 4th ed. Supplement, 1973–1987.* By M. Marlene Martin and Timothy J. O'Leary. 3 vols. New Haven: Human Relations Area Files, 1990. See also entry under Murdock, George Peter, in this section.

Murdock, George Peter. *Ethnographic Bibliography of North America.* 4th ed. 5 vols. New Haven: Human Relations Area Files, 1975. See also entry under Martin, M. Marlene, in this section.

Vane, Sylvia Brakke. *California Indians: Primary Resources, a Guide to Manuscripts, Artifacts, Documents, Serials, Music and Illustrations.* By Sylvia Brakke Vane and Lowell John Bean. Rev. ed. Menlo Park, CA: Ballena Press, 1990.

Waldman, Carl. *Who Was Who in Native American History: Indians and Non-Indians from Early Contacts Through 1900.* New York: Facts on File, 1990.

Databases
North American Indians. St. Paul, MN: Quanta Press, Inc. Available on CD-ROM from the provider.

AMERICAN INDIAN STUDIES VIDEOS
Geronimo and the Apache Resistance
The Spirit of Crazy Horse
Surviving Columbus
Winds of Change (2-part series)
(All of these titles are available from PBS Video, Alexandria, VA.)

c. Asian-American studies

Asian Americans: Comparative and Global Perspectives. Shirley Hune et al., eds. Pullman, WA: Washington State Univ. Press, 1991.

Asian Americans Information Directory. 1st ed. Karen Backus and Julia C. Furtlaw, eds. Detroit: Gale, 1992–present.

Chan, Sucheng. *Asian Americans: An Interpretive History.* Boston: Twayne, 1991.

Haseltine, Patricia. *East and Southeast Asian Material Culture in North America: Collections, Historical Sites, and Festivals.* New York: Greenwood, 1989.

Kim, Hyung-chan. *Asian American Studies: An Annotated Bibliography and Research Guide.* New York: Greenwood, 1989.

ASIAN-AMERICAN JOURNALS
Amerasia Journal
Asian Week
East Wind
Transpacific: The Asian American Magazine

ASIAN-AMERICAN VIDEOS
The Chinese Americans: The Early Immigrants
A Family Gathering
I'm Not Prejudiced But . . . Korean Immigrants in Black Neighborhoods
(All of these titles are available from PBS Video, Alexandria, VA.)

d. African-American studies

Books
Black Americans Information Directory. 1st ed. (1990–91)–present. Detroit: Gale, 1990–present. Biennial.
Black Leaders of the Nineteenth Century. Leon Litwack and August Meier, eds. Urbana: Univ. of Illinois Press, 1988.
The Black Resource Guide. R. Benjamin Johnson, ed. Washington, DC: Black Resource Guide, Inc., 1981–present. Annual.
Cantor, George. *Historic Landmarks of Black America.* 1st ed. George Cantor, ed. Detroit: Gale, 1991.
Contemporary Black Biography. Barbara Carlisle Bigelow, ed. 2 vols. Detroit: Gale, 1992–present. Published twice a year.
Hornsby, Alton. *Chronology of African-American History: Significant Events and People from 1619 to the Present.* 1st ed. Detroit: Gale, 1991.
Index to Black Periodicals. Boston: G. K. Hall, 1984–present. Annual. Formerly: *Index to Periodical Articles By and About Blacks.*
The Negro Almanac: A Reference Work on the African American. Compiled and edited by Harry A. Ploski and James Williams. 5th ed. Detroit: Gale, 1989.
Schomburg Center for Research in Black Culture. *Bibliographic Guide to Black Studies.* Boston: G. K. Hall, 1975–present. Supplement to New York (City) Public Library. *Schomburg Collection of Negro Literature and History. Dictionary Catalog.*
Stevenson, Rosemary M., comp. *Index to Afro-American Reference Sources.* New York: Greenwood, 1988.
Who's Who Among Black Americans. Detroit: Gale, 1976–present. Biennial. Also available on diskette and magnetic tape from Gale.
Databases
Gale Biographies. Detroit: Gale. Corresponds to, among other publications, *Who's Who Among Black Americans and Black Writers.* Available on-line from Mead Data Central, Inc., Dayton, OH.
Newspaper Abstracts Ondisc. Louisville, KY: UMI/Data Courier. Includes *Black Newspaper Index.* Available on CD-ROM from University Microfilms International (UMI), UMI Ondisc, Ann Arbor, MI. Also available on magnetic tape (1984–88) from UMI.

AFRICAN-AMERICAN JOURNALS
(*Indicates title available on-line from DIALOG in a full-text format.)
Black Scholar
Crisis
*Ebony
Journal of Black Studies
Journal of Negro History

AFRICAN-AMERICAN VIDEOS
Eye on the Prize (6-part series)
Eye on the Prize—Part II (8-part series)
Roots (6 programs)
Roots of Resistance—A Story of the Underground Railroad
(All of these titles are available from PBS Video, Alexandria, VA.)

e. Hispanic-American Studies

Books
The Chicano Index. Berkeley: Chicano Studies Library Publications Unit,
    1989–present. Annual. Supersedes the *Chicano Periodicals Index*, providing in-
    dexing to books, anthology articles, reports, and other documents as well as
    journal articles. See also *Chicano Database on CD-ROM* in databases section.
Chicano Periodicals Index. 6 vols. Boston: G. K. Hall, 1981–1989. Superseded by *The
    Chicano Index.* See also entry *Chicano Database on CD-ROM* in databases section.
Garcia-Ayvens, Francisco. *Chicano Anthology Index: A Comprehensive Author, Title, and
    Subject Index to Chicano Anthologies, 1965–1987.* Comp. and ed. by Francisco
    Garcia-Ayvens. Berkeley: Chicano Studies Library Publications Unit, Univ. of
    California, 1990.
Graham, Joe Stanley. *Hispanic-American Material Culture: An Annotated Directory of Col-
    lections, Sites, Archives, and Festivals in the United States.* New York: Greenwood, 1989.
HAPI, Hispanic American Periodicals Index. Los Angeles: UCLA Latin American Cen-
    ter Publications, 1970/74–present. Annual.
The Hispanic Almanac. 2d ed. Washington, DC: Hispanic Policy Development Proj-
    ect, 1990.
Hispanic Americans Information Directory. Detroit: Gale, 1990–present. Biennial.
Meier, Matt S. *Dictionary of Mexican American History.* By Matt S. Meier and Feliciano
    Rivera. Westport, CT: Greenwood, 1981.
Meier, Matt S. *Mexican American Biographies: A Historical Dictionary, 1836–1987.* New
    York: Greenwood, 1988.
Statistical Handbook on U.S. Hispanics. Compiled and edited by Frank L. Schick and
    Renee Schick. Phoenix: Oryx Press, 1991.
Databases
The Chicano Database on CD-ROM. Berkeley, Univ. of Calif., Chicano Studies Library.
    Supersedes the *Chicano Periodicals Index*, providing indexing to books, anthol-
    ogy articles, reports, and other documents as well as journal articles. Available
    from the provider.

HISPANIC-AMERICAN JOURNALS
Aztlan
Hispanic
La Opinion (newspaper)
Latino Studies Journal
Nuestro

HISPANIC-AMERICAN VIDEOS
An American Story With Richard Rodriguez
Los Mineros

New Harvest, Old Shame
(All of the titles are available on PBS Video, Alexandria, VA.)

B-7 High technology

Books

Advances in Automation and Robotics: Theory and Applications. G. N. Saridis, ed. Greenwich, CT: JAI Press, 1985–present. Annual.

Computer & Control Abstracts. London: Institution of Electrical Engineers, 1969–present. Monthly. Material for 1989–present issued also on CD-ROM as part of *INSPEC Electronics & Computing.*

Computer Literature Index. Phoenix: Applied Computer Research, 1971–present. Quarterly, with annual cumulation.

Computers and Computing Information Resources Directory. Detroit: Gale, 1987–present. Annual.

———. *Supplement.* Detroit: Gale, 1987–present.

Computing Information Directory: A Comprehensive Guide to the Computing Literature. Compiled and edited by Darlene Myers Hildebrandt. 7th ed. Colville, WA: Hildebrandt, Inc., 1990.

Cortada, James W. *A Bibliographic Guide to the History of Computing, Computers, and the Information Processing Industry.* New York: Greenwood, 1990.

Covington, Michael A. *Dictionary of Computer Terms.* By Michael Covington and Douglas Downing. 3d ed. Hauppauge, New York: Barron's, 1992.

Electronics Engineers Reference Book. Edited by F. F. Mazda; with specialist contributions. 6th ed. London: Butterworths, 1989.

Encyclopedia of Artificial Intelligence. Stuart C. Shapiro, editor-in-chief. 2nd ed. 2 vols. New York: Wiley, 1992.

Encyclopedia of Computer Science and Technology. Jack Belzer et al., executive eds., 23 vols. New York: M. Dekker, 1975–1990. Kept up-to-date by supplementary volumes and by a companion title, *Encyclopedia of Microcomputers* (see below).

Encyclopedia of Electronics. By Stan Gibilisco and Neil Sclater. 2d ed. Blue Ridge Summit, PA: TAB Professional and Reference Books, 1990.

Encyclopedia of Microcomputers. Allan Kent et al., executive eds. 9 vols. New York: M. Dekker, 1988–1992. To be complete in 12 vols. plus supplements.

Freeman, Alan. *The Computer Glossary.* 5th ed. New York: AMACOM, 1991.

The Handbook of Artificial Intelligence. Avron Barr et al., eds. Stanford, CA: HeurisTech, 1981–present. Work in progress. Vols. 4- published by Addison-Wesley, Reading, MA.

Handbook of Theoretical Computer Science. Jan van Leeuwen, ed. 2 vols. New York: Elsevier, 1990.

Hordeski, Michael F. *The Illustrated Dictionary of Microcomputers.* 3d ed. Blue Ridge Summit, PA: TAB Professional and Reference Books, 1990.

McGraw-Hill Personal Computer Programming Encyclopedia: Languages and Operating Systems. William J. Birnes, ed. 2nd ed. New York: McGraw-Hill, 1989.

Microcomputer Index. Santa Clara, CA: Microcomputer Information Services, 1980–present. Quarterly. A periodical index, with abstracts. Also available online from DIALOG.

Microsoft Press Computer Dictionary. Contributors, Jo Anne Woodstock, et al. Redmond, WA: Microsoft Press, 1991.

The Software Encyclopedia. New York: Bowker, 1985–present. Issued in 2 vols. 1985/86–present. Updated annually. See also entry under *Microcomputer Software Guide Online.*

<u>Databases</u>

Advanced Manufacturing Technology (AMT). Fort Lee, NJ: Technology Insights, Inc. Available on-line from DIALOG.

INSPEC. Stevanage, Herts., Eng. Citations to journal articles and research papers. Available on-line from DIALOG; also available on CD-ROM as *INSPEC Ondisc* from University Microfilms International, Ann Arbor, MI.; and on magnetic tape from Institution of Electrical Engineers, Stevanage, Herts., Eng.

Microcomputer Software Guide Online. New Providence, NJ: Bowker. Available on-line from DIALOG; also available on CD-ROM as part of *Children's Reference Plus* from Bowker. See also entry under *The Software Encyclopedia.*

Robotics. New Providence, NJ: Bowker A&I Publishing. A bibliography, with abstracts. Available on-line from DataStar, London; also available on CD-ROM as part of *Supertech Abstracts Plus* from Bowker and on magnetic tape from Bowker.

HIGH TECHNOLOGY JOURNALS

(*Indicates title is available on-line in full-text format from DIALOG.)
Artificial Intelligence
*Byte
*CAD/CAM Update
*Datamation
*Incider A+
*MacWorld
*PC Magazine
*Robotics Today

HIGH TECHNOLOGY VIDEOS

Artificial Intelligence
Computer Aided Design
Computer Aided Manufacturing
How Computers Work: A Journey Into the Walk-Through Computer
Semiconductor Devices
(Consult *The Video Source Book,* 11th ed., 1990, for information on these videos.)

B–8 History

a. World history

<u>Books</u>

Barzun, Jacques. *The Modern Researcher.* By Jacques Barzun and Henry F. Graff. 5th ed. Fort Worth: Harcourt Brace Jovanovich, 1992.

Boorstin, Daniel J. *The Discoverers: A History of Man's Search to Know His World and Himself.* New York: Random, 1983.

The Cambridge Ancient History. 3d ed. London: Cambridge Univ. Press, 1970–present. Eight volumes of this important set have been published.

The Cambridge Medieval History. 2d ed. Planned by J. B. Bury; H. M. Gwatkin and J. P. Whitney, eds. London: Cambridge Univ. Press, 1975–present. Eight volumes of this indispensable set have been published.

Cook, Chris. *Dictionary of Historical Terms.* 2d ed. New York: Peter Bedrick, 1990.

Durant, Will and Ariel. *The Story of Civilization.* 11 vols. New York: Simon, 1935–1975. A monumental work of enduring worth, written in a readable style.

Encyclopedia of Asian History. Prepared under the auspices of The Asia Society; Ainslie T. Embree, editor-in-chief. 4 vols. New York: Macmillan, 1988.

Fritze, Ronald H. *Reference Sources in History: An Introductory Guide.* By Ronald H. Fritze et al. Santa Barbara, CA: ABC-CLIO, 1990.

Great Historians of the Modern Age: An International Dictionary. Lucian Boio, editor-in-chief. New York: Greenwood, 1991.

Historical Abstracts, Parts A & B. Santa Barbara, CA: ABC-CLIO, 1955–present. Quarterly. Available on-line from DIALOG; also available on CD-ROM from ABC-CLIO.

Kohn, George C. *Dictionary of Historic Documents.* Introduction by Leonard Latkovski. New York: Facts on File, 1991.

The New Cambridge Modern History. 14 vols. Cambridge: Cambridge Univ. Press, 1957–79. Another seminal title in the Cambridge history series.

Ritter, Harry. *Dictionary of Concepts in History.* Westport: Greenwood, 1986.

Steinberg, S. H. *Historical Tables, 58 B.C.–A.D. 1985.* 11th ed., updated by John Paxton. New York: Garland, 1986.

Strayer, Joseph R., ed. *Dictionary of the Middle Ages.* New York: Scribner's, 1982–present. A projected 12-vol. set of monumental proportions.

The Times Atlas of World History. Geoffrey Barraclough, ed. 3d ed. Norman Stone, ed. Maplewood, NJ: Hammond, Inc., 1991.

Worldmark Encyclopedia of the Nations. 7th ed. 5 vols. New York: Worldmark Press, 1988.

Databases

Read More About It. Ann Arbor, MI: Pierian Press. Available on magnetic tape from the producer.

Time Table of History: Business, Politics & Media. New York: SONY Electronic Publishing Co. Available on CD-ROM from the producer (SONY Data Discman).

WORLD HISTORY JOURNALS
The Historian
History Today
Journal of Modern History
Journal of the History of Ideas

WORLD HISTORY VIDEOS
Castle
Cathedral
Odyssey (14-part series)
Pyramid
(All of these titles are available from PBS Video, Alexandria, VA.)

b. American history

Books

Album of American History. James Truslow Adams, editor-in-chief. 6 vols. New York: Scribner, 1981. *Supplement, 1968–1982.* New York: Scribner, 1985.

America, History and Life. Santa Barbara, CA: ABC-CLIO, 1964–present. "Article abstracts and citations of reviews and dissertations covering the United States and Canada." Published three times a year. Also available on-line from DIALOG and on CD-ROM from ABC-CLIO.

American Reformers: An H. W. Wilson Biographical Dictionary. Alden Whitman, ed. New York: H. W. Wilson, 1985.

The Annals of America. Chicago: Encyclopaedia Britannica, 1968–1987.

Dictionary of American History. Rev. ed. 8 vols. New York: Scribner, 1976–1978.

Documents of American History. Edited by Henry Steele Commager and Milton Cantor. 10th ed. 2 vols. Englewood Cliffs, NJ: Prentice-Hall, 1988.

Encyclopedia USA: The Encyclopedia of the United States of America Past & Present. R. Alton Lee, ed. 12 vols. Gulf Breeze, FL: Academic International Press, 1983–1990.

Historical Times Illustrated Encyclopedia of the Civil War. Patricia L. Faust et al., eds. New York: Harper, 1986.

Kane, Joseph Nathan. *Facts About the Presidents: A Compilation of Biographical and Historical Information.* 5th ed. New York: H. W. Wilson, 1989.

National Geographic Society. *Historical Atlas of the U.S.* Washington, DC: National Geographic Society, 1988.

Databases

The American Civil War. New York: SONY Electronic Publishing Co., SONY Data Discman. Available on CD-ROM from the producer.

WESTLAW™ Bicentennial of the Constitution Database. St. Paul, MN: West Publishing Co., WESTLAW. Available on-line from WESTLAW.

U.S. History on CD-ROM. Parsippany, NJ: Bureau of Electronic Publishing.

U.S. Presidents. St. Paul, MN: Quanta Press. Available on CD-ROM from the producer.

USA Wars—Vietnam. St. Paul, MN: Quanta Press. Available on CD-ROM from the producer.

AMERICAN HISTORY JOURNALS

*American Heritage
American Historical Review
American History Illustrated
Civil War Times Illustrated
Journal of American History
(*Indicates title is available on-line in full-text format from DIALOG.)

AMERICAN HISTORY VIDEOS

The American Experience (continuing series)
The Civil War (9-part series)
Making Sense of the Sixties (6-part series)
(All of these titles are available from PBS Video, Alexandria, VA.)

B–9 Literature

Books

a. General

Abrams, M. H. *A Glossary of Literary Terms.* 5th ed. New York: Holt, Rinehart and Winston, 1988.

Abstracts of English Studies. Boulder, CO: National Council of Teachers of English, 1958–present. Quarterly. Frequency varies.

Bartlett, John. *Familiar Quotations.* 16th ed. Edited by Justin Kaplan et al. Boston: Little, Brown, 1992.

Black Literature Criticism: Excerpts From Criticism of the Most Significant Works of Black Authors Over the Past 200 Years. James P. Draper, ed. 3 vols. Detroit: Gale, 1992.

Black Writers: A Selection of Sketches From Contemporary Authors. 1st ed. Linda Metzer et al., eds. Detroit: Gale, 1989. Also available on diskette and magnetic tape from Gale.

Bracken, James K. *Reference Works in British and American Literature.* 2 vols. Englewood, CO: Libraries Unlimited, 1990–1991.

Columbia Dictionary of Modern European Literature. 2d ed. Jean-Albert Bede and William B. Edgerton, general ed. New York: Columbia Univ. Press, 1980.

Contemporary Authors: A Bio-Bibliographic Guide to Current Writers. Detroit: Gale, 1962–present.

Contemporary Dramatists. 4th ed. With a preface by Ruby Cohn; D. L. Kirkpatrick, ed. Chicago: St. James, 1988.

Contemporary Literary Criticism. Detroit: Gale, 1973–present.

Contemporary Novelists. 5th ed. Lesley Henderson, ed. Chicago: St. James, 1991.

Contemporary Poets. 5th ed. Tracy Chevalier, ed. Chicago: St. James, 1991.

Dictionary of Literary Biography. Matthew J. Bruccoli, editorial director. Detroit: Gale, 1978–present.

A Dictionary of Modern Critical Terms. Rev. and enl. ed. Roger Fowler, ed. London: Routledge & K. Paul, 1987.

Drama Criticism. Detroit: Gale, 1991–present. Irregular. Four volumes have been published.

Encyclopedia of World Literature in the 20th Century. Rev. ed. Leonard S. Klein, general ed. 4 vols. New York: Ungar, 1981–1984.

Essay and General Literature Index. Bronx, NY: H. W. Wilson, 1900/33–present. Semi-annual, with annual and five-year cumulations. Also available on-line from WILSONLINE, on CD-ROM from WILSONDISC, and on magnetic tape from WILSONTAPE.

European Writers. George Stade, editor-in-chief. 14 vols. New York: Scribner, 1983–1991.

The Feminist Companion to Literature in English: Women Writers From the Middle Ages to the Present. Virginia Blain et al., eds. New Haven; Yale Univ. Press, 1990.

Good Reading: A Guide for Serious Readers. 23d ed. Arthur Waldhorn et al., eds. New York: Bowker, 1989.

Hazen, Edith P. *The Columbia Granger's Index to Poetry.* 9th ed. Edith P. Hazen and Deborah J. Fryer, eds. New York: Columbia Univ. Press, 1990.

Hispanic Writers: A Selection of Sketches from Contemporary Authors. 1st ed. Bryan Ryan, ed. Detroit: Gale, 1990. Also available on diskette and magnetic tape from Gale.

Holman, C. Hugh. *A Handbook to Literature.* By C. Hugh Holman and William Harmon. 6th ed. New York: Macmillan, 1992.

Kuntz, Joseph M. *Poetry Explication: A Checklist of Interpretation Since 1925 of British and American Poems.* By Joseph M. Kuntz and Nancy C. Martinez. 3d ed. Boston: G. K. Hall, 1980.

Literature Criticism From 1400 to 1800. James E. Person, Jr., ed. Detroit: Gale, 1984–present.

Magill's Literary Annual. Englewood Cliffs, NJ: Salem, 1977–present.

Masterplots II. Drama Series. Frank Magill, ed. 4 vols. Pasadena, CA: Salem, 1990.

MLA International Bibliography of Books and Articles on the Modern Languages and Literature. New York: Modern Language Association of America, 1921–present. Also available on-line from WILSONLINE, H. W. Wilson Co., and on CD-ROM from the same company.

Poetry Criticism. Robyn V. Young, ed. Detroit: Gale, 1991–present. Biannual.

Research Guide to Biography and Criticism. Walton Beacham, ed. 6 vols. Washington, DC: Research Pub., 1985–1991.

Short Story Criticism. Detroit: Gale, 1988–present. Annual.

Spanish American Women Writers: A Bio-Bibliographical Source Book. Diane E. Martinez, ed. New York: Greenwood, 1990.

Wakeman, John. *World Authors, 1950–1970.* New York: H. W. Wilson, 1975. Continued by volumes for 1970–1975 and 1975–1980, also published by H. W. Wilson.

Walker, Warren S. *Twentieth Century Short Story Explication: New Series.* Hamden, CT: Shoe String Press, 1993.

b. American literature

American Literary Scholarship. Durham, NC: Duke Univ. Press, 1965–present.

American Women Writers: A Critical Reference Guide from Colonial Times to the Present. Lina Mainiero, ed. 4 vols. New York: Ungar, 1979–82.

Annals of American Literature, 1602–1983. Richard M. Ludwig and Clifford A. Nault, Jr., eds. New York: Oxford, 1986.

Blanck, Jacob. *Bibliography of American Literature.* Comp. by Jacob Blanck for the Bibliographical Society of America. New Haven, CT: Yale Univ. Press, 1955—present. 9 vols. have been published.

The Cambridge Handbook of American Literature. Jack Salzman, ed., with Cameron Bardick. New York: Cambridge Univ. Press, 1986.

Columbia Literary History of the United States. Emory Elliott, general ed. New York: Columbia Univ. Press, 1988.

Concise Dictionary of American Literary Biography. 6 vols. Detroit: Gale, 1987–1989.

Gerhardstein, Virginia B. *Dickinson's American Historical Fiction.* 5th ed. Metuchen, NJ: Scarecrow, 1986.

Kellman, Steven G. *The Modern American Novel: An Annotated Bibliography.* Pasadena, CA: Salem, 1991.

Leitch, Vincent B. *American Literary Criticism From the 30s to the 80s.* New York: Columbia Univ. Press, 1988.

Literary History of the United States. Robert E. Spiller, et al., eds. 4th ed., rev. 2 vols. New York: Macmillan, 1974.

Notable Women in the American Theatre: A Biographical Dictionary. Alice M. Robinson et al., eds. New York: Greenwood, 1989.

Reference Guide to American Literature. 2d ed. Introductions by Lewis Leary and Warren French; D. L. Kirkpatrick, ed. Chicago: St. James, 1987.

c. British literature

Annals of English Literature, 1475–1950: The Principal Publications of Each Year. 2d ed. Oxford: Clarendon, 1961.

British Novelists, 1660–1800. Martin C. Battestin, ed. 2 vols. Detroit: Gale, 1985.

British Writers. Ian Scott-Kilvert, general ed. 7 vols. New York: Scribner, 1979–1984.

The Cambridge Guide to Literature. Rev. ed. Ian Ousby, ed; foreword by Margaret Atwood. Cambridge: Cambridge Univ. Press, 1992.

The Cambridge Guide to World Theatre. Martin Banham, ed. Cambridge: Cambridge Univ. Press, 1988.

The Cambridge History of English Literature. A. W. Ward and A. R. Waller, eds. 15 vols. Cambridge: Cambridge Univ. Press, 1918–1930. This set, along with *The Oxford History of English Literature* (see entry below), form a pair of invaluable cornerstones for the study of English literature. The first work is updated by: Sampson, George. *The Concise History of English Literature.* 3d ed. Cambridge: Cambridge Univ. Press, 1970.

Concise Dictionary of British Literary Biography. 8 vols. Detroit: Gale, 1991–1992.

Cyclopedia of World Authors II. Frank N. Magill, ed. 4 vols. Pasadena, CA: Salem, 1989.

English Novel Explication: Criticism to 1972. Helen H. Palmer and Anne Jane Dyson, comps. Hamden, CT: Shoe String, 1973. Supplements *The English Novel, 1578–1956,* by I. F. Bell and D. Baird.

English Novel Explication. Supplement. 4 vols. Hamden, CT: Shoe String, 1976–1990.

Gray, Martin. *A Chronology of English Literature.* Burnt Mill, Eng.: Longman, 1989. Supplements II–IV.

Kunitz, Stanley. *European Authors, 1000–1900: A Biographical Dictionary of European Literature.* Stanley J. Kunitz and Vineta Colby, eds. New York: H. W. Wilson, 1967.

Marcuse, Michael J. *A Reference Guide for English Students.* Berkeley: Univ. of Calif. Press, 1990.

The New Cambridge Bibliography of English Literature. George Watson, ed. 5 vols. Cambridge: Cambridge Univ. Press, 1969–1977.

The New Moulton's Library of Literary Criticism. Harold Bloom, general ed. 11 vols. New York: Chelsea House, 1985–1990.

The Oxford History of English Literature. Oxford: Clarendon, 1945–present. Eleven volumes have been published in this most indispensable set.

William Shakespeare: His World, His Work, His Influence. John F. Andrews, ed. 3 vols. New York: Scribner, 1985.

Databases

DiscLit: American Authors. Boston: G. K. Hall. Available on CD-ROM from OCLC Online Computer Library Center, Inc., Dublin, OH.

Literary Forum. Columbus, OH: CompuServe Information Service. Available on-line from the producer.

Magill Book Reviews. Pasadena, CA: Salem Press. Available on-line from Dow Jones News/Retrieval (/Books), Princeton, NJ.

Quotations Database. New York: Oxford Univ. Press—Oxford Electronic Publishing. Available on-line from DIALOG.

The Riverside Shakespeare. Orem, VT: Electronic Text Corp. Available on diskette from the producer.

Walt Whitman. Orem, VT: Electronic Text Corp. Available on diskette from the producer.

LITERATURE JOURNALS
American Literature
Cambridge Quarterly
Journal of Modern Literature
Modern Fiction Studies
PMLA
World Literature Today

LITERATURE VIDEOS
Discovering Hamlet
Moyers: The Power of the Word (6-part series)
Writer's Workshop (15-part series)
(All of these titles are available from PBS Video, Alexandria, VA.)

B–10 Music

Books
Anderson, James. *The Harper Dictionary of Opera and Operetta.* 1st U.S. ed. New York: Harper & Row, 1990.

Annals of the Metropolitan Opera Guild: The Complete Chronicle of Performances and Artists: Chronology, 1883–1985. New York: Metropolitan Opera Guild, 1989.

Baker, Theodore. *Baker's Biographical Dictionary of Musicians.* 8th ed. Revised by Nicolas Slonimsky. New York: Schirmer, 1992.

Boardman, Gerald M. *American Musical Theatre: A Chronicle.* 2d ed. New York: Oxford Univ. Press, 1992.

Cohen, Aaron I. *International Encyclopedia of Women Composers.* 2d ed., rev. and enl. 2 vols. New York: Books & Music USA, 1987.

Contemporary Musicians. Michael L. LeBlanc, ed. 6 vols. Detroit: Gale, 1989—present. Published twice yearly.

Duckles, Vincent H. *Music Reference and Research Materials: An Annotated Bibliography.* By Vincent H. Duckles and Michael A. Keller. 4th ed. New York: Schirmer, 1988.

Ewen, David. *Composers Since 1900.* New York: H. W. Wilson, 1969.

———. *First Supplement.* New York: H. W. Wilson, 1981.

Ewen, David. *Great Composers, 1300–1900: A Biographical and Critical Guide.* New York: H. W. Wilson, 1966.

Gammond, Peter. *The Oxford Companion to Popular Music.* New York: Oxford Univ. Press, 1991.

The Harmony Illustrated Encyclopedia of Rock. Mike Clifford, consultant. 7th ed. New York: Harmony, 1992.

Heintze, James R. *Early American Music: A Research and Information Guide.* New York: Garland, 1990.

International Who's Who in Music and Musicians' Directory. Cambridge, Eng.: Melrose, 1975–present.

LePage, Jane Weiner. *Women Composers, Conductors, and Musicians of the Twentieth Century: Selected Biographies.* 3 vols. Metuchen, NJ: Scarecrow, 1980–1988.

Music Index. Detroit: Information Coordinators, 1949–present. Monthly, with annual cumulations. An important periodical index.

Musical America. International Directory of the Performing Arts. Great Barrington, MA: ABC Leisure Magazines, 1974–present. Annual.

The Musical Woman: An International Perspective. Westport, CT: Greenwood, 1984—present. An ongoing series chronicling the achievements of women in music.

The New Grove Dictionary of American Music. H. Wiley Hitchcock and Stanley Saide, eds. 4 vols. New York: Grove's Dictionaries of Music, 1980.

The New Grove Dictionary of Jazz. Barry Kernfeld, ed. 2 vols. London: Macmillan, 1988.

The New Grove Dictionary of Music and Musicians. Stanley Sadie, ed. 20 vols. London: Macmillan, 1980. A comprehensive reference source on all aspects of music since 1450.

The New Grove Dictionary of Musical Instruments. Stanley Sadie, ed. 3 vols. London: Macmillan, 1984.

The Oxford History of Music. 10 vols. New York: Oxford Univ. Press, 1954–1900. An extremely important, basic set.

Popular Music: An Annotated Index of American Popular Songs. Detroit: Gale, 1974–present. Annual.

Popular Music, 1980–1984. Bruce Pollock, ed. Detroit: Gale, 1986.

Shapiro, Nat. *Popular Music, 1920–1979: A Revised Cumulation.* Nat Shapiro and Bruce Pollock, ed. 3 vols. Detroit: Gale, 1985.

Shemel, Sidney. *This Business of Music.* By Sidney Shemel and M. William Krasilovsky. Rev. and enl. 6th ed. New York: Billboard, 1990.

Slonimsky, Nicolas. *Music Since 1900.* 5th ed. New York: Schirmer, 1993.

Stedman, Preston. *The Symphony: A Research and Information Guide.* New York: Garland, 1990–present. One volume has been published.

Thomsett, Michael C. *Musical Terms, Symbols, and Theory: An Illustrated Dictionary.* Jefferson, NC: McFarland, 1989.

Waters, William J. *Music and the Personal Computer: An Annotated Bibliography.* New York: Greenwood, 1989.

<u>Databases</u>

Music Directory Plus. New Providence, NJ: Bowker. Available on CD-ROM from Bowker Electronic Publishing, New Providence, NJ.

Music Information Service. Fort Lauderdale, FL: Music Information Service. Available on-line from CompuServe Information Service, Columbus, OH.

Music Library: Musical Sound Recordings. Dublin, OH: OCLC Online Computer Library Center, Inc. Available on CD-ROM from OCLC.

Music Literature International. New York: International RILM Center. Available on-line from DIALOG. Also available on CD-ROM under the title *RILM Abstracts* from National Information Services Corp., Baltimore, MD.

MUSIC JOURNALS
Downbeat
Music Quarterly
Opera News
Stereo Review

MUSIC VIDEOS
American Patchwork: Songs and Stories About America (5-part series)
Good Mornin' Blues
Pinchas Zuckerman and the St. Paul Chamber Orchestra
(All of these titles are available from PBS Video, Alexandria, VA.)

B–11 Mythology/Classics

Ancient Writers: Greece and Rome. T. James Luce, editor-in-chief. 2 vols. New York: Scribner, 1982.

Atlas of Classical History. Richard J. A. Talbert, ed. New York: Macmillan, 1985.

Bell, Robert E. *Women of Classical Mythology: A Biographical Dictionary.* Santa Barbara, CA: ABC-CLIO, 1991.

Brewer, Ebenezer Cobham. *Brewer's Dictionary of Phrase and Fable.* By Ivor H. Evans. 14th ed. New York: Harper & Row, 1989.

Bulfinch, Thomas. *Bulfinch's Mythology.* Introduction, notes, and bibliography by Richard P. Martin. Illustrations by Sabra Moore. New York: HarperCollins, 1991.

Civilization of the Ancient Mediterranean: Greece and Rome. Michael Grant and Rachel Kitzinger, eds. 3 vols. New York: Scribner's, 1988.

Classical and Medieval Literature Criticism. Detroit: Gale, 1988–present. Annual.

Frazer, James George. *The Golden Bough: A Study in Magic and Religion.* 3d ed. 9 vols. New York: St. Martin's, 1990.

Hamilton, Edith. *Mythology.* Steele Savage, illus. Boston: Little, Brown, 1942.

Howaston, M. C. *The Oxford Companion to Classical Literature.* 2d ed. New York: Oxford Univ. Press, 1989.

Humanities Index. Bronx, NY: H. W. Wilson. Available on-line from WILSONLINE; also available on CD-ROM through WILSONDISC and on magnetic tape through WILSONTAPE.

Man, Myth, & Magic: The Illustrated Encyclopedia of Mythology, Religion, and the Unknown. Richard Cavendish, editor-in-chief. New ed., ed. and comp. by Yvonne Deutsch. 12 vols. New York: Marshall Cavendish, 1983.

Mythical and Fabulous Creatures: A Source Book and Research Guide. Malcolm South, ed. New York: Greenwood, 1987.

New Larousse Encyclopedia of Mythology. Introduction by Robert Graves. New ed. New York: Crescent, 1989.

Walker, Barbara G. *The Woman's Dictionary of Symbols and Sacred Objects.* San Francisco: Harper & Row, 1988.

Databases

Arts & Humanities Search. Philadelphia: Institute for Scientific Information. Available on-line from DIALOG.

MYTHOLOGY/CLASSICS JOURNALS
Classical Bulletin
Classical Quarterly
Greece and Rome
Parabola

MYTHOLOGY/CLASSICS VIDEOS
Moyers: Joseph Campbell and the Power of Myth (6-part series)
(Available from PBS Video, Alexandria, VA.)

B–12 Philosophy

Books

The Concise Encyclopedia of Western Philosophy and Philosophers. J. O. Urmson and Jonathan Ree, eds. New ed., completely rev. London: Unwin Hyman, 1989.

Copleston, Frederick C. *A History of Philosophy.* 9 vols. Westminster, MD: Newman Bookshop, 1946–1975.

The Directory of American Philosophers. Bowling Green, OH: Philosophy Documentation Center, Bowling Green State Univ., 1963–present. Biennial.

The Encyclopedia of Eastern Philosophy and Religion: Buddhism, Hinduism, Taoism, Zen. Ingrid Fischer-Schreiber et al., ed. Boston: Shambala, 1989.

Encyclopedia of Ethics. Lawrence C. Becker, ed. 2 vols. New York: Garland, 1992.

The Encyclopedia of Philosophy. Paul Edwards, editor-in-chief. Reprinted. 8 vols. in 4. New York: Macmillan, 1972.

Grimes, John A. *A Concise Dictionary of Indian Philosophy: Sanskrit Terms Defined in English.* Albany, NY: State Univ. of New York Press, 1989.

The Handbook of Western Philosophy. G. H. R. Parkinson, general ed. New York: Macmillan, 1988.

Handbook of World Philosophy: Contemporary Developments Since 1945. John R. Burr, ed. Westport, CT: Greenwood, 1980.

International Directory of Philosophy and Philosophers. 1st–6th ed. Bowling Green, OH: Philosophy Documentation Center, Bowling Green Univ., 1965–present. Companion volume to *The Directory of American Philosophers.*

Kersey, Ethel M. *Women Philosophers: A Bio-Critical Source Book.* New York: Greenwood, 1989.

The Oxford Companion to the Mind. Richard L. Gregory, ed., with the assistance of O. L. Zangwill. New York: Oxford Univ. Press, 1987.

The Philosopher's Index. Bowling Green, OH: Philosophy Documentation Center, Bowling Green Univ., 1967–present. Quarterly. "An international index to philosophical periodicals." Also available on-line and CD-ROM from DIALOG.

Sparkes, A. W. *Talking Philosophy: A Wordbook.* London: Routledge, 1991.

Tice, Terrence N. *Research Guide to Philosophy,* by Terrence N. Tice and Thomas P. Slavens. Chicago: American Library Assn., 1983.

World Philosophy: Essay-Reviews of 225 Major Works. Frank N. Magill, ed. 5 vols. Englewood Cliffs, NJ: Salem, 1982.

Databases

Arts & Humanities Search. Philadelphia: Institute for Scientific Information. Available on-line from DIALOG.

Humanities Index. Bronx, NY: H. W. Wilson. Available on-line from WILSONLINE, on CD-ROM from WILSONDISC, and on magnetic tape from WILSONTAPE (all produced by H. W. Wilson).

Religion and Ethics RoundTable. Rockville, MD: GE Information Services (GEIS). Available on-line from GEnie (General Electric Network for Information Exchange).

PHILOSOPHY JOURNALS
American Philosophical Quarterly
International Philosophical Quarterly
Journal of Philosophy
Journal of the History of Ideas
Mind

PHILOSOPHY VIDEOS
A Confucian Life in America With Tu Wei-ming
Mortal Choices With Ruth Macklin, pt. 1
Moyers: Facing Evil
(All these titles are available from PBS Video, Alexandria, VA.)

B–13 Psychology

Books
Annual Review of Psychology. Stanford, CA: Annual Reviews, 1950–present.

Beere, Carole A. *Sex and Gender Issues: A Handbook of Tests and Measures.* New York: Greenwood, 1990.

Campbell, Robert Jean. *Psychiatric Dictionary.* 6th ed. New York: Oxford Univ. Press, 1989.

Child Development Abstracts and Bibliography. Chicago: Univ. of Chicago Press, 1927–present. Published three times a year.

The Encyclopedia of Human Development and Education: Theory, Research, and Studies. R. Murray Thomas, ed. New York: Pergamon, 1990.

A History of American Psychology in Notes and News, 1883–1945: An Index to Journal Sources. Ludy T. Benjamin, Jr. et al., eds. Millwood, NY: Kraus International, 1989.

International Encyclopedia of Psychiatry, Psychology, Psychoanalysis, & Neurology. Benjamin B. Wolman, ed. 12 vols. New York: Produced for Aesculapius Publishers by Van Nostrand Reinhold, 1977. Updated by Progress volume, 1983–present.

Mental Measurements Yearbook. Lincoln, NE: Buros Institute of Mental Measurements, Univ. of Nebraska—Lincoln, 1985–present. Available on-line from BRS Information Technologies (MMYD), McLean, VA.

PsycBooks: Books and Chapters in Psychology. Arlington, VA: American Psychological Assn., 1987–present. Each annual consists of five volumes.

Psychological Abstracts. Washington, DC: American Psychological Assn., 1927—present. See also *PsycINFO* and *PsycLIT* in Databases section.

Sutherland, N. S. *The International Dictionary of Psychology.* New York: Continuum, 1989.

Tests: A Comprehensive Reference for Assessments in Psychology, Education, and Business. 3d ed. Richard C. Sweetland and Daniel J. Keyser, general eds. Austin, TX: Pro-Ed, 1991.

Treatment of Psychiatric Disorders: A Task Force Report of the American Psychiatric Association. 4 vols. Washington, DC: The Association, 1989.

Women in Psychology: A Bio-Bibliographic Sourcebook. Agnes N. O'Connell and Nancy Felipe Russo, eds. New York: Greenwood, 1990.

<u>Databases</u>

Human Sexuality. Shady, NY: Clinical Communications, Inc. Available on-line from CompuServe Information Service (HUMAN), Columbus, OH.

Mental Health Abstracts. Alexandria, VA: IFI/Plenum Data Co. Available on-line from DIALOG.

PsyComNet. New York: PsyComNet. Available on-line from GEnie (General Electric Network for Information Exchange), Rockville, MD.

PsycINFO. Washington, DC: American Psychological Assn. Available on-line from DIALOG. Also available on magnetic tape from the producer. See also *PsycLIT in this section.*

PsycLIT. Norwood, MA: Silver Platter Information, Inc. Available on CD-ROM from the producer. See also entry under *PsycINFO* in this section.

PSYCHOLOGY JOURNALS
(*Indicates title is available on-line in a full-text format from BRS Information Technologies, McLean, VA.)
(**Available on-line [full-text] from DIALOG.)
American Journal of Psychiatry
American Psychologist
Behavioral Science
Journal of Abnormal and Social Psychology
Psychological Perspectives
Psychology of Women Quarterly
**Psychology Today*

PSYCHOLOGY VIDEOS
Broken Minds
Child Abuse: The Perfect Crime
Death and Dying: A Conversation With Elisabeth Kubler-Ross, M.D.
The Mind (9-part series)
(All of these titles are available from PBS Video, Alexandria, VA.)

B–14 Religion

<u>Books</u>

The Anchor Bible. Introd., translation, and notes. Garden City, NY: Doubleday, 1964–present. In progress. A monumental set.

The Anchor Bible Dictionary. David Noel Freedman, ed. 6 vols. New York: Doubleday, 1992.

The Cambridge History of Judaism. W. D. Davies and Louis Finkelstein, eds. New York: Cambridge Univ. Press, 1984–present. In progress; to be in 4 vols.

Critical Review of Books in Religion. Atlanta: Journal of the American Academy of Religion and the Journal of Biblical Literature, 1988–present. Annual.

Encyclopaedia Judaica. 16 vols. Jerusalem: Encyclopaedia Judaica, 1972.

————. *Supplement.* Jerusalem: Encyclopaedia Judaica, 1982?–present. Decennial.
————. *Year Book.* Jerusalem: Encyclopaedia Judaica, 1973–present. Annual.
The Encyclopedia of Islam. New ed. Prepared by a number of leading Orientalists. Leiden, the Netherlands: Brill, 1954–present. In progress.
Encyclopedia of Religion. Mircea Eliade, editor-in-chief. 16 vols. New York: Macmillan, 1987.
Encyclopedia of the American Religious Experience: Studies of Traditions and Movements. Charles H. Lippy and Peter W. Williams, ed. 3 vols. New York: Scribner, 1988.
Illustrated Dictionary and Concordance of the Bible. Geoffrey Wigoder et al., eds. New York: Macmillan, 1986.
The International Standard Bible Encyclopedia. Fully rev. Geoffrey W. Bromiley et al., eds. 4 vols. Grand Rapids, MI: W. B. Eerdmans, 1979–1988.
MacGregor, Geddes. *Dictionary of Religion and Philosophy.* New York: Paragon, 1989.
Mead, Frank Spencer. *Handbook of Denominations in the United States.* New 9th ed. Revised by Samuel S. Hill. Nashville: Abingdon, 1990.
Melton, J. Gordon. *The Encyclopedia of American Religions.* 3d ed. Detroit: Gale, 1989.
Mercer Dictionary of the Bible. Watson E. Mills, general ed. Macon, GA: Mercer Univ. Press, 1990.
New Catholic Encyclopedia. Prepared by an editorial staff at the Catholic Univ. of America. 18 vols. New York: McGraw-Hill, 1967–1989.
The Oxford Dictionary of the Christian Church. 2nd ed. F. L. Cross and E. A. Livingstone, eds. New York: Oxford Univ. Press, 1974.
Peters, Francis E. *Judaism, Christianity, and Islam: The Classical Texts and Their Interpretation.* 3 vols. in 1. Princeton, NJ: Princeton Univ. Press, 1990.
Religion Index One. Periodicals. Rev. and expanded ed. *of the Index to Religious Periodical Literature.* Chicago: American Theological Library Assn., 1949–present. Also available on-line as *Religion Index* from DIALOG, on CD-ROM as *Religion Indexes* from H. W. Wilson through WILSONDISC and on magnetic tape from H. W. Wilson through WILSONTAPE.
Religious Leaders of America. Detroit: Gale, 1991–present. Triennial.
The Sacred Books of the East. Translated by various Oriental scholars. F. Max Muller, ed. 50 vols. Oxford: Clarendon, 1879–1910.
Who's Who in Religion. Chicago: Marquis Who's Who, 1975/76–present.
Yearbook of American and Canadian Churches. Nashville: Abingdon, 1973–present.
Databases
Bible (King James Version). Nashville: Thomas Nelson. Available on-line from DIALOG.
Catholic News Service. Washington, DC: Catholic News Service. Available on-line from NewsNet, Inc. (CNOI), Bryn Mawr, PA.
Global Jewish Database. Ramat-Gan, Israel: Bar-Ilan Univ. Available on-line from Institute for Computers in Jewish Life, Chicago.
Religion and Ethics RoundTable. Rockville, MD: GE Information Services (GEIS). Available on-line from GEnie (General Electric Network for Information Exchange), Rockville, MD.

RELIGION JOURNALS
America
Christian Century
Journal of Biblical Literature
Journal of Religion

Religious Studies
Tikkun

RELIGIOUS VIDEOS
Hanukkah: Let There Be Lights
Islam
Moyers: God and Politics (3-part series)
Ocean of Wisdom
(All of these titles are available from PBS Video, Alexandria, VA.)

B–15 Science

<u>Books</u>
Album of Science. I. B. Cohen, general ed. New York: Scribner's, 1978–present. In progress.
American Men & Women of Science. 17th ed. 8 vols. New York: Bowker, 1989–1990. Irregular. Also available on-line from DIALOG and on CD-ROM as part of *SciTech Reference Plus* from Bowker Electronic Publishing, New Providence, NJ.
Annual Review of Information Science and Technology. Medford, NJ: Learned Information, Inc., 1966–present.
Asimov, Isaac. *Asimov's Chronology of Science and Discovery.* New York: Harper & Row, 1989.
Cambridge Dictionary of Science and Technology. Peter M. B. Walker, general ed. New York: Cambridge Univ. Press, 1990.
Dictionary of Scientific Biography. Charles Coulston Gillispie, editor-in-chief. 18 vols. in 10. New York: Scribner, 1980–1990. Beginning with vol. 15, issued as supplements.
———. *Supplement II.* Frederic L. Holmes, editor-in-chief. New York: Scribner's, 1990.
Encyclopedia of Physical Sciences and Engineering Information Sources [by] Steven Wasserman et al., eds. Detroit: Gale, 1989.
General Science Index. Bronx, NY: H. W. Wilson, 1978–present. A periodical index to 106 English-language periodicals. Monthly except June and December, plus an annual cumulation. Available on-line from WILSONLINE, on CD-ROM from WILSONDISC, and on machine-readable tape from WILSONTAPE (all from H. W. Wilson).
Herzenberg, Caroline L. *Women Scientists from Antiquity to the Present: An Index.* West Cornwall, CT: Locust Hill, 1986.
History of Technology. London: Mansell, 1976–present. Annual. In progress.
Lincoln, Roger J. *The Cambridge Illustrated Dictionary of Natural History* by R. J. Lincoln and G. A. Boxshall. New York: Cambridge Univ. Press, 1987.
McGraw-Hill Encyclopedia of Science & Technology: An International Reference Work. 7th ed. 20 vols. New York: McGraw-Hill, 1992. Also available on-line (6th ed.) from WESTLAW (EST) (West Publishing Co., St. Paul, MN) with the title *McGraw-Hill CD-ROM Science & Technical Reference Set*; and on CD-ROM from McGraw-Hill.
Magill's Survey of Science. Physical Science Series. Frank N. Magill, ed. 5 vols. Pasadena, CA: Salem, 1992.
Marshall Cavendish Illustrated Encyclopedia of Plants & Earth Sciences. 10 vols. New York: Marshall Cavendish, 1988.

Parkinson, Claire L. *Breakthroughs: A Chronology of Great Achievements in Science and Mathematics, 1200–1930.* Boston: G. K. Hall, 1985.

Science Citation Index. Philadelphia: Institute for Scientific Information, 1961–present. "An international interdisciplinary index to the literature of science." Published bi-monthly with an annual cumulation. See also *SciSearch* in Databases section.

Van Nostrand's Scientific Encyclopedia. 7th ed. Douglas M. Considine, ed. 2 vols. New York: Van Nostrand Reinhold, 1980.

Weather Almanac. 6th ed. Frank E. Bair, ed. Detroit: Gale, 1992.

<u>Databases</u>

International Who's Who in Science. St. Andrews, Scotland: Longman Cartermill, Ltd. Available on-line from the producer.

Science Citation Index® Compact Disc Edition. Philadelphia: Institute for Scientific Information (ISI). Available on CD-ROM from ISI. See *SciSearch* in this section.

SciSearch. Philadelphia: Institute for Scientific Information. Corresponds in coverage to *Science Citation Index.* Available on-line from DIALOG. See also *Science Citation Index® Compact Disc Edition* in this section.

SciTech Reference Plus. New Providence, NJ: Bowker Electronic Publishing. Available on CD-ROM from the producer.

SCIENCE JOURNALS

(†Indicates title is available on-line in a full-text format from BRS Information Technologies, McLean, VA.)

(††Indicates title is available on-line in a full-text format from DIALOG.)

American Scientist

Bulletin of the Atomic Scientists

†*Nature*

††*New Scientist*

††*Science News*

††*Scientific American*

SCIENCE VIDEOS

Acid Rainbows

Discover: The World of Science (continuing series)

The Earth Explored (14-part series)

Out of the Fiery Furnace (7-part series)

(All of these titles are available from PBS Video, Alexandria, VA.)

B–16 Social sciences

<u>Books</u>

An American Profile—Opinions and Behavior, 1972–1989. Detroit: Gale, 1990–present. In progress.

Annual Review of Sociology. Palo Alto, CA: Annual Reviews, 1975–present.

Barker, Robert L. *The Social Work Dictionary.* 2d ed. Silver Spring, MD: National Assn. of Social Workers, 1991.

Boudon, Raymond. *A Critical Dictionary of Sociology* by Raymond Boudon and Francois Bourricaud. Chicago: Univ. of Chicago Press, 1989.

Encyclopedia of Sociology. Edgar F. Borgatta, editor-in-chief; Marie L. Borgatta, managing ed. 4 vols. New York: Macmillan, 1992.

Handbook of Sociology. Neil J. Smelser, ed. Newbury Park, CA: Sage, 1988.

International Encyclopedia of the Social Sciences. 19 vols. New York: Macmillan, 1979–1991.

Li, Tze-Chung. *Social Science Reference Sources: A Practical Guide.* Rev. and enl. 2d ed. New York: Greenwood, 1990.

London Bibliography of the Social Sciences. London: Mansell, 1929–present. Irregular. In progress.

PAIS International In Print. New York: Public Affairs Information Service, 1991–present. An important periodical index; includes listing of books, government documents, pamphlets, and reports as well. International in scope. Published monthly, with an annual cumulation. Also available on-line from DIALOG as *PAIS International* and on CD-ROM and magnetic tape from the publisher.

The Social Science Encyclopedia. Rev. and repr. Adam Kuper and Jessica Kuper, eds. New York: Routledge, 1989.

The Social Sciences: A Cross-Disciplinary Guide to Selected Sources. Nancy L. Herron, general ed. Englewood, CO: Libraries Unlimited, 1989.

Social Sciences Citation Index. Philadelphia: Institute for Scientific Information, 1973–present. Published quarterly. See *Social SciSearch* in Databases section. Also available on CD-ROM from the producer.

Social Sciences Index. Bronx, NY: H. W. Wilson, 1974–present. An important periodical index. Published quarterly, plus an annual cumulation. Available on-line from WILSONLINE, on CD-ROM from WILSONDISC, and on machine-readable tape from WILSONTAPE—all from H. W. Wilson.

Sociological Abstracts. San Diego, CA: Sociological Abstracts, 1953–present. Bimonthly, with an annual cumulative index. Also available on-line from DIALOG and on magnetic tape from the publisher. See entry *Sociofile* under Databases section.

Databases

Social SciSearch. Philadelphia: Institute for Scientific Information. Available on-line from DIALOG.

Sociofile. Norwood, MA: Silver Platter Information, Inc. Available on CD-ROM from the producer.

SOCIAL SCIENCES JOURNALS

American Behavioral Scientist
American Journal of Sociology
International Social Science Journal
Social Forces
Social Research

SOCIAL SCIENCES VIDEOS

America Becoming
The Information Society
Murder in America
New Harvest, Old Shame
(All of these titles are available from PBS Video, Alexandria, VA.)

B–17 Women's studies

Books
Carter, Sarah. *Women's Studies: A Guide to Information Sources.* By Sarah Carter and Maureen Ritchie. Jefferson, NC: MacFarland, 1990.
The Continuum Dictionary of Women's Biography. New expanded ed. Jennifer S. Uglow, comp. and ed. New York: Continuum, 1989.
Feminist Periodicals: A Current Listing of Contents. Madison: Office of the Women's Studies Librarian-at-Large, Univ. of Wisconsin System, 1981–present. Quarterly.
Handbook of American Women's History. Angela Howard Zophy, ed. Frances M. Kavenik, associate ed. New York: Garland, 1990.
Humm, Maggie. *The Dictionary of Feminist Theory.* Columbus: Ohio State Univ. Press, 1990.
Jackson, Guida. *Women Who Ruled.* Santa Barbara, CA: ABC-CLIO, 1990.
Notable American Women, 1607–1950: A Biographical Dictionary. Edward T. James, ed. 3 vols. Cambridge, MA: Belknap Press of Harvard Univ. Press, 1971.
Notable Black American Women. Jessie Carney Smith, ed. Detroit: Gale, 1992.
Statistical Handbook of Women in America. Cynthia Taeuber, comp. and ed. Phoenix: Oryx, 1991.
Statistical Record of Women Worldwide. Linda Schmittroth, comp. and ed. Detroit: Gale, 1991.
Watson, G. Llewellyn. *Feminism and Women's Issues: An Annotated Bibliography and Research Guide.* By G. Llewellyn Watson with the assistance of Janet P. Sentner. 2 vols. New York: Garland, 1990.
Women Studies Abstracts. Rush, NY: Rush Pub. Co., 1972–present. Quarterly.
Women's Studies Encyclopedia. Helen Tierney, ed. New York: Greenwood, 1989—present. In progress.
Databases
Marketing to Women. Boston: Marketing to Women, Inc. Available on-line from NewsNet, Inc., Bryn Mawr, PA.
Women: Partners in Development. New York: CD Resources. Available on CD-ROM from the producer.

WOMEN'S STUDIES JOURNALS
(†Indicates title is available on-line in a full-text format from DIALOG.)
Feminist Studies
New Directions for Women
Resources for Feminist Research Signs
†*Women's Sports & Fitness*

WOMEN'S STUDIES VIDEOS
A Baby Maybe?
Women and Creativity
Women of the World (7-part series)
(All of these titles are available from PBS Video, Alexandria, VA.)

Index